APPLYING THE RASCH MODEL: FUNDAMENTAL MEASUREMENT IN THE HUMAN SCIENCES

APPLYING THE RASCH MODEL: FUNDAMENTAL MEASUREMENT IN THE HUMAN SCIENCES

Trevor G. Bond
Christine M. Fox

Illustrations by Tami Schultz

 LAWRENCE ERLBAUM ASSOCIATES, PUBLISHERS

2001   Mahwah, New Jersey   London

Lawrence Erlbaum Associates, Inc., Publishers
10 Industrial Avenue
Mahwah, New Jersey 07430

Cover design by Kathryn Houghtaling Lacey

Library of Congress Cataloging-in-Publication Data
Bond, Trevor G.
  Applying the Rasch model : fundamental measurement in the human sciences /
Trevor G. Bond & Christine M. Fox; illustrations, Tami Schultz.
    p.   cm.
  Includes bibliographical references and index.
  ISBN 0-8058-3476-1 (cloth : alk. paper)   ISBN 0-8058-4252-7 (pbk : alk. paper)
  1. Psychology—Statistical methods.   2. Social sciences—Statistical methods.
  3. Psychology—Research—Methodology.   4. Social sciences—Research—
Methodology.   I. Fox, Christine M.   II. Title.
BF39.B678   2001
150'.7'27—dc21
                                                                00-061704
                                                                  CIP

Books published by Lawrence Erlbaum Associates are printed on acid-free paper,
and their bindings are chosen for strength and durability.

Printed in the United States of America
10   9   8   7   6   5

Contents

Preface

To insist on calling these other processes measurement adds nothing to their actual significance, but merely debases the coinage of verbal intercourse. Measurement is not a term with some mysterious inherent meaning, part of which may be overlooked by the physicists and may be in course of discovery by psychologists. It is merely a word conventionally employed to denote certain ideas. To use it to denote other ideas does not broaden its meaning but destroys it: we cease to know what is to be understood by the term when we encounter it; our pockets have been picked of a useful coin.

—Guild (1938)

No doubt we are not the first authors to end up writing a volume considerably different from the one we set out to write. In terms of the method adopted and the research examples used, the ideas for this book have been crystallizing slowly in the first author's mind for the past 5 years. The need for such a book became more and more obvious, when, at the end of each presentation made at some conference, yet another colleague would approach and ask for a 10-min summary of what all this Rasch modeling was about. Then each time a colleague or new student wanted to undertake research using the Rasch model, it usually involved reteaching, yet again, an introduction to Rasch methodology to another beginner. This book then was designed to be a simple solution to this frustration of the repetition, a textbook to introduce the "how" of Rasch measurement to those who already already had thought at least a little about the "why."

Of course, actually writing the book is not quite as simple as developing a good plan for its structure and content. Moreover, without the active collaboration and expertise of the second author, this book still would be merely just that—a good plan for its structure and content.

Of course, the book continually changed as we tried to write it. What started out as a textbook about the how and why of Rasch analysis in developmental psychology gradually changed its focus as we tried to amplify the "why" section of the book to include a greater focus on the fundamental measurement aspect of the project. All the while we grappled with the demands of colleagues that we attempt to broaden the scope of our examples beyond the narrowly defined realm of developmental psychology.

Our observation is that the human sciences, particularly for those who have been driven by the quantitative research methods developed in psychology, are at the turn of the millennium, in a period that Kuhn would describe as a crisis. Whereas at the beginning of our writing we saw Rasch modeling as a very important methodologic contribution to data analysis in the fields of developmental and educational psychology, as we neared the end of the writing process, we realized that we had undertaken a much more important task. Without a technique that delivers the possibility of genuine, interval-scale, linear measurement of individual variables, data analysis in the human sciences will be condemned to the sort of number-crunching gymnastics that we in the past have mistaken for what other scientists call measurement.

These next few pages will serve by way of introduction to acquaint you, the reader, with the backgrounds, experiences, and motivations that brought us to the Rasch measurement orientation that we want to share with you.

Trevor G. Bond

Unfortunately, I have been conducting empirical research in psychological problems long enough to have some history in this matter. The subtext of my published and unpublished research is the quest to find some suitable way of analyzing my developmental data in an effort to find as much as I can about the phenomena I am studying. The core of my research has focused on the acquisition of mature forms of thinking during adolescence. My general problem involved finding a way to show that the test of formal thinking I had developed was the same, empirically, as what Inhelder and Piaget (1958) had developed in their ground breaking research. However, it is quite evident from my work with colleagues in developmental, educational, and general psychological research that the concepts with which I was grappling are central to the work that many of us are doing in psychology and the other human sciences. Therefore, although much of the data used in this book for illustrative purposes addresses the research questions on which I and my colleagues have worked, we try to make it clear to the reader that the applications are very widespread in all these fields. Indeed, almost every time I go to a conference presentation that features the Rasch approach to the objective measurement of human variables, I am amazed at the inventiveness of my colleagues in using the Rasch model to address previously unapproachable questions in human research. The uses of Rasch measures to certify medical professionals, to measure customer satisfaction, to detect eating disorders, to estimate posthospitalization rehabilitation, and to make international comparisons of educational achievement, for example, show the widespread potential of these fundamental measurement principles in research with humans.

In my own work at test development, I had used a pretty conventional approach toward statistical analyses. I developed a bank of potential multiple-choice test items based on the rather prescriptive theoretical reasoning provided by the classic text in the field (Inhelder & Piaget, 1958). I argued the construct validity of each and every item meticulously and, in keeping with the conventional wisdom of the time, used point-biserial correlations to help guide me in the refinement and selection of the 35 items that composed the final Bond's Logical Operations Test (BLOT). (The BLOT has point biserials ranging from approximately 0.3 to more than 0.6.)

To check the internal reliability of the test, I used Cronbach's alpha (α = 0.89). For a second indicator of reliability (i.e., of stability over time), I used Pearson's r to correlate test and retest scores ($r = 0.91$; $p < 0.001$; $n = 91$) over an interval of 6 weeks. The big problem came with trying to demonstrate that the ability shown when students completed the BLOT was the same ability as that shown when these same children were given cognitive development subscale allocations based on their problem solving in Piagetian interview situations. The rank order nature of the data prompted me, very predictably, to use Spearman's rho to show the correlation between test and task performances ($r_s = 0.93$; $p < 0.0005$; $n = 30$). I must say that I was very happy with the results in their own terms. You can see from the indications in parentheses that the statistics were quite good.

One thesis examiner undermined my whole satisfaction with this work by arguing that the BLOT and the Piaget tasks could be measuring one whole developmental stage level apart and still produce that high rho result. Given that I had conducted all the interviews personally and knew what had gone into the development of the BLOT, the qualitative and quantitative results had confirmed for me that I really was on to something, but it seemed that the quantitative evidence did not do sufficient justice to the qualitative strengths of the research work.

Luckily, I am persistent (a nice way of saying pigheaded and opinionated), or I would have given up on this style of empirical research, as many others did at that time, would not eventually have realized the errors of conventional wisdom about data analysis in the social sciences, and would not have written this book with Christine Fox. I had 1,000 cases of what I was convinced were pretty good data, and I wanted to be able to reveal their strengths and details in quantitative terms. Or is it just that a poor workman always blames his tools?

Eventually, I realized that my problems raised one very fundamental question of all well-informed psychological research, in which testing, or what is generally called measurement, takes place. Although the questions raised in this volume should come into sharp focus readily for those actually involved in test development, these questions also must become the concern of everyone involved in testing or measuring human abilities. There is nothing so practical as a good theory, and I contend that practical measurement should always start with that: a good theory. For these purposes, I assert that we need a more or less clearly articulated theory or conception of what it is we are setting out to measure, and, of course, why we are bothering to measure it.

That substantive psychological theory (or taxonomy of educational outcomes, profile of rehabilitation, and so on) might be well articulated in a definitive textbook on the subject; might result from years of research, reading, or thinking in the area; or might be defined already in an existing test instrument. Most of us then would be in a position to argue on some sort of theoretical grounds as to why certain items or indicators should be included in a test or checklist and why others should not, on the basis of our chosen theoretical perspective. Christine Fox suggests later that many of her colleagues do not have explicitly elaborated theories concerning the variables they are intent on measuring, but it is immediately clear that for many of them, their item writing is guided by some implicit concept of how their ideas are effective in practice.

A key question then in the analysis of the data is, "How well have my theoretical intentions been empirically realized?" The related question of course is, "How can I tell?" Are the items working together in a way that is explained by the theory? Moreover, does this test of the underlying construct work together with other established or accepted tests in a way that is consistent with the theoretical explanations?

Therefore following the examiner's critique of the analyses in my thesis, I continued to work on the analysis of the data in a part-time sort of way. Naturally, I really worked with Guttman scaling for quite a while, which was the wisdom of the time. Guttman was *the* way for developmental data. I found that I could never include all 35 BLOT items in a true Guttman scale, but I thought there could be enough information in the results to corroborate the existing correlation results. It was possible to construct many pretty good Guttman scales of 10 or 12 items from the original BLOT data set, and many of the items fitted many of the scales.

Anyone who has worked with the Guttman model realizes that its expectations for steplike development of sequential skills are unrealistically strict. There are two sorts of problems. First, Guttman scales expect machine-like precision of responses, in the way that all "classical" or "true-score" statistics do. Each and every person must respond perfectly correctly to items in order of difficulty until his or her ability runs out. Then the person must respond incorrectly to every other item that is more difficult.

Easy → → Difficult
✔ ✔ ✔ ✔ ✔ ✔ X X X X
is allowed,

but
✔ ✔ ✔ ✔ X ✔ X X X X
(a little lack of recent practice of skill 5) is not;

nor is
✔ ✔ ✔ ✔ ✔ X X ✔ X X
(a little educated guestimation);

nor is
X ✔ ✔ ✔ ✔ ✔ ✔ X X X
(a slow, or nervous, start).

We all know that human performance is almost never machine-like and perfect, and most of us know that machines are not perfect performers, especially if you own a personal computer! What would be the point of the Olympic Games if human performance were machine-like and perfect? However, the Guttman model expects machine-like and perfect stepwise progression, as do all the true-score models. Why then are we using it as the model for developmental acquisition of human abilities? We are following conventional wisdom, of course.

The second problem with the Guttman scale relates to including items of similar difficulty in the same scale: You may include either of them but you may not include both. If you are a pragmatist, that is okay. Just dump one! But if you have good theoretical reasons for including both items, then you cannot make a Guttman scale! Simple! Could there be two skills of similar difficulty such that some people can do A but not B, whereas others can do B but not A? Could it be that sometimes I will be able to do A but not B, whereas at other times I will be able to do B but not A? Of course it could. Human life is like that! But not under Guttman principles! I have no problems with the key ideas underlying Guttman's breakthrough concept of orderly development. It is remarkably good. However, the mathematical expression of these ideas do not meet our realistic expectations of what human performance actually is like.

When I came across the first mention of ordering theory in the literature, it seemed as though my search for a statistical method was over. The authors and users of ordering theory seemed to address exactly the problem that I thought I had: How can a number of interrelated Guttman-type scales be incorporated into one hierarchy? It would be possible to show a number of alternative branching paths through a large set of items. I even went so far as to get a FORTRAN listing of an ordering theory analysis program from an overseas colleague and to punch-card it in Australia so I could analyze the BLOT data. It sort of worked. Some items appeared as apparently important nodes in the branches and consequently appeared in a number of paths, whereas others appeared in one path only. Other items of similar difficulty offered alternative paths between the nodes.

Luckily, Mark Wilson and Geoff Masters were in the audience the day I made my ordering theory presentation at an Australian Association for Research in Education (AARE) conference and invited me to their subsequent workshop on Rasch modeling. The questions I appeared to be asking were well answered by Rasch methodology, they claimed, and I had many more questions that only Guttman scaling and ordering theory couldn't begin to address. Indeed, one reason for resorting to correlational and factor analyses in human research is to demonstrate the coherence of tests, and consequently to show that a single ability underlies performance on two or more tests or scales. An American colleague had shown that three Piagetian tasks provided a unifactorial solution under factor analysis (Lawson, 1979). In a point-scoring mood, I had copied his argument to show that the three Piagetian tasks and the BLOT as well also produced a unifactorial solution (i.e., measured a single ability; Bond, 1980). This was good enough in itself, but as long ago as 1941, Ferguson had successfully argued that where item difficulties varied greatly in a data set, the two- or three-factor solutions might merely be an artifact of the large difficulty range alone. Yet, the concept of unidimensionality, represented by the unifactorial solution in factor analysis, remains an important touchstone in psychological research.

A look at the following little two-by-two matrix will show the total possible ways that members of a sample might perform on two items from a test. Suppose we make this a developmental test suitable across a good range of development. (It could just as easily be an achievement test in mathematics or a checklist item on a customer satisfaction scale.) Item P is one of the easier items, whereas item Q requires much more of that ability.

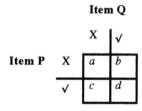

Matrix of possible relations between two test items.

Then:

  a = those students who get both items wrong

  b = those students with easier item wrong, but harder item right

  c = those students with easier item right, but harder item wrong

  d = those students who get both items right.

In the calculation of correlations that are the basis of factor analysis solutions, the results of students in cells *a* and *d* (both wrong or both right) contribute to an increase in the correlation coefficient, whereas the results of students in cells *b* and *c* (wrong/right and right/wrong) detract from the mathematical expression of the relation between the two items. This is fair enough if we are only trying to show that the two items are tapping exactly the same ability. However, in a developmental scale, and in many other human performance scales, the ability shown by item P could be a precursor to the ability underlying item Q. However, it might appear later, perhaps under greater stress, or it might be learned in the next grade, and so on. Therefore, the progression that we explicitly expect, XX, then X✔, and finally ✔✔, has as its second step X✔, easier item right but harder item wrong. However, because of unquestioned conventional wisdom, the observations of X✔ count against the statistical indices that many of us have used to evaluate the success of our empirical efforts.

During my first full year as a full-time researcher, a sabbatical with Michael Shayer and his team at King's College at the University of London, we ran DICOT (Masters, 1984), a little Rasch analysis software program, on a tiny BBC-2 microcomputer. For two committed empirical researchers with decades of experience between us, we found results that were amazing. Using the Rasch model with data sets that we knew pretty well by then, we found out more than we had thought possible. First, we had evidence of a single dimension in each of the data sets. We found that the order of the items along that dimension was revealed, as well as the amount by which the items varied in difficulty. Then we found that the performances of the students we had tested also were displayed on the same single dimension as the items, and with similar meaningful ability distances revealed between the students. The following little example illustrates the idea of what we found:

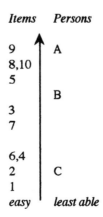

Difficulty levels for 10 items and ability levels for three persons along a single continuum.

These 10 imaginary items are plotted along a single dimension according to their difficulty: Item 9 is the hardest, whereas items 6 and 4 are at the same difficulty level. Person A is the most clever person on this test of 10 items, having scored 9/10. By looking at the items, we can conclude that person A probably missed item 9, the most difficult one. Person B, with a score of 6/10, is likely to have missed the top four (difficult) items (5, 8, 10, and 9), whereas the least able of these persons, C, will have scored 2 out of 10, and probably from the group of four easy items only. These relations are easy to read because Rasch modeling plots persons and items along the same single dimension. (Here are some extra questions to try: What is most likely: person C succeeds on item 7; B succeeds on item 5; or A succeeds on 9? Which item is B more likely to get right, 3 or 5? Which items are all persons likely to find as the easiest? the hardest?) Just imagine your favorite data set represented like that: 35 items and 1,000 persons. Both Shayer and I were impressed!

However, the world never stops still long enough for me to catch up with it. I continually found that as I was getting my mind around these fundamental measurement concepts, the theoreticians were developing their ideas and potential applications faster than I could follow unaided. I have been very fortunate to enjoy almost uninterrupted access to some of the best minds in the business to help me solve my measurement problems and to answer my naïve questions! Mark Wilson from Berkeley has always had a predisposition for the particular problems posed by developmental questions. Geoff Masters and his colleagues from the Australian Council for Educational Research (Peter Congdon, in particular) always shared the insights they had acquired from their experiences with *very* large samples, and, like most others in the field, I can attribute my best lessons and best arguments in measurement to Ben Wright at the University of Chicago.

One of the most fruitful areas for debate and discussion has been how the rationales supporting the use of Rasch modeling for developmental, and education data in particular, and psychological and human sciences data in general became more explicit. I had been drawn originally to Rasch modeling for clearly pragmatic reasons; it provided so much useful, confirmatory information about my research data. However, it became obvious that the superiority of Rasch measurement techniques over many of the statistical analyses most of us learn in quantitative methodology classes was not accidental.

First, the philosophy and mathematical theory underlying Rasch modeling are clearly in empathy with what many of us practicing researchers are trying to discover from our research data. Second, the Rasch-based techniques I was using had very firm bases in general principles of mathematics and measurement that have been expounded gradually by some of the world's leading figures in these fields during the past century. Many philosophers, theoreticians, and mathematicians in the 20th century, for example, Thurstone, Guttman, Loevinger, Kolmogorov, Levy, and Luce and Tukey, among others, independently have elucidated the fundamental basic principles of a mathematically sound and scientifically rigorous measurement theory particularly well adapted to the social sciences.

In keeping with the arguments of Michell (1990), it seems that the majority of psychologists have missed the significance of the Luce and Tukey (1964) description of *conjoint measurement* as the path to the meaningful quantification of psychological variables. Recent examination of Rasch's model by Brogden (1997), Fisher and Wright (1994), Karabatsos (1998), and Wright (1997), among others, has demonstrated the strong connection between the Rasch measurement model and conjoint measurement theory. Therefore, it is not just some dogmatic belief in Rasch modeling that holds it as superior in the analyses we discuss in this volume. The fundamental underlying mathematical principles, what some researchers have called *probabilistic conjoint measurement*, are the keys to the success of this approach. The Rasch family of models happens to be a very compact, efficient, and effective form of what measurement in the human sciences should always be like.

Christine M. Fox

Given that my research experience differs somewhat from that of Bond, I address the key advantages of the Rasch model from my own perspective. Whereas Bond has been using the Rasch model to represent developmental theory empirically, I have been using the Rasch model in consulting with instrument developers across a variety of disciplines, many of whom have no obvious theoretical basis for their measures. Many of the colleagues with whom I work share common assumptions about constructing measures, and I show them how the Rasch model addresses each of these assumptions. Bond's historical perspective relates how, as an empirical researcher, he discovered numerous problems with traditional approaches to analyzing developmental data (e.g., Guttman scaling, ordering theory). Because my perspective stems more from experience in consulting colleagues on the mechanics of test development, I can add to this introduction by highlighting some key features of the Rasch model that I point out to these colleagues as we progress through the test development process.

I have been studying and applying principles of educational and psychological research, measurement, and statistics for the past 12 years. I typically characterize my background as that of an applied generalist. My work is applied in the sense that I act as liaison between statisticians and researchers in disciplines such as health education, counseling psychology, higher education, and early childhood, helping them to choose, analyze, and interpret a variety of statistical analyses. I am a generalist, however, in that I do not specialize only in statistical applications. I also teach, consult, and publish on topics related to research design, evaluation, and measurement.

My interest in the Rasch model, which began during my doctoral training, has steadily increased over the past 5 years. During this time, the bulk of my teaching load has consisted of graduate-level statistics classes. Although I enjoy helping students make connections among various statistical concepts, I often become frustrated when interpreting the results. As I verbalized the conclusions represented by numbers on a computer output, I too often realized that these interpretations were based on simplistic inferences from poorly conceptualized measures. Of course, we as a class had taken the time to check our data carefully and to match our statistical analysis with both our scale of measurement and our research question. However, we had not *first* adequately operationalized our construct such that we could make any sensible claims about relations among variables! How then could the class intelligently discuss statistical results without adequate empirical evidence for the construct we were purporting to measure?

Common Assumptions in Measurement Practice

Operationalizing and then measuring variables are two of the necessary first steps in the empirical research process. Statistical analysis, as a tool for investigating relations among the measures, then follows. Thus, interpretations of analyses can be only as good as the quality of the measures. Why then are students and researchers seemingly unconcerned about how they measure those constructs? I do not mean to suggest that these people do not put care into their research. On the contrary, I see much meticulous work performed every day, and in every discipline. However, what I am suggesting is that the same care that goes into literature reviews, formulation of hypotheses, and choice of statistical analysis is not given to the fundamental question of *measurement* as well. I am suggesting that sound measurement is the piece of the puzzle on which accurate inferences are hinged, and hence it is this very piece on which careful thought and analysis must be placed.

Let us investigate some of the assumptions being made when typical scale development practice is used. First, a researcher develops a group of items intended to assess a construct. After administering these items to a sample of respondents, the responses are aggregated to form a total scale value. For example, suppose a researcher develops an eating disorder scale, wherein high total scores would indicate persons with more eating disorder problems and low total scores would indicate persons with fewer problems. Items are scored on a 5-point scale: 1 (strongly disagree), 2 (disagree), 3 (neutral), 4 (agree), and 5 (strongly agree). We shall imagine that a few of the items looked like this:

	SD	D	N	A	SA
1. I vomit regularly to control my weight.	1	2	3	4	5
2. I count the fat grams of the food I eat.	1	2	3	4	5
3. I exercise solely to burn calories.	1	2	3	4	5

If the rating scale responses for one individual were 2, 4, and 5, respectively, traditional practice would consist of assigning this person a score of 11 on the eating disorder scale. This 11 then would be used as the "measure" in subsequent statistical analyses. Another individual who responded 5, 5, and 1 also would receive the same score of 11. Two assumptions are being made by summing the ratings in this way: (a) Each item contributes equally (i.e., is valued equally) to the measure of the eating disorder construct, and (b) each item is measured on the same interval scale. Let us take each assumption in turn.

According to the first assumption, treating items equally implies that all items are of identical importance in the assessment of the construct. It seems nonsensical to treat these three qualitatively different items as equal contributors to a total eating disorder scale. For example, strong agreement with the first item indicates a greater problem than does strong agreement with the third item. Also, it could be argued that item 2 is a fairly low-level concern with respect to eating issues. Thus, when items represent different levels on a given construct (i.e., different levels of severity), should the data not be analyzed so that the total score reflects this "value" of the item's contribution to the total scale value? Surely a response of "strongly agree" on item 1 should contribute more to an overall eating disorder score than an answer of "strongly agree" to item 2.

The second assumption is that of an equal interval scale. The addition of rating scale categories 1 through 5 implies that the distance between each scale point is uniform both within and across items. Let us take the first item on the fictitious eating disorder scale. It is very likely that the rating categories of "agree" and "strongly agree" are very close to one another (psychologically) for the respondents. Likewise, "disagree" and "strongly disagree" might be perceived as close. Thus, if I mapped the psychological distance between rating scale points for that item, it might look like this:

1. I vomit regularly to control my weight.   SD   D   N   A   SA

This spacing illustrates how the psychological leap from endorsing disagreement (D) to endorsing agreement (A) can be quite large (i.e., one either vomits regularly or does not vomit regularly), but how the subtle gradations within agreement (A or SA) or disagreement (D or SD) categories are not so clear-cut. For example, for a respondent who did not regularly vomit to control weight (item 1), it would be fairly easy to check either "disagree" or "strongly disagree" because the psychological distance between those two choices is very close. However, it would be much more difficult for that respondent to check "agree" or "strongly agree." That is, the psychological distance between agreement and disagreement categories is quite large in this example.

This lack of linearity within items also can be manifested across items. That is, the value of distances between the rating scale categories might differ for each item. For example, A and SA may be a short psychological "leap" for some items, but not for others. The practice of summing raw item ratings to form a total score ignores this phenomenon, and is yet another compromise in the precision of measurement when total raw scores are treated as measures of the construct. Therefore, our three-item eating disorder scale might be more accurately conceptualized like this as a consequence:

1. I vomit regularly to control my weight.   SD   D   N   A   SA
2. I count the fat grams of the food I eat.   SD   DN   A SA
3. I exercise solely to burn calories.   SD   DN   A   SA

In understanding the need to use a measurement model that addresses these assumptions commonly made in practice, researchers can begin to treat measurement with as much rigor as they treat other aspects of the research process. The Rasch model provides not only a mathematically sound alternative to traditional approaches, but its application across disciplines can be understood easily by nonpsychometricians when they struggle to operationalize their research constructs. Furthermore, the results produce measures that adequately represent one's construct with a replicable and meaningful set of measures. Without this foundation for empirical investigations, good research design and advanced statistical analyses are of little use in advancing knowledge. How accurate are conclusions about any psychological phenomenon when the phenomenon has not even been *measured* carefully in the first place?

Applications of Measurement Principles Across Disciplines

As a consultant to other faculty in my college, I have been steadily increasing the frequency with which I introduce the Rasch model as a help in the investigation of research problems. I typically begin by inquiring about the construct the researchers intend to measure, for example, obtaining sample items and descriptions of persons they think would "score high" on this measure and those who would "score low." I then work with them to rough out their items across a line of inquiry. That is, I ask them to identify which items they expect are easier to answer, and which are more difficult to answer. These decisions, which aid the researchers in explicating the construct of interest, typically are based on either theory or experience and aimed at getting them to make their theories or conceptualizations of the variable explicit.

Completely skipping mathematical explanations, I then analyze the results for them. Output from the Rasch analysis informs the researcher of the empirical hierarchy of items, as estimated by the computer program. Together we compare this hierarchy to the one hypothesized in advance, discussing any discrepancies between the two. In addition to this information, items that do not fit along this continuum, persons who do not respond in expected ways, and gaps along the line of inquiry are clearly identified for future iterations of item writing.

The receptiveness to this process has been overwhelming. Researchers who previously knew little of measurement have been telling their colleagues of the interpretability and usefulness of this analysis. As Bond expressed earlier in this preface, they "found out more than they thought possible." The following sections discuss some of the ideas encompassed by the Rasch model that are readily accepted as commonsense guidelines to nonpsychometricians across a variety of disciplines.

The Idea of Measuring a Single Variable. The Rasch model is based on the idea that data must conform to some reasonable hierarchy of "less than/more than" on a single continuum of interest. For example, if one is assessing the motivation of teachers working with families of special needs children, the assumption is that some teachers are more motivated than others. We do not have a variable unless people express individual differences on the characteristic being measured. By attempting to measure this variable, the researcher is implicitly acknowledging that although teachers have many important and distinctive characteristics, only one characteristic can be meaningfully rated at a time, conceptualizing the variable as a continuum of "more than/less than." Investigators always have some preconceived implicit notion of a meaningful hierarchy, even in the absence of an explicit theory, and when they make explicit to themselves the idea of a hierarchy, they are taking the first step in both understanding their construct and writing a set of items that will measure a range of motivation, ability, agreement, satisfaction, and so forth on that continuum.

Translating this idea into a mathematical model is a simple process. The Rasch model uses the traditional total score (e.g., the sum of the item ratings) as a starting point for estimating *probabilities* of responding. The model is based on the simple idea that all persons are more *likely* to answer easy items correctly than difficult items, and all items are more likely to be passed by persons of high ability than by those of low ability. You will recall that Bond's questions about the earlier Rasch scale example were asked in the form of "what was *most likely.*" This terminology also can be altered to reflect the language relevant to self-reports or behavioral data measured on rating scales. For example, the term "high item difficulty" can be replaced by the term "difficult to endorse," and "high person ability" can be replaced by the term "agreeability." Thus, persons who have high total scores on the variable in question are more agreeable overall than persons with low scores. Likewise, items that receive lower ratings are more difficult to endorse than items that receive higher ratings.

This idea of measuring a single variable is depicted with a map of persons and items on the same scale. Our example illustrated this with persons A, B, and C responding to items 1 through 10. This illustration clearly shows that the test developer can clearly identify (a) which items are more difficult than others and which persons are more able than others, (b) gaps along the continuum where items are missing, and (c) how well the difficulties of the items are matched to the abilities of the sample.

Validity Indices.   Rasch analysis provides two sets of general guidelines to help the researcher to determine the validity of a set of measures. First, the researcher must assess whether all the items work together to measure a single variable. The researcher originally had constructed the items to form a hierarchy, but this assumption must be empirically tested. Similarly, each person's response pattern must be examined, that is, assessed to determine whether the person was responding in an acceptably predictable way given the expected hierarchy of responses (Wright & Stone, 1979).

When taking a test or completing a survey, some respondents might, for example, occasionally guess at the answers, work so slowly that they do not finish in the allotted time, or misinterpret the directions. Surely, the researcher would not want to place trust in the total scores for those individuals. Likewise, some particular items might not be working well with the bulk of the test items: They might be tapping a different construct from the other items, or they might be written so ambiguously that the responses are inconsistent. Such items would show as not measuring the single construct under investigation, and hence should be rewritten or excluded. The point is that the Rasch model provides estimates for each item and each individual separately. These tell the researcher the relative value of every one of the person measures and item difficulty estimates. The investigator can flag these particular persons or items for closer inspection, perhaps giving the individuals additional testing or rewriting the questions, but certainly not blindly interpreting the total raw score for all persons on all items as the total construct measure!

A second way to assess the validity of a test is through examination of the item ordering. This involves matching the empirical hierarchy with the theoretical/experiential basis for item development. Inconsistencies between the two must be examined carefully, with consideration that the source of the problem might stem from either the theoretical basis or the empirical results.

These guidelines used in constructing meaningful measures challenge researchers to explicate the form that a useful measure of any single construct might take. Examination of the data analysis then supports some ideas and questions others. For example, what might originally have been thought of as the "best" item may in fact measure people less precisely than expected. Additionally, items that do not work well might highlight research assumptions, misconceptions about the construct, or problems in the operationalization of the theory. The point here is that the construction of measures is an iterative process that encourages thoughtful investigation. Engagement in this process results in a set of measures both more meaningful to the researcher and more valid in its inferences.

Implications for the Practice of Measurement. The Rasch approach
to investigating measures illustrates an appreciation of the dialectical nature of
the measurement process: Theory informs practice, and practice informs theory.
It is indeed very difficult to escape the traditional statistics mind-set, which depends on arbitrary and more-or-less inviolable cutoffs such as $p < 0.05$ or $p <$
0.01 as the deciding point for truth or falsehood in human research, as the point
at which we "reject" or "fail to reject" the null hypothesis.

From our viewpoint, every item you write puts either the theory, your understanding of it, or your ability to translate it into an empirical indicator on the
line. Tossing out items might be fine if you have trawled up a huge bunch of
"possible" items and are looking for the "probables" to keep in your test. However, if you have developed items that encapsulate for you the very essence of
the theory or construct to which you are attached, then all the items are
probables. In fact, you might consider all of them as somehow indispensable!
Thus, whereas your theory tells you how to write the item, the item's performance should tell you about your theory, your understanding of it, or your item-
writing skills. Under these circumstances, you do not want to trash an item, a
bunch of items, or your theory because $p > 0.05$, for heaven's sake! You want to
find out what went wrong. You want your items to be the best possible reflection of your theory and your ability to translate it into practice, and you want
your items to tell you about your theory, whether it is good enough, whether
some bits need rejigging, or whether it is time to toss it and get a new theory.
The measurement model you see in this text invites you to enter into a dialectical process in which theory informs practice via measurement and practice
informs theory via measurement.

We all understand one of the principles underlying post-Popperian falsi-
ficationism: If P then Q; not Q, then not P. The conventional wisdom goes thus:
If (theory) P is true, then (practical outcome) Q is true as its consequence. We
look around and find not-Q (i.e., practical outcome Q is false). We then conclude that theory P must be false as well. This is the received view of falsifi-
cationism as often applied in the human sciences.

One crucial question that we overlook asks: *Who* decides that Q is the critical
practical consequence of theory P? If an item in a test is the expression of Q and
the item fails to measure up, is the theory wrong? Is the interpretation of theory
to practice amiss? Is the item just poorly written? or Did we give it to the wrong
sample? In test construction, theory P has a number of related Q consequences:
Q_1 (an interpretation into practice), Q_2 (a well-constructed item), Q_3 (administration to an appropriate sample), and so on. Typically, we do not see ourselves at
fault (e.g., my poor understanding or interpretation of the theory; my far-fetched
practical outcome; my substandard item writing; my poor sample selection; or,
even, my poor choice of data analysis technique). Instead, we lay the blame on
(i.e., disprove) the theory.

Moreover, most worthwhile theories of the human condition are necessarily complex—just as humans are complex. As some of its important consequences, very useful complex theory P is likely to have propositions such as Q, R, S, T, U, V, and the like, some aspects of which, say, Q_3, S_3, T_4, and V_5, might be argued as having measurable, empirical consequences. Therefore, finding V_5 to be false *does not* require the ditching of theory P. With a complex theory P, which has a number of interrelated consequences as shown earlier, what we need is to establish a dialogue between the theoretical aspects of our investigations and our realization of those theoretical intentions as they are manifested in practice. This can be achieved by the informed use of the principles of measurement that we espouse in this textbook.

In the following chapters, we flesh out the principles and applications of the Rasch model, using computer applications of real data sets to illustrate the main points. Throughout the chapters, we more fully address the themes presented in this preface: order (e.g., unidimensionality, hierarchy) and amount (interval measurement), the substantive meaning of the construct (and the implications of its operationalization), and the dialectic between theory and practice.

ACKNOWLEDGMENTS

Of course, despite all the work that we have put into writing and editing our textbook, we must acknowledge that we have benefited substantially from the input of our colleagues and our students in order to be able to bring our plans to fruition. A string of long-suffering and intelligent students have demanded from us clearly expressed conceptualizations of Rasch modeling principles. Indeed, teaching them has been the single greatest stimulus to the clarity of the ideas that we express in the next dozen or so chapters. In particular, we thank Carla Drake, Jacqui Russell, Lorna Endler, Bev Stanbridge, David Lake, Kellie Parkinson, Marcia Ditmyer, Tina Ughrin, Tom Mcloughlin, Tony Miller, Svetlana Beltyukova, and Daniel Cipriani for the questions they have asked of us. One of the particularly useful outcomes of being involved in the research projects of our colleagues has been the interaction required in tapping the almost limitless measurement resources of the Rasch model to address what began as the data analysis problems of our colleagues. Noteworthy in that regard have been the interactions with Gino Coudé, Gerald Noelting, Jean Pierre Rousseau, Michael Shayer, Bill Gray, Theo Dawson, John King, Ulrich Müller, Willis Overton, Bryan Sokol, Chris Lalonde, Dick Meinhard, and Jonas Cox.

It seems as though the writing of this book necessarily implies some sort of criticism directed at the other Rasch-based texts currently available. On this count, we must plead guilty with extenuating circumstances. The major textbooks in the field, those by Andrich (1988), McNamara (1996), Wright and

Masters (1982), and Wright and Stone (1979), are well suited to their purposes, and we have found them to be wonderful resources for our own work. Indeed, we find key passages in each of these texts to be wonderful models of conceptual clarity. Our focus here has been somewhat different. We have tried to communicate these ideas in a fresh and practical way to those who are not enamored with a mathematical disposition to research life. In this, we must thank our Rasch-author colleagues for the help they have inadvertently given us. We have also benefited from the generous and unstinting support of Rasch colleagues around the world. Although it would be impossible to list all those who have helped us in this regard, the following are particularly noteworthy examples of generous collegiality: Peter Congdon, Geoff Masters, Mike Linacre, Margaret Wu, Ray Adams, Mark Wilson, George Karabatsos, and Richard Smith. Like almost every Anglophone who gets hooked by the Rasch measurement bug, we must acknowledge a debt greater than we realize to Ben Wright for his long-term, committed, patient expounding of Georg Rasch's ideas, as well as for his exemplary collegial mentoring of our work.

You will see in the body of the text that a number of the research colleagues have contributed segments of their own research to be included as exemplars of the analyses we describe. That usually involved their effort to seek out suitable research reports, discuss the interpretation of their work with us, and then review our attempts to communicate their ideas to our audience. Our thanks go to Gerald Noelting, Theo Dawson, George Engelhard, Karen Draney, and Mark Wilson.

Dick Meinhard, William Fisher, and Tina Ughrin gave critical feedback to early drafts of key chapters, and Leslie Smith and Kurt Fisher supported presentations of the ideas that now form parts of chapter 2.

A number of our graduate students from the University of Toledo have made very practical and substantial contributions to this publication. Both Lei Yu and Song Yan have worked diligently at the construction of the glossary, and have provided research assistance to us during important writing phases. Lei also developed the chapter 5 instructions for the Excel spreadsheet that originated with Peter Congdon. Tami Schultz used her time and considerable information technology skills to produce the illustrations that now grace these pages. The original illustrations for the early chapters looked as though they had been drawn with "a thumbnail dipped in tar." Jolene Miller took control of the reference list, collating the various e-mail messages, electronic lists, and scraps of paper that we generated to produce the verified list at the end of the book. Jolene then constructed both the subject and author indexes; our heartfelt thanks.

This book could not have been completed without the support of the University of Toledo during the time when Trevor Bond visited as Distinguished Visiting Professor in the College of Education. Acting assistant dean, Bill Gray, who has been a colleague of both authors, applied for research funding to facilitate Bond's visit, organized office space, and personally provided accommodation and transport for the duration. Leave to undertake a Special Studies Program funded by James Cook University provided the much-needed break from teaching and administrative tasks, which allowed Bond the opportunity to collaborate with Fox to complete the writing and editing tasks.

We also thank Richard Smith in his role as founding editor of both the *Journal for Outcome Measurement* and the *Journal of Applied Measurement*. He has given those working in Rasch measurement an opportunity to submit articles for consideration in an academic journal that is disposed toward, rather than prejudiced against, Rasch-based research. We trust that our readers will be able to apply the knowledge they have gained from the following chapters to a critical appreciation of the research work published under Smith's guiding editorial hand. Our thanks go to the members of the Rasch Special Interest Group (SIG) of the American Educational Research Association, and the contributors to the Rasch listserve who continue to challenge and support our developing concepts of the Rasch modeling role. The organizers and participants involved with the biennial International Objective Measurement Workshops and the Midwest Objective Measurement Seminars continue to be both critical and supportive at the same time, a credit to the idea of academia as open critical inquiry. Grudging thanks to those colleagues who demanded a 10-minute summary of Rasch modeling at the end of conference presentations. Now you can go and read the book!

Fortunately, one colleague stands head and shoulders above even all these. William Fisher supported this book from the moment he heard about the project. He challenged and encouraged us to expand our self-imposed horizons and to write for a more general audience. He helped us when we struggled, and then took on the invidious task of being a "critical friend" by critiquing the whole draft manuscript in record time before we sent it to the publishers.

Although we at every point have argued that the basis of scientific measurement is grounded explicitly in substantive theory, we have avoided trying to teach these theories to our readers. We presume they will have theories of their own to which they are attached. Those doubting our devotion to construct validity could turn to the original research reports on which our worked examples are based. The worked examples are just that: examples that show the key features of the Rasch family of measurement models. We have made our data available to you (see Appendix B). You are encouraged to access the Rasch software of your choice and to use our control files to analyze the data for yourselves.

In the end, however, we must admit that, despite all the opportunities that we have had to benefit from the input of our students and colleagues, the responsibility for the errors and inadequacies that remain lies entirely with us.

—*Trevor G. Bond*
—*Christine M. Fox*

APPLYING THE RASCH MODEL:
FUNDAMENTAL MEASUREMENT
IN THE HUMAN SCIENCES

1

Why Measurement Is Fundamental

Researchers in the quantitative tradition in the human sciences typically fail to realize their potential to produce high-quality, experimental science. This is evidenced by their explicit lack of rigor when measuring human variables. Although researchers in commerce and engineering routinely trust their physical measures (e.g., attributes such as weight, mass, volume, and length are deemed consistent and accurate), to date this has not been demanded of psychological measures as well. Without deliberate, thoughtful, and scientific construction of measures, psychosocial research will continue to progress slowly. The results of efforts so far are flawed conclusions about critical issues such as children's education, the diagnosis and treatment of patients with mental illness, and the certification of physicians, to name a few. The quality of the inferences made, and hence subsequent policy and training decisions, hinge directly on the scientific quality of the measures used.

What psychologists and others in the human sciences have been effective at doing, however, is applying sophisticated statistical procedures to their data. Although statistical analysis is a necessary and important part of the scientific process, and we in no way would ever wish to replace the role that statistics play in examining relations between variables, the argument throughout this book is that quantitative researchers in the human sciences are too narrowly focused on statistical analysis, and not concerned nearly enough about the quality of the measures on which they use these statistics. Therefore, it is not the authors' purpose to replace quantitative statistics with fundamental measurement, but rather to refocus some of the time and energy used for data analysis on the construction of quality scientific measures.

THE CURRENT STATE
OF PSYCHOLOGICAL MEASUREMENT

The psychological definition of measurement differs from that used in the physical sciences. It is based on Stevens' (1946) definition of *measurement* as the "assignment of numerals to objects or events according to a rule" (Michell, 1997). This definition, coupled with complete ignorance of the fact that for an attribute (construct) to be measurable it must possesses an additive structure (Michell, 1999), has led psychologists to ignore not only the structure of quantitative attributes, but also the importance of the falsifiability of current "measurement" practices based on Stevens' approach.

What then happens in practice is that psychometricians, behavioral statisticians, and their like conduct research as if the mere assignment of numerical values to objects suffices as scientific measurement (Michell, 1997). This is evidenced by such widespread practices as summing values from responses to a Likert scale and treating the total score as if it were a measure. The lack of empirical rigor in such a practice is indefensible. Numbers are assigned to response categories to produce ordinal-level data, after which these numbers are summed to produce a total score. This total score then is used in subsequent statistical analyses. The ordinal data are treated as if they were interval-level data, and no hypotheses are tested to acknowledge that this particular assignment of numbers represents a falsifiable hypothesis. Hence, the additive structure of these quantitative attributes is summarily ignored. Quantitative researchers in the human sciences need to stop analyzing raw data or counts, and instead analyze measures.

THE CONSTRUCTION
OF SCIENTIFIC MEASURES

Scientific measures in the social sciences must hold to the same standards as do measures in the physical sciences if they are going to lead to the same quality of generalizations. That is, they must be objective abstractions of equal units. Measures must meet these criteria to be both reproducible and additive. These are basic requirements for any scientific quantitative attributes.

Objectivity, the key to scientific measurement, requires that the measure assigned to the attribute/construct be independent of the observer. This is not the case with traditional psychological measures (in the Stevens tradition), in which measures are confounded with the sample of respondents. As defined by classical test theory, the difficulty of an item is defined as the proportion of people passing an item. This definition alone tells us that the difficulty of an item depends directly on the distribution of the abilities of the persons who responded to the item. Imagine this logic in the physical sciences, telling a person that the height of 6 feet on a ruler depends on what the person is measuring!

Traditional test theory in the social sciences thus confounds the item calibration and the measurement of the attribute. Measurement instruments must first be created, and the units calibrated, so that we all agree on the reproducibility of their locations. Only then are we justified in using these instruments to measure how tall, heavy, anxious, bright, or stressed a person is. The construction of clocks, thermometers, or the Richter scale illustrates the point. These instruments had a long history of careful calibration before they ever were reliably used to measure time, temperature, or the magnitude of an earthquake. The fact that the Richter scale was named after an American seismologist who helped to devise a scale for measuring the strength of earthquakes points to the historical practice of deliberately constructing scales for measuring.

How then do researchers go about constructing objective measures in the human sciences? Some common physical measures such as weight can serve as examples. Weight is a fiction, a useful abstraction that partially solves the problem of different-size products in trade and commerce. Weight is divided into equal units so we can use the same measurement criterion or "ruler" every time we want to buy produce, for example. Weight, as we know it today, has been so useful in producing reliable estimates of amount only because, over time, groups of people deliberately decided to create a set of units, with the goal of advancing fair practice in trade and commerce. The same can be said for volume, mass, and length. This is exactly what needs to be done in the social sciences. Abstractions of equal units must be created and calibrated over sufficiently large samples so that we are confident in their utility. Then these abstractions can be used to measure attributes of our human subjects.

OBSERVATION VERSUS INFERENCE

Once psychologists have created objective measures, abstractions of equal units that represent a particular quantitative attribute, they too will have reproducible measures, just as in the physical sciences. Only then can inferences regarding underlying constructs, rather than descriptions of superficial raw data, be made. The goal is to create abstractions that transcend the raw data, just as in the physical sciences, so that inferences can be made about constructs rather than mere descriptions about raw data.

Measurement in the Stevens tradition chains our thinking to the level of raw data. Under the pretense of measuring, psychologists describe the raw data at hand. They report how many people answered the item correctly (or agreed with the item), how highly related one response is to another, and what the correlation is between each item and total score. These are mere descriptions. Although psychologists generally agree on what routinely counts as "measurement" in the human sciences, this usage cannot replace measurement as it is known in the physical sciences. Yet the flurry of activity surrounding all these statistical analyses, coupled with blind faith in the attributions of numbers to events, have blinded psychologists, in particular, to the inadequacy of these methods. Michell (1997) is quite blunt about this in his article entitled "Quantitative Science and the Definition of Measurement in Psychology," in which psychologists' "sustained failure to cognize relatively obvious methodological facts" is termed *"methodological thought disorder"*(p. 374).

When we ask a child to stand against a yardstick or step onto a scale, we are depending on a replicable instrument to help us make inferences about an abstraction. The abstractions in this example are height and weight, respectively, yet we do not typically think of them as abstractions because we are so used to them in our daily lives. Yet in the human sciences, we clearly are dealing with abstractions (e.g., perceived social support, cognitive ability, and self-esteem), so we need to construct measures of abstractions, using equal units, so that we can make inferences about constructs rather than remain at the level of describing our data.

SCALE CONSTRUCTION
IN THE PHYSICAL SCIENCES

Many who work in the human sciences reject completely the idea of trying to measure any human attributes at all. They regard all human attributes as too complicated to be subjected to the insulting process of reductionism to mere numbers. Numbers can be used in descriptions of objects, but they may not be used in relation to subjects. Of course, most psychometricians do not share such qualms. Psychometricians have spent more than a century trying to quantify a whole range of somewhat intangible human traits. However, they often regard the precise objective measurement that has been the touchstone of the physical sciences as being far beyond their own meager reach.

At least part of this outlook has come about because human scientists remain quite ignorant as to how physical measures came into being. They remain unaware of how much time, money, and effort still are committed to the construction, calibration, and maintenance of the measurement units we routinely use every day. Moreover, most of us think that physical measures are absolutely precise when they are routinely imprecise. We regard physical measures as error free, when in fact systematic and random errors are acknowledged by those who specialize in their use. Yet, we always double and triple check our measurement of linear dimensions when the fit has to be "just so," but then rely on a "one-shot" achievement test from last year, for example, to place young Mary into a reading group at school. If quantitative researchers in the human sciences see the attainment of such quality measures as beyond their grasp, it is perhaps because, on the one hand, we overestimate the quality of our physical measures while, on the other hand, we underestimate the quality of the tools we currently have for constructing and maintaining objective measures in the human sciences.

A brief historical look at the experimental techniques of Galileo will help us to understand how time might have been measured in the era before clocks, whereas the problems of measuring time at the beginning of the 21st century will show that the task still is not yet taken for granted. It also is rather helpful to look at how temperature has been conceptualized and measured, because much historical information about this relatively recent development in physical science methods is available to inform us about the procedures involved. Although measuring the passage of time is crucially fundamental to many of the physical and human sciences, we tend to forget that most of us see time as measured by the angular distance that a sweep second hand might move around a stopwatch dial.

Galileo's *Two New Sciences* reported how he substituted rolling balls down an inclined plane for his previous experiments with free-falling objects. This allowed him more control of the experimental situation. In particular, it allowed him the opportunity of making more precise measurements. In the 17th century, however, there were no set standards for the measurement of length, so Galileo resorted to arbitrary units, which he replicated along the rolling track to standardize his estimates of length. To estimate the intervals of time required for the balls to traverse the marked sections of track, he collected the volume of water that spurted through a narrow pipe in the base of a large elevated container. The water collected for any interval then was weighed on a very accurate beam balance. The differences between the weights and the ratios between them allowed for the estimation of the relative time intervals. Of course, the process of weighing also was somewhat indirect: Equality of the weights in opposing pans of the balance beam was inferred from the level beam—the moments of force around the central pivot point were held to be equal when equal weights were suspended from equal arms in the absence of friction. What an interesting set of inferential leaps and scientific theories underlies this attempt to measure equal intervals of the time construct (Sobel, 1999).

The construction of the thermometer was developed in a similar manner. What began as human sensations of "hot" and "cold" eventually evolved into the field of thermometrics (i.e., the measurement of temperature). Early records of attempts to construct temperature scales date back to A.D. 180, with Galen mixing equal quantities of ice and boiling water to establish a "neutral" point for a seven-point scale having three levels of warmth and three levels of coldness. Techniques slowly improved throughout the centuries. Scientists in the 17th century, including Galileo, are credited with the early successful work in this area. Santorio of Padua first reported using a tube of air inverted in a container of water, so that the water level rose and fell with temperature changes. Subsequently, he calibrated the scale by marking the water levels at the temperatures of flame and ice. Necessarily, these instruments ignored the systematic errors caused by changes in the volume of the glass and the liquid that occurred during the instrument's use. Neither could contemporaries explain why different liquids behaved in different ways to produce estimates of temperature.

The famous Celsius and Fahrenheit scales, each named for its originator, merely set two known temperature points (e.g., ice and boiling points) and divided the scale into equal units or degrees (e.g., 100). Robert Hooke of the Royal Institute in London defined a scale in which 1° Fahrenheit was defined as "a change of 1/10,000 in the volume of a given body of mercury" and used one fixed calibration point. Despite the publication of detailed construction and calibration instructions, Hooke's attempts at temperature measurement had little influence at the time. Although measures of temperature proliferated, Hooke-based temperature measures often did not match measures based on other models, such as the transfer of heat from one liquid to another, or those based on expansion-of-air models. (This sounds familiar. It seems as though there is still hope for psychometrics.)

In approximately 1850, Lord Kelvin's theoretical structure, known as thermodynamics, was accepted as the standard practice and used for 75 years. His additive model posited that the addition of heat units to a given body would change the temperature of that body by that same number of units. This property held regardless of where on the scale the units of heat were added. This measure of heat was based on hydrogen because it was determined that hydrogen provided the best approximation at that time of his model based on the behavior of an ideal gas.

Twentieth-century work has added to Kelvin's hydrogen expansion thermometer (e.g., platinum resistance thermometers and platinum/rhodium thermocouples; Choppin, 1985) to measure temperature changes outside the precision range of the Kelvin scale. Although we commonly use the approximate estimates of temperature provided by mercury and alcohol thermometers, and although we control refrigerators, air conditioners, and car cooling systems with bimetallic strips, even the best temperature-measurement devices based on the models described here show inconsistencies between the various methods at different temperatures.

What we can learn from the process of thermometer construction is that the construction of a reproducible measurement system is always under revision. There is no one true model, and no model comes without imprecision. Working glass thermometers were useful in medicine long before we figured out why they worked, yet these very same thermometers, on which life-and-death decisions are sometimes made, are next to useless for many other temperature-measurement uses. We even have to know how and where to position the medical glass thermometer for it to be fully useful. Yet working within that imprecision, acknowledging it, and proceeding to construct measures despite imprecision, is critical to the advancement of science. Even incorrect models, as long as they are based on the creation of additive structures, are very useful in solving current scientific problems. (This brief coverage relies heavily on the work of Choppin, 1985.)

One of the cover stories in the June 2000 issue of *Discover* magazine reports, in layperson's terms, the difficulties that currently beset those who maintain watch over the world's time. Although the passage of time was previously marked by sunrise and sunset, and more recently by pendulum clocks, which also are calibrated against the rotation of the earth, inconsistencies in our planet's shape and movement make it unreliable as a basis for the measurement of time. From 1967, the standard definition of the period of 1 second moved to the atomic scale based on the radiation of the cesium 133 atom. Although the $650,000 cesium clock in Boulder, Colorado, estimates the passing of 1 second with almost unbelievable precision, it does not directly keep time. The keeping of the international time standard is the responsibility of the Paris Observatory. Moreover, it is based on an average. The time estimates of more than 200 atomic clocks from around the world are routinely collected, averaged, and fed back to the originating laboratories so that the computer-generated records on the passage of time at each laboratory can be adjusted regularly for the local clock's deviation from the world average, even if it is somewhat after the fact (Klinkenborg, 2000). We could wonder what such a well-funded and well-coordinated international effort might produce in terms of measuring just one key human attribute.

THE RASCH MODEL

The previous examples illustrate not only the necessity for creating universal scales of equal intervals, but also the imprecision inherent in this process. Scientific measurement begins with an idea of what we want to measure, whether it be time, temperature, social status, or achievement. For those working in the human sciences, the realization of these ideas often comes in the form of item writing "aimed at eliciting signs of the intended variable in the behavior of the persons" (Wright & Stone, 1979).

In the human sciences, we currently have only one readily accessible tool to help us construct objective, additive scales: the Rasch model. This model can help transform raw data from the human sciences into abstract, equal-interval scales. Equality of intervals is achieved through log transformations of raw data odds, and abstraction is accomplished through probabilistic equations. Finally, unlike other probabilistic measurement models, the Rasch model is the only one that provides the necessary objectivity for the construction of a scale that is separable from the distribution of the attribute in the persons it measures.

The ideas of fundamental measurement are not new to the human sciences. In 1926, Thorndike expressed the need for an equal-interval scale in which "zero will represent just not any of the ability in question, and 1, 2, 3, 4, and so on will represent amounts increasing by a constant difference" (Thorndike, 1926, p. 4). Thurstone's "absolute scale" (1925, 1927) approximated an equal-interval scale. However, it was not objective because it was dependent on the ability distribution of the persons using the scale (Wright & Stone, 1979).

In 1947, Loevinger noted the need for objectivity in measurement by saying that "an acceptable method of scaling must result in a derived scale which is independent of the original scale and of the original group tested" (Loevinger, 1947, p. 46). This sentiment was reiterated by Gulliksen (1950) and Tucker (1953), and later by Angoff (1960), who said that "a test which is to have continued usefulness must have a scale which does not change with the times, which will permit acquaintance and familiarity with the system of units, and which will permit an accumulation of data for historical comparisons" (p. 815). Despite these expressions of inadequacy throughout the history of psychometrics, the Stevens tradition has remained predominant, with psychologists suffering from what Michell (1997) coined as "methodological thought disorder."

Current methods for constructing objective, empirical approximations of abstract concepts are based on logistic distributions (Wright & Stone, 1979). In the 1960s, Georg Rasch proposed a simple logistic model (Andrich, 1988) as the basis for constructing objective measures in psychology as he "became aware of the problem of defining the difficulty of an item independently of the population and the ability of an individual independently of which items he has actually solved" (Rasch, 1960, p. viii). Rasch and others inspired by his groundbreaking work then went on to develop a family of probabilistic models to solve this very problem.

When we analyze our data using a Rasch model, we get an estimate of what our construct might be like if we were to create a ruler to measure it. The Rasch model provides us with useful approximations of measures that help us understand the processes underlying the reason why people and items behave in a particular way. These approximations help us to solve problems that cannot be solved currently with any other model. It is therefore our intention in this book to demonstrate the utility of the Rasch model, the only model to date that provides the tools for approximating objective reproducible additive measures in the human sciences.

2

Important Principles of
Measurement Made Explicit

Although this volume is about using a particular version of one approach to the quantitative analyses of data from the human sciences, it raises a number of problems and principles endemic to the investigation of almost any human performance. It seems reasonable to suggest that both qualitative and quantitative analyses of developmental observations are designed to yield summaries of those observations. The aim is to produce a shortened account of the results from the investigation sufficient to communicate the essence of the empirical data in a meaningful, useful, or valid way. Although it currently is the fashion to criticize quantitative approaches to developmental, psychological, and other human research for their reductionism, it is obvious that all analyses do more or less injury to the phenomena under investigation.

Admittedly, the summary of any complex human behavior in exclusively quantitative terms makes the reductionism obvious to all but the most hardened empiricist. The written summary of the same act in several sentences, or even paragraphs, also misses the mark in similar but perhaps less obvious ways. Neither the score of 93/100 nor a paragraph of suitably purple prose can adequately capture the experience of tasting an extraordinary wine. Each misses the point completely. But each summary (quantitative or qualitative) can effectively summarize aspects of the experience sufficiently for others to be tempted into purchasing and drinking a bottle of the same wine!

As we try to record an event to share with others, the original experience is damaged in a multitude of ways: via the orientation of the investigator, the adequacy of the observation schedule, the validity of the observations, and the completeness of the set of observations, and all this, before we look at the adequacy of the particular analytical devices along with the care and rigor of their use. The very act of focusing on any aspect of human experience immediately relegates all other aspects toward oblivion. The authors would argue that both quantitative and qualitative approaches have the same starting point, in observation. The extent of this common ground becomes evident in later chapters, where a synthesis of quantitative and qualitative approaches is demonstrated.

"All that can be observed is whether or not the specified event occurs, and whether the data recorder (observer or respondent) nominates (any particular) category as their observation" (Wright, 1996, p. 3). This is the basis of the results for all our investigations. The respondent might tick "false" on a response sheet, write a paragraph, or produce a journal. The observer might record that an appropriate word was inserted into a space in a sentence, note that "a" was the correct response to item 17, or compose a particular phrase or statement to correspond to an identified segment of a video or journal record. In essence, all of our observations can be so depicted, whether qualitative or quantitative analyses are intended.

In the case of simple observations, the investigator might make a qualitative decision about whether the event was absent or present, whether it did or did not occur. As part of a more complex schedule, the investigator might decide whether a particular event was absent, whether it occurred to some extent or to a greater extent, or whether a complete display of the appropriate behavior was observed. In this way, all of our investigatory observations are qualitative, and the classification or identification of events deals with data at the nominal level. When we start counting these events or observations, we apply a mathematical value to these events. This counting is the beginning of an expressly quantitative approach. Even in the first instance (presence/absence), we are dealing with ordinal data because we hold the presence of an event (a tick, a mark in the correct box, a "yes") as more valuable than the absence of that event (a cross, a mark in the wrong box, or a "no"). In the second instance (none/some/more/all) our data are much more evidently ordinal. Our counting of observations or events always remains on those levels. It is our attempt to make meaningful measures of those observations that constructs an interval scale, in which the distances between counts are made equal and meaningful. As a consequence, any analytical model that implicitly or explicitly makes assumptions about "interval" or "ratio" relations between the data points does so unjustifiably. Wright and Linacre (1989) developed these points more fully.

Recognizing the presence/absence of behavior and ordering observations along a none/some/more/all continuum presumes that some underlying theory is guiding those observations. Unfortunately, for many researchers in the human sciences, that theory often remains as implicit. Much of the research reported as exemplars in this volume shares common origins in expressly articulated explicit psychological theories.

PRINCIPLES OF MEASUREMENT

Any investigator's record of qualitative observations represents nominal categories. The investigator might then score these observations to organize them into a stepwise order of precedence according to the theoretical model used to generate the observational schedule. This presumption or expectation of meaningful ordering of data is at the very heart of any of those conceptions of humans that have developmental origins.

As a useful starting point, quantitative summarizing of qualitative observations can be achieved by simply assigning 1 (or ✔) for the presence of an occurrence and 0 (or X) for its absence, so that the data summary for person A across all items is recorded as a row:

A   111000011001   or   ✔ ✔ ✔ X X X X ✔ ✔ X X ✔

The data summary for item d across all persons is recorded as a column:

d
0   or   X
1   ✔
0   X
1   ✔
0   X
1   ✔
0   X
0   X
1   ✔
1   ✔
0   X
0   X
0   X
0   ✔

A teacher's record book or a complete record of a sample's performances on the items of a developmental test could look just like this. Typically, our preference for focusing on the performance of the persons rather than investigating the performance of the items has us rushing to express the results of the investigation as a raw score total for each person. We often do not make even that same crude summary for items. Therefore, in the matrix shown as Table 2.1, the last column entry for each person is the total raw score. We often use this raw score as the estimate of the person's ability on the test.

In keeping with a guiding principle adopted for the writing of this book, the authors have selected from some data actually collected to answer substantive questions from developmental or educational psychology. The data for chapter 2 are taken from a test generated by a group of primary school teachers (Bond, 1996; Parkinson, 1996). The test was designed to make explicit the school's

TABLE 2.1

Data Matrix for 14 Selected Persons (A–N) on 12 Selected Items (*a–l*)

Persons	*a*	*b*	*c*	*d*	*e*	*f*	*g*	*h*	*i*	*j*	*k*	*l*	Raw Score
A	✔	✔	✔	X	X	X	X	✔	✔	X	X	✔	6
B	✔	X	✔	✔	X	X	X	X	✔	X	X	X	4
C	✔	✔	✔	X	✔	X	X	✔	✔	✔	✔	✔	9
D	✔	X	✔	✔	X	X	X	X	✔	X	X	✔	5
E	X	✔	✔	X	X	✔	X	✔	✔	✔	✔	✔	8
F	✔	✔	✔	✔	X	X	X	✔	✔	X	X	✔	7
G	✔	X	✔	X	X	✔	X	X	✔	X	✔	✔	6
H	✔	X	✔	X	X	X	X	X	X	X	X	✔	3
I	✔	✔	✔	✔	X	X	X	✔	✔	X	X	✔	7
J	✔	✔	✔	✔	✔	✔	✔	✔	✔	X	✔	X	10
K	✔	X	✔	X	X	✔	X	X	✔	X	✔	✔	6
L	X	✔	✔	X	X	✔	X	✔	✔	✔	✔	✔	8
M	X	X	X	X	X	X	X	X	X	X	X	X	0
N	✔	✔	✔	✔	✔	✔	✔	✔	✔	✔	✔	✔	12

math curriculum requirements for dealing with area-based concepts. Questions at the lower level required students to color the surface of, say, a square. Others required computations based on formulas such as area = length × breadth, and area = side^2. Advanced skills were tested by questions requiring calculations based on several formulas, added or subtracted, to give area measures of complex figures.

What then might we infer from the data matrix shown in Table 2.1? Of course, we can see that quite a range of person performances, from 0/12 (all wrong, person M) to 12/12 (all correct, person N), is evident. However, from this information alone, we cannot immediately draw any conclusions about the items, or about the interactions between the items and the persons.

Because the following steps (often implicit or omitted) can show us a lot about our data and introduce some crucial features of Rasch analysis, we should take each of them in turn. The authors would argue that researchers (and teachers) could learn a great deal about their testing procedures by taking time regularly to inspect their raw data in the following fashion. A simple spreadsheet on a microcomputer will do the job. The data matrix (i.e., the result of the theory-driven qualitative observations) can be arranged so that the items are ordered from least to most difficult and the persons are ordered from least to most able (Table 2.2). The higher up the table one goes, the more able the persons (person N: 12/12). The further right across the table one goes, the more difficult the items (item *g*: only two persons are successful). The table then reveals some properties about the observations that will help to guide future data collection and the data analysis.

TABLE 2.2
Selected Data Matrix With Persons Arranged According to Ability
(From Top to Bottom) and Items Arranged by Facility (From Left to Right)

Persons	Items												Ability
	c	i	a	l	b	h	k	d	f	j	e	g	
N	✔	✔	✔	✔	✔	✔	✔	✔	✔	✔	✔	✔	12
J	✔	✔	✔	X	✔	✔	✔	✔	✔	X	✔	✔	10
C	✔	✔	✔	✔	✔	✔	✔	X	X	✔	✔	X	9
E	✔	✔	X	✔	✔	✔	✔	X	✔	✔	X	X	8
L	✔	✔	X	✔	✔	✔	✔	X	✔	✔	X	X	8
I	✔	✔	✔	✔	✔	✔	X	✔	X	X	X	X	7
F	✔	✔	✔	✔	✔	✔	X	✔	X	X	X	X	7
K	✔	✔	✔	✔	X	X	✔	X	✔	X	X	X	6
A	✔	✔	✔	✔	✔	✔	X	X	X	X	X	X	6
G	✔	✔	✔	✔	X	X	✔	X	✔	X	X	X	6
D	✔	✔	✔	✔	X	X	X	✔	X	X	X	X	5
B	✔	✔	✔	X	X	X	X	✔	X	X	X	X	4
H	✔	X	✔	✔	X	X	X	X	X	X	X	X	3
M	X	X	X	X	X	X	X	X	X	X	X	X	0
Facility	13	12	11	11	8	8	7	6	6	3	3	2	

The simple task of ordering data from least to most occurrences (for persons and for items) is likely to show that the theoretical model used for the collection of the qualitative observations has not produced results entirely as anticipated. Usually, the first use of a test will not yield a complete set of distinctively useful observations. In the case of the observation schedule or items, some items might have no observations of presence (i.e., all zeroes were recorded, meaning every child "failed" on that item). Other items might not discriminate between the persons in the sample observed (i.e., all ones were recorded, meaning every child "passed" on that item). These items should be discarded from that data set because they are not useful discriminators of the substantive sequence under investigation with this particular sample. Subsequently, these items should be examined closely and perhaps improved or used in other appropriate scales or with other samples.

Similarly, some persons might have no observations showing presence of the anticipated behaviors (all zeroes, meaning they "fail" all items; e.g., person M), or they might be more capable than this observation schedule predicted (all ones, meaning they "pass" all items; e.g., person N). The results for these persons should be discarded also as inadequate. It is not possible to make satisfactory descriptions showing the progress of these persons along the continuum revealed by this qualitative observation schedule. All we can conclude definitively is that the persons had either too little ability to score on this test or more ability than needed for this test.

This procedure is not meant to disregard our intention to record that one child got everything right, or that another failed on all items for a particular sample or purpose. Rather, it reminds us that these results are quite insufficient for estimating ability. It should tell us that the next time, when we construct subsequent versions of such a test, we will need to include some easier as well as some more difficult items of this sort to cover properly the range of abilities shown in a sample such as the one under investigation.

The authors' claim is that qualitative inspection of the data is a necessary prerequisite to meaningful quantitative analysis and, hence, should always precede it. We have discovered already how valuable information about the match or mismatch between the persons observed and the items used to observe them could guide our next investigation of this ability. We have been cautioned about the inadequate information we have about persons (in this case, persons M and N). Strictly speaking, we should remove these cases from the data matrix and follow up with some extra data collection for these two. It is now revealed that we have some less-than-useful items (in this case, item c). With the nonscoring person M removed from the matrix, item c is correctly answered by all. It might be a useful item for less able children, but not for this sample. For our next use of this test, we also have a guide to the difficulty level of further useful items.

The next step is to calculate item difficulties and person abilities (expressed as the fraction n/N, the item or person raw score divided by the total possible score). These fractions show more readily the ordinal relations among abilities on the one hand and among difficulties on the other, allowing us to make crude comparisons between the dispersions of difficulties and abilities in the observations (Table 2.3). The routine procedure in education circles is to express each of these n/N fractions as a percentage and to use them directly in reporting students' results. We will soon see that this commonplace procedure is not justified. In keeping with the caveat we expressed earlier, these n/N fractions are regarded as merely orderings of the nominal categories, and as insufficient for the inference of interval relations between the frequencies of observations.

Just as theories about humans would predict, the data displayed in Table 2.3 show substantial variation in the presence of the targeted ability in the sample observed. They also show considerable variation in the facility or difficulty of the items that represent the observation schedule. Indeed, the very concept of a variable has variation at its heart. Immediately, the developmental nature of these observations is obvious in the way the presence of the observations (1's) change to absences (0's) in the direction of increasing difficulty of the items ($\rightarrow$) and in the direction of decreasing ability of the persons ($\downarrow$).

Even at this level, the arrangements of some data points should cause us to reflect on the nature of these children's development made evident by these empirical manifestations of the underlying theoretical ideas. We should focus now on the patterns of success and failure revealed in the data matrix. Only of passing concern is the evidence showing that the intersection of the patterns of "suc-

TABLE 2.3
Selected Ordered Data Matrix for Items
and Persons With Sufficient Information

Persons	*i*	*a*	*l*	*b*	*h*	*k*	*d*	*f*	*j*	*e*	*g*	Ability	n/N%
J	1	1	0	1	1	1	1	1	0	1	1	9	82
C	1	1	1	1	1	1	0	0	1	1	0	8	73
E	1	0	1	1	1	1	0	1	1	0	0	7	64
L	1	0	1	1	1	1	0	1	1	0	0	7	64
I	1	1	1	1	1	0	1	0	0	0	0	6	55
F	1	1	1	1	1	0	1	0	0	0	0	6	55
K	1	1	1	0	0	1	0	1	0	0	0	5	45
A	1	1	1	1	1	0	0	0	0	0	0	5	45
G	1	1	1	0	0	1	0	1	0	0	0	5	45
D	1	1	1	0	0	0	1	0	0	0	0	4	36
B	1	1	0	0	0	0	1	0	0	0	0	3	27
H	0	1	1	0	0	0	0	0	0	0	0	2	18
Facility	11	10	10	7	7	6	5	5	3	2	1		
n/N%	93	83	83	58	58	50	42	42	25	17	08		

cess" and "difficulty" has a small zone of unpredictability associated with it. Typically, 1's do not change to 0's in a rigid, steplike fashion, either for persons or for items. It is reasonable to suggest that this pattern of responses reflects recently acquired or yet-to-be consolidated developmental abilities that might not be fully reliable in their display. Therefore, the data contained in the shaded cells of Table 2.3 should delay us no further.

Unlike the data patterns that display small zones of unpredictability, "unexpected" observations of presence (1) or absence (0) that seem more out of place (cells with data in bold type) are of greater concern. These unexpected observations will be of greater or lesser concern depending on their number and their location in the data matrix. Persons who score well on difficult items despite low overall total scores might have done so by guessing or cheating. Similarly, poor scores on easy items despite high overall total scores might indicate lack of concentration or guessing. Of course, the presence of other unexpected idiosyncratic circumstances, including particular person–item interactions, is always a possibility.

This brings to our attention an important principle guiding our use and interpretation of observational schedules and tests. Although some students (see student A) perform in a strictly orderly fashion (raw score of 5 for student A means exactly the 5 easiest items correct and the 6 hardest items incorrect), our observations of most human behaviors rarely show rigid steplike patterns of progression. The vagaries of our observational abilities, and those of human performance, ensure that rigid adherence to even precisely defined developmental sequences is the exception rather than the rule.

Similarly, items that precisely separate more able from less able students, as items *i*, *e*, and *g* appear to do, also are rare. It is more plausible that the sequence will be more or less predictable: that the likelihood of getting any question correct increases in line with the person's raw score. Of course, the lower a person's raw score is, the lower the likelihood of the person getting any question correct, or of meeting any of the observational criteria. Predicting success or failure is most hazardous where the 0's meet the 1's for any student. Obviously, in such cases, the response is almost equally likely to be successful or unsuccessful. A prediction of success is determined by how far the item is embedded in the student's zone of success. The further the item is embedded in the student's zone of success (the 1's), the more likely it is that the student will succeed on that item. Conversely, the likelihood of failure increases the further the item is embedded in the student's zone of failure (the 0's).

The pattern for person A is almost too good to be true, but a closer look at the response patterns of the students gaining raw scores of 6 or 7 is illuminating. The patterns for persons I and F are quite orderly enough according to the general principle of increased likelihood of success and failure just outlined. How could anyone who has sat for or written a test quibble about the little reversal of items *k* and *d*? The response patterns for persons E and L, however, do not match our expectations as easily. Although the unexpected failure on item *d* might be overlooked, the unexpected failure on very easy item *a* starts us wondering whether E's and L's understandings of area are directly comparable with those of C and I. However, we are not likely to be so equivocal when we try to interpret the success/failure patterns of person K. The responses of K are so erratic and unpredictable in comparison with the general orderliness that is evident in the rest of the data matrix that it would be unfair to say that a raw score of 5 is a fair summary of K's ability to solve area problems.

The same argument can be just as readily applied to the performance patterns of items or observations. Responses to items *b* and *h* seem orderly enough. It is possible to predict with a good deal of success any student's overall likelihood of doing well or poorly on the whole area test just by looking at that student's performance on items *b* and/or *h*. But in looking at item *d*, we see that it not only is a more difficult item but that the responses to it are so erratic, it is practically impossible to predict who will be successful with it and who will not. Success on item *d* should be highly predictable for about the most able one third of the group, but the response pattern tells us that the difficulty rating for this item (0.42) cannot be taken at face value: High scorers C, E, and L failed on *d*, whereas low scorers D and B were successful. Something else is going on with this item, something different from the general response pattern that we see in the whole data matrix for area.

The next part of this procedure shows the inadequacy of treating raw scores of ability and difficulty directly as measurement scales. To illustrate the point, the ability fractions have been taken from Table 2.3 and their locations plotted along a continuum to see how the items and persons disperse (Fig. 2.1, left). Of course, the raw score fraction (0.45) corresponds exactly to the same raw score expressed as a percentage (45%). Many teachers and university professors would recognize the pattern shown for person abilities. They regularly see their students' results in this format as they go through the process of assigning grades. However, it is much less common for teachers or researchers to give even this very basic treatment to the test questions they use to produce these student grades.

The problem with using raw score fractions or percentages is that this procedure tends to clump students around the middle scores and does not adequately contrast the results of the more able and less able students. Earning a few extra marks near the midpoint of the test results, say from 48 to 55, does not reflect the same ability leap required for a move from 88 to 95 at the top of the test or from 8 to 15 at the bottom. The real problem here is that we routinely mistake the distances between fraction or percentage scores as having direct meaning, when all we really may infer from these data is the ordering of the persons or the items. We need a sound way of interpreting the size of the gaps between the scores, so that we are able to say, for example, "Betty shows more ability than Bill on this test, and by this much."

A simple mathematical procedure for better representing the relative distances between the raw scores has been available since the work of Thurstone in the 1920s. This procedure involves converting a raw score summary to its natural logarithm. Although such mathematical transformations to produce linear measures abound in the physical sciences, we have tended to avoid them, or even to be suspicious of them, in the human sciences. In addition to transforming the score from a merely ordinal scale to a mathematically more useful interval scale, a log odds scale avoids the problem of bias toward scores in the middle of the scale, and against persons who score at the extremes.

The first step in this procedure is to convert the raw score percentage into its success-to-failure ratio or odds. A raw score of 60% becomes odds of 60 to 40; 90% becomes 90 to 10; 50% becomes 50 to 50; and so on. Then a spreadsheet command, or even many handheld calculators, can perform the elementary function of converting scores to their natural log odds. For person L (64% or odds of 64 to 36), we enter 64/36, push the log function, and read off the result (+0.58). Try a few of these to get the hang of it: Ability odds of 55 to 45 for F become a log value of +0.20, and the odds of 45 to 55 for G become a value of −0.20. Using the data from the matrix, try a few other values or use a more familiar set of results to see what happens.

We have included the logarithmic transformation of the person data on the righthand side of Fig. 2.1. The relative placements (i.e., the ordinal relations) are, of course, the same as those on the left. The all-important order remains the same. However, looking at the positions for the lower achievers on this test (those below the 50% level), we can observe that the distances between the per-

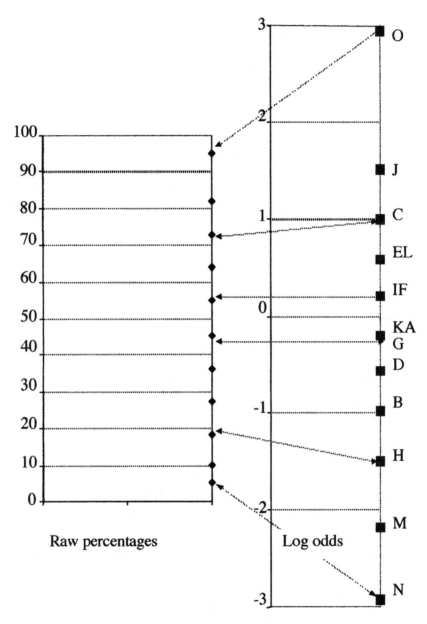

FIG. 2.1.   Relative abilities of persons A–H shown in raw percentages (left) and as log odds (right). More extreme persons' locations (M = 10%, N = 5%, and O = 95%) are added for purposes of illustration only.

son locations have been stretched out. The distances between D, B, and H (each only one raw score apart) are now considerably larger than the gaps between F, L, and C (each one raw score apart as well). Now the scale we have for plotting the person and item locations has the properties of an interval scale, whereby the value of the scale is maintained at any position along that scale. It is only with an interval scale that we can begin to say how much more able Betty is than Bill, instead of merely saying that she is more able. Moreover, the effect becomes much more marked if we introduce some more extreme person abilities into these figures: A person with a 95% raw score becomes located at +2.94 on the log ability scale, whereas the low score of 10% translates as −2.2 and 5% becomes −2.94. The argument is that this wider distribution of person locations more fairly represents the increase in ability required to move from a score of 90% to a score of 95% as considerably greater than the ability difference between, say, a score of 50% and a score of 55%.

Up to this point, we have attempted to show that for a model to be useful for investigating aspects of the human condition represented in developmental and other theories, it needs to incorporate the following properties:

It should be sensitive to the ordered acquisition of the skills or abilities under investigation (i.e., it should aim at uncovering the order of development or acquisition).

It should be capable of estimating the developmental distances between the ordered skills or persons (i.e., it should tell us by how much T is more developed, more capable, or more rehabilitated than S).

It should allow us to determine whether the general developmental pattern shown among items and persons is sufficient to account for the pattern of development shown by every item and every person.

The reader will not be very much surprised if we now go on to demonstrate that analyses based on Rasch measurement are particularly suited to investigations in the wide range of human sciences on exactly these grounds.

3

Basic Principles of the
Rasch Model

This chapter presents a developmental pathway analogy to explain the basic concepts of the Rasch model. Although the analogy is obviously and directly applicable to observations in developmental psychology, its relevance for the other measurement situations in the human sciences in which the Rasch model should be used is detailed in the following chapters.

THE DEVELOPMENTAL PATHWAY
ANALOGY

Let us imagine a segment in children's development. Anything will do, for example, the progressive attainment of the skills in drawing a reasonable human form or the progress toward realizing that two differently shaped glasses contain the same amount of juice. Although our underlying developmental theory for either of these two examples might define a single sequence of development that could be represented by the arrow in Fig. 3.1, we would not expect our recorded observations of the development to be as perfect or precise as a straight line. Instead, what we need to be able to do is build a measurement tool (a set of tasks, a list of assessment criteria, or a series of questions) that will be empirically useful enough in practice to make a meaningful assessment of children's development of that ability.

What then will be good enough? Such a tool must represent our best effort to acknowledge both the role of that straight line in measurement theory and the diversions from this straight path that exist in the empirical reality of practice. Only the user will be able to tell that by experience, but the criteria by which usefulness can be gauged are built into the Rasch model and demonstrated in our analogy.

Whereas the arrow represents the unattainable ideal, the circular stepping-stones in Fig. 3.1 represent a selection of the items (L, M, N, . . . , U) in our test or observation schedule. The steps at the bottom of the path will suit the beginners, and those at the top will be reached only by the most developed children. Therefore, the different intermediary stepping-stones along the way will be useful for the varied levels of development we expect among the test takers. The distance of the step from the bottom of the path (A) represents its difficulty relative to the other items. This is our representation of item difficulty: closer to the bottom is easier, further is more difficult. The idea is that each child will progress along the steps as far as the child's ability (development) will carry him or her. The child will use (master) the steps until the steps become too difficult. How far any child moves along the pathway will be our estimate of the child's development or ability. We have used little squares to represent how far each of the children has moved along the pathway. This is our representation of person ability.

This map of item and person relationships we have used to represent the developmental pathway analogy contains a lot of basic information that is central to Rasch measurement, but which can be readily gleaned by attending to the basic difficulty/ability concepts mentioned earlier. Please look carefully at Fig. 3.1 and try to answer the following questions (with reasons). All the answers can be derived directly from the figure without any extra knowledge of Rasch modeling. First, take a look at the positions of the round stepping-stones (item locations).

Is item S (much) more difficult or (much) less difficult than item N?

Which item is the most likely to be failed by the students?

Which item is the most likely to be passed by the students?

Now take a look at the positions of the squares that represent the person locations on the developmental pathway (the item–person map of abilities and difficulties). With the Rasch model, the principles about items work with exactly the same logic for persons. According to developmental pathway representation of these data in Fig. 3.1,

Is Bill (much) more able or (much) less able than Bob?

Which student is revealed as least able on this test?

Is Bill likely to have answered item U correctly?

What would be more unexpected, that Bill will miss item S or item M?

Mike scored 1 on the test. Which item is most likely to be the one he got right?

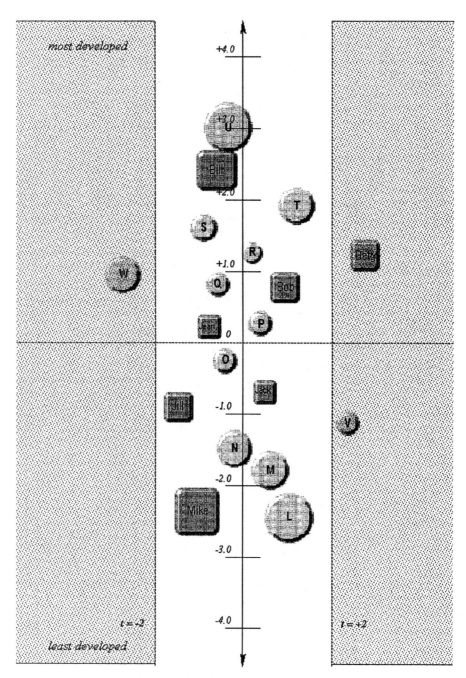

FIG. 3.1. Developmental pathway.

The dotted lines in Fig. 3.1, where white meets shaded, are meant to represent the edges of the pathway. Stepping-stones within these boundaries can been seen as useful steps on this particular pathway. Locations outside the boundaries cannot be interpreted meaningfully with regard to this pathway. Therefore,

Which items are not usefully located on the pathway in their present forms?

Which person is traveling to the beat of a different drum?

Is Bob's ability well measured by this test?

Jill scored 3 on the test. Which items are most likely to be those she got right?

From the representation of persons and items on the map, item S is much more difficult than item N, whereas item U is the toughest on this test. Most of these children will not succeed on item U. Item L, however, is very easy, in fact, the easiest on this test. Most children will get L correct. The map shows that Bill is considerably more able than Bob on this test. There is a fair-size gap between the two. Bill is not likely to have succeeded on item U. Persons who succeed on U usually need more ability than Bill shows. Bill has much more ability than required to succeed on item M. For Bill, missing M would be a rare, but not impossible, event. However, because item S is much tougher, much closer to Bill's ability level, we should not be surprised if Bill misses items such as S from time to time.

Stepping-stones V and W are not located well enough on our pathway to be useful as they are, whereas Betty has not used the pathway in the same manner as the others. Bob's location fits well between the dotted control lines, so he has performed according to the model's expectations, and thus is well measured. Jill is most likely to have succeeded with L, M, and N. Her location shows that she is more able than necessary to answer L, M, and N correctly at most administrations of this test.

In developing any test, our aim would be to put enough stepping-stones along the path to represent all the stepping-points useful for our testing purposes, between little development (A) and much development (Z). Of course, to do that, we would need to collect observations from enough suitable persons. Good data analysis requires more items and many more persons than we have included in Fig. 3.1. We have merely selected some illustrative examples here. Also, with our emphasis on building and defining a pathway, we have concentrated on items and (unforgivably) tended to ignore persons at this point. Let us now turn our attention to some specific ideas and guidelines that will aid us in accomplishing this task.

Unidimensionality

Underlying the ideas about measuring development that have been raised so far is an important implicit principle. Unfortunately, this principle is so taken for granted in our use of measurement tools for size, weight, temperature, and the like that when it is made explicit, it causes concern for researchers in the human sciences who perhaps have not thought the matter through. In attempting to measure the physical attributes of objects, people, or the weather, scientists and laypeople alike take care to measure just one attribute of the target at a time. A rectangular solid has many attributes (e.g., length, breadth, height, weight, volume, density, and even hardness, to name a few), but all attempts to make meaningful estimations of the object under scrutiny focus on only one attribute at a time. This focus on one attribute or dimension at a time is referred to as *unidimensionality*.

Similarly, for people height, weight, age, waist measurement, and blood pressure all are estimated separately. Perhaps we could envision a new scale for person size that incorporated both height and girth by starting with a tape measure at the toes, winding it around the left knee and right hip, under the left armpit, and up behind the head. No doubt we could become well practiced and reasonably accurate in making this measurement. We could perhaps even find some uses for it. But people designing airplane seats, hotel beds, and hatchways in submarines would soon revert to taking independent measures of, say, height and width in a sample of intended users, in which the dimensions are not confused with each other.

Another analogy illustrates confusions that can occur when two measures are confounded into one estimate. As we all know, the general practice for clothing manufacturers has been to establish sizes for their products to help consumers choose appropriate garments. This type of estimation system for determining generic shoe size as 9, 9½, 10, and so on confounds the two important attributes of shoe and foot size: the length and the width. On the other hand, for example, there have been very popular sizing systems for shoes in the United Kingdom, the United States, and Australia based on an alternative "fractional fitting" principle in which all shoes come in a variety of lengths and widths: 9A (quite narrow) . . . 9C . . . 9EE (very wide indeed). A little knowledge and experience with this system, in which the two key attributes, length and breadth, are estimated and reported separately, allows for much more confidence in predicting shoe size suitability.

The fractional fitting system has given way under the pressures of mass production, but one major U.S. running-shoe manufacturer boasts its "many widths for every shoe length" models, and specialist shoe manufacturers still use the system. However, even this system has its problems. For one, our confidence in this measurement system is lessened when in certain situations we determine that a particular shoe does not match the expectations we have of the shoe size scale. Similarly, the feet of some individuals do not match the model adequately, so that every shoe-buying attempt remains a tortuous, almost arcane process that relies more on persistence and chance than on anything at all "scientific."

Of course, even something as apparently simple as human foot and shoe size is oversimplified by the fractional fitting focus on length and width dimensions.

Athletes, medical rehabilitation patients, and others who have specialist shoe needs, also take into account the height of the foot arch, the curve of the sole, and the height of the heel to get a better compromise between foot and shoe. Foot size is remarkably complex, and a single size scale that confuses length and width means "try before you buy" every time, even with sandals. Estimating the length and width dimensions separately makes the foot–shoe match much easier for most. It is sufficient for the task most of the time. Even so, we all recognize that foot size, like most physical and psychological attributes, is always much more complex than what we can capture through separate estimates of distinct attributes. Although the complexity of what we are measuring appears to be lost, it is through measuring one attribute at a time that we can develop both useful and meaningful composite descriptions.

We all are aware that the complexity of human existence can never be satisfactorily expressed as one score on any test. We can, however, develop some useful quantitative estimates of some human attributes, but we can do that only for one attribute or ability at a time. Confusing a number of attributes into a single generic score makes confident predictions from that score more hazardous and the score a less useful summary of ability or achievement. But carefully constructed tests that make good measurement estimates of single attributes might be sufficient for a number of thoughtfully decided purposes. For specialist or difficult situations, collecting more good estimates of other appropriate attributes is essential. Of course, qualitative data might be used to complement the quantitative results. Human beings are complex, multidimensional creatures to be sure. But whereas using height as a measure of a person is an obvious and unforgivable reductionism, in many cases useful predictions can be made about the suitability of doorway heights based on that estimate alone. And we would be naïve to think that this would be sufficient for every person.

The meaning of the estimates of person ability and item difficulty in the data matrix we have used thus far (see chapter 2) will be meaningful only if each and every question contributes to the measure of a single attribute (e.g., the ability to solve area problems). If the intention of teachers who measure this ability is not well implemented in each of the items, we might find that other attributes of the children's abilities are included in the measure and hence produce less meaningful test results. For example, one item might be predominantly a test of language comprehension. Another item might focus too much on interpretation of a complex geometrical drawing. Still another might be so poorly written that children find it difficult to understand the requirement of the examiner, and so on. Then, of course, the children must cooperate with the teachers' intention as expressed in the test. To the extent that they replace strategies based on the understanding of area with other strategies based on, say, simple recall, guessing, cheating, carelessness, use of a calculator, and so forth, the estimate of that child's ability to solve area problems will be confounded with other attributes not intentionally measured by the teachers. The resultant measure then is uninterpretable to the extent that these other abilities, and not the understanding of area, are manifested in the children's responses. It is here that the principles of unidimensionality require that our analytical procedures must incorporate a test of the degree to which persons and items fit our idea of the ideal unidimensional line.

Item Fit

A good measurement process in education, psychology, or the other human sciences will allow for the estimation of one ability at a time, and will not, intentionally or unintentionally, confuse two or more human attributes into one measure or score. Each of the items should contribute in a meaningful way to the construct/concept being investigated. It will be helpful here to reflect explicitly on how the Rasch model focuses on the key developmental ideas of "construct validity" and "order" introduced in the Preface. First, *construct validity* focuses on the idea that the recorded performances are reflections of a single underlying construct: the theoretical construct as made explicit by the investigator's attempt to represent it in items or observations, and by the human ability inferred to be responsible for those performances. The data matrix that relates the items and the persons together in a coherent, integrated way is more likely to represent (i.e., fit) the construct under examination satisfactorily than one in which the relations appear serendipitous.

Of course, detecting this confusion might not be an easy matter, but for teacher-made tests and early drafts of potentially large-scale tests, it is useful to sit down with a few selected examinees after the test marking has been done to work through the questions with each examinee in turn to help determine the extent to which the intentions of the test writer are revealed in the students' responses. Of course, the ordered data matrix, as shown in chapter 2, would be a very good device for deciding which students and which questions might be worth closer scrutiny. Items or persons that do not adhere to the expected ability/difficulty pattern would be good starting points. That way, the quantitative and qualitative aspects of investigation get a chance to work together to improve test design.

Because visual inspection of a data matrix typically is not sufficient for assessing the impact of individual items or persons, Rasch analysis provides fit statistics designed to aid the investigator in making a number of interrelated decisions about the data (Smith, 1991a, 1992, 2000; Smith & Miao, 1994; Wright & Masters, 1982; Wright & Stone, 1979). Rasch analysis provides indicators of how well each item fits within the underlying construct. This is a crucial aid for the investigator assessing the meaning of the unidimensional construct. That is, fit indices help the investigator to ascertain whether the assumption of unidimensionality holds up empirically. Items that do not fit the unidimensional construct (the ideal straight line as shown in Fig. 3.1) are those that diverge unacceptably from the expected ability/difficulty pattern (see chapter 2). Therefore, fit statistics help to determine whether the item estimations may be held as meaningful quantitative summaries of the observations (i.e., whether each item contributes to the measurement of only one construct).

Notice in Fig. 3.1 that the steps (e.g., items, L, M, N) do not lie precisely along the theoretical straight line. We might get some of our items/observations close to perfect, but our aim is to place them close enough to the theoretical straight line to be good practical indicators of the hypothetical path from A to Z. Suppose we are developing a test of fundamental math skills. Items such as L, M, and N (easy items) might be simple addition problems, whereas items T and U (difficult items) might be long-division problems. Stepping-stone items that are not close enough to the centerline to be part of this path, such as items V and W in our drawn example, most likely do not follow this pattern. Perhaps these two items contain story problems that confound reading ability with math ability. The fit statistics then would indicate that these two items might be included better in some other related pathway. They will not be a useful part of the A–Z developmental pathway until they fit a bit better. Perhaps we could try rewriting those items or expressing them some other way the next time we use this test. We could replace them or use them in some other test. At this stage, however, it would be more appropriate not to count the results of items V and W in any child's test score. Our measure of children's math ability would be more meaningful if these results were not counted.

To help us decide which items to include in our pathway, we could put a dotted line on each side of, and parallel to, our straight line as a check that the fit of our steps to the path is good enough for our purposes (e.g., something like 95% confidence lines). Indeed, some Rasch software outputs report item fit data in a graphic form, in just this way.

In each case, the analytical output would provide greater detail on how each item or performance met, or failed to meet, the model's expectations. Clearly, items whose estimations do not sufficiently "fit" the model require further investigation. Test construction and testing are always done for good reasons. Presumably then, there would always be sound theoretical grounds for including all of the items in a schedule and for using that schedule to make observations of any particular person. Important insights into the theory or its expression in practice are likely outcomes of such deliberations. Our theories guide us in deciding what sort of items we should use and with whom we should use them. This Rasch-informed method can be contrasted with the often-used procedure of generating a huge net of possible items, and then trawling through very large, supposedly normal samples to find a set of items with acceptable statistical characteristics.

The Rasch model incorporates a theoretical idealization (or construct, or fiction) of the data's interrelations, an unachievable state that is mathematically represented as the ideal straight line shown in Fig. 3.1. The Rasch model represents the concept of perfect "one attribute at a time" measurement, and hence we want to see whether reality (our data) adheres to that concept of a straight measurement line. (Psychometricians also refer to this fiction, or underlying construct, as a latent trait.) Conversely, if the chief contention of this volume is accepted, then the outcomes of Rasch modeling can also reveal the suitability of the observation schedule as an expression of the substantive human sciences theory in empirical practice. That is, we can take the conventional approach and see this as a test of whether our data fit with our fiction. However, it is more useful if we complement this use with the idea of whether our construct, as expressed in developmental or other theory, fits with our data. Ideally, theory informs practice and practice informs theory, dialectically.

Difficulty/Ability Estimation and Error

In developing the mathematical representation of the straight line, the Rasch model specifically addresses the conception of order, an idea fundamental to any account of developing human ability and basic to the idea of measuring more or less of any human condition. Whereas order obviously is important in psychological theories of child development, it also is central to the arrangement of cells in a Likert response scale, easily detected in medical rehabilitation settings, and directly relevant to academic achievement where the difficulty of questions varies. Specifically, in the Rasch model, performances are attributed relative importance in proportion to the position they hold on the measurement continuum. For example, correctly worked-through long-division problems are attributed more importance in the assessment of advanced mathematical skill than correctly worked-through simple addition problems. The Rasch model thus incorporates an algorithm that expresses the probabilistic expectations of item and person performances when one construct is held to underlie the developmental sequence represented by the observation schedule (Wright & Stone, 1979).

When a data matrix reflects a successful attempt to implement a theoretically guided line of inquiry with a sample for whom that inquiry was appropriate, then a number of propositions are supportable. Two key propositions are as follows:

> Persons who are more able/more developed have a greater likelihood of correctly answering all the items in the observation schedule (e.g., in Fig. 3.1, Bill is more likely than Bob to answer all the items correctly).
>
> Easier items are more likely to be answered/reached correctly by all persons (e.g., both Bob and Bill are more likely to answer L correctly than P, and more likely to answer P correctly than S).

These propositions are necessary for expressing unidimensionality of data, and they explicitly illustrate the concept of order in establishing that unidimensionality.

Based on this logic of order, the Rasch analysis software programs perform a logarithmic transformation on the item and person data to convert the ordinal data to yield interval data. These transformations represent the estimation of person ability and item difficulty detected in the data set (i.e., item and person placement along the single line of inquiry). Actual item and person performance probabilities determine the interval sizes. They are not introduced as a priori assumptions of the investigator, or of the analytical algorithm. To the extent that the set of observations adheres sufficiently to Rasch's mathematical model of expectations, it is held to be unidimensional (i.e., the single difficulty/ability continuum is sufficient to explain the patterns of item/person performances).

These person ability and item difficulty estimates, having been subjected to a log transformation, are displayed in computer output along a *logit* (log odds unit) scale. The logit scale is an interval scale in which the unit intervals between the locations on the person–item map have a consistent value or meaning. The Rasch model routinely sets at 50% the probability of success for any person on an item located at the same level on the item–person logit scale. Because Bob's logit ability estimate is equal to item Q's difficulty estimate, Bob has a 50% chance of passing this item, for which he is equally matched. The probability of his success increases to 75% for an item that is 1 logit easier (perhaps item O) or decreases to 25% for an item that is 1 logit harder (perhaps item T). The investigator now has more detailed information than that provided by just the data matrix alone on which to make judgments concerning the items, the persons, and the substantive theory that guided the investigation.

But how do we interpret the accuracy of these estimates? What is the good of item and person estimates if we do not know how good they are? Often our best intentions to realize our theoretical ideas as observation schedules or items go astray. Yes, the stepping-stones along the pathway might be located at an exact point along the pathway, but our figure gives each one a size as well. The difficulty location of any test item (stepping-stone) is located at a point, but always has a zone of imprecision, or error, associated with it. Small stepping-stones (small error) suggest that we can locate their difficulty rather precisely. With the larger stepping-stones (larger errors), the item locations are not as precise. Figure 3.1 shows that some of the items overlap, particularly at the extremes of the path where errors of location tend to be larger.

Figure 3.1 shows that items O, P, Q, R, and S have relatively little error associated with their difficulty estimates, because ability estimates for a number of our test candidates (Jill, Jack, Jean, Bob, and Bill) are close to or targeted near the same level as those items. Thus, if items Q, R, and S are, say, multiplication problems, this means that the ability of both Bill and Bob includes capabilities at or near the ability to solve multiplication problems. Hence their responses provide us with enough information to estimate the difficulty of those items more accurately. Items L, M, N, and U, on the other hand, have relatively large errors associated with their estimates. Because very few persons in our sample have ability levels equal to the difficulty estimates of these items (i.e., the bulk of our sample is too competent for the simple addition problems, but not up to the demands of item U), estimating the difficulty of such items involves a bit more guesswork, so we are left with more imprecision.

Each person's ability location on the map has an error estimate as well. Note that Bill's square is a bit larger than Bob's. Bill's ability estimate contains more uncertainty because there are not as many items in our observation schedule targeted at his level of ability. Bob, on the other hand, has more items close to his ability level, thereby providing more detailed information to estimate his ability level accurately. Mike has only one, or perhaps two, items directly relevant to him, so his ability estimate will be clouded by a larger error estimate.

All this does not mean that the stepping-stones provided to measure some human ability along some pathway under investigation represent all or the only steps along that path. Development occurs, or ability develops, independently of our observing it in some organized manner via a test or observation schedule. The items we use are chosen for any one of a number of pragmatic/theoretical reasons from the almost endless population of possible relevant items. Therefore, a child's walk along the pathway can be pictured in any reasonable way: as little steps, large steps, skipping, or a mixture of these. However, the record of development produced by our observation of it, via a test or checklist, will depend on which stepping-stones the child succeeded in using and which the child did not use on the day of the test to progress as far as possible down the developmental pathway.

Measurement of any human performance and the estimation of any ability depends on the cooperation of the subject being tested. We tend to assume that the person being examined cooperates with our intention, as revealed by the test instructions and items. However, we all know about some notorious practices of test takers that subvert our measurement intentions. Sometimes respondents just guess at some or all of the answers. Sometimes they copy from neighbors. Sometimes they even bring notes to crib. They also have been known to have lapses in concentration, give up partway through the testing, try to remember formulaic responses to problem-solving tests, and so on. Some even appear less than entirely motivated to complete our clever tasks or do not speak the test language well enough.

Despite all these well-known problems, we as psychologists, teachers, health professionals, and examiners tend to ignore the problems and just count the number of correct steps taken on the pathway (i.e., the raw score) as the indicator of ability. This is a time-honored strategy, but it could stand some serious reconsideration. A developmental pathway is useful only to the extent that the vast majority of respondents use it in demonstrably similar ways. Betty, who scores 6/10 (getting L, O, R, S, T, and U correct on our test in Fig. 3.1), is not showing the same development as Bob who scores a raw score of 5/10 by using steps L,

M, N, O, and *Q.* Therefore, if we want to plot Bob and Betty somewhere on the pathway, we must credit Bob with five, and Betty with six answers correct. We can locate Bob on the pathway well within the dotted lines, showing that his performance pattern fitted our developmental expectations sufficiently well. Betty is located outside the pathway's dotted lines (i.e., her response pattern does not fit the model). That is a warning to us: Even though she scores 6/10, her pattern for scoring those six marks was not orderly enough for us to claim that her performance fitted our expectations. Something else has contributed to Betty's score. We should not take 6/10 at face value as an indicator of Betty's development. If our developmental path is set up according to Rasch's specifications, then we will want to check out Betty's result: Is she a guesser? Were the items she missed biased against her? Did she lose concentration on easy items that did not engage her? Of course, we cannot tell that from her score alone, but her misfitting location off the pathway suggests that 6/10 is not a representative score for her, and that we need to find out more.

Reliability

Now, suppose the investigator did not provide enough steps along the pathway. The first consequence would be that the locations of the steps would be less precise. More good items give more precise locations than fewer good items. Because we do not have many steps to separate the varying levels of development in our example, the children would tend to be distributed along the steps in clumps. This would not be a problem if the test were designed to provide merely a coarse-grained picture of the development being recorded. However, if we are involved in "high-stakes" testing to certify the sufficient development of skills in a critical medical setting, or to allow just certain schoolchildren to move on in a particular educational direction as the result of some testing/recording procedure, then coarse-grained measures will not suffice. The representation of the developmental pathway, as test items or tasks, would require many more stepping-stones (items), each with a quite precise location, so that any person's location on the path could be located precisely and with confidence. This would be of utmost importance at the point along the pathway where the "developed enough/not developed enough" decision is to be made (i.e., at the high-stakes cutoff score).

The Rasch measurement model provides indices that help the investigator to determine whether there are enough items spread along the continuum, as opposed to clumps of them, and enough spread of ability among persons. The *person reliability index* indicates the replicability of person ordering we could expect if this sample of persons were given another set of items measuring the same construct (Wright & Masters, 1982). That is, given another set of items purported to measure the same construct, will Bill still be estimated as being more able than Bob, and Bob more able than Jean? Person reliability is enhanced by small error in ability estimates, which in turn is affected by the number of targeted items. Then in the make-believe example represented in Fig. 3.1, we would expect person reliability to be fairly low. What we do have working for us in terms of person reliability is that our items are targeted at the ability level of our sample. This gives us confidence in our ability estimates. However, the shortcoming with this pathway example is the lack of many additional persons spread along the ability continuum. Person reliability requires not only ability estimates well targeted by a suitable pool of items, but also a large-enough spread of ability across the sample so that the measures demonstrate a hierarchy of ability/development (person separation) on this construct (Fox & Jones, 1998). Therefore, high person reliability means that we have developed a line of inquiry in which some persons score higher and some score lower, and that we can place confidence in the consistency of these inferences.

The *item reliability index* indicates the replicability of item placements along the pathway if these same items were given to another sample with comparable ability levels. For example, if other persons were given these same items, would the item estimates remain stable? For example, would item P still be more difficult than item N? In Fig. 3.1, we would expect a very low item reliability index because there are not enough people in the example at the lower ability levels. Therefore, items L through P, for example, do not have enough information (and hence have large errors) to pinpoint their exact difficulty level accurately. We would need more children with lower math ability in the sample to better estimate the location of these easier items. Therefore, from high item reliability, we can infer that we have developed a line of inquiry in which some items are more difficult and some items are easier, and that we can place confidence in the consistency of these inferences.

CONCLUSIONS

The Rasch model provides a mathematical framework against which test developers can compare their data. The model is based on the idea that useful measurement involves examination of only one human attribute at a time (unidimensionality) on a hierarchical "more than/less than" line of inquiry. This line of inquiry is a theoretical idealization against which we can compare patterns of responses that do not coincide with this ideal. Person and item performance deviations from that line (fit) can be assessed, alerting the investigator to reconsider item wording and score interpretations from these data.

Each item difficulty and person ability is estimated on a logit scale, and each of these estimates has a degree of error associated with it. Estimation error decreases as information about difficulty and ability increases (i.e., when items and persons are appropriately targeted with the sample of items and persons at hand). These error estimates, coupled with item and person reliability estimates, indicate the stability and replicability of the item and person estimates. This information then guides the researcher in knowing how better to interpret and modify measures in the human sciences.

How then would these developmental pathway features be represented in a Rasch analysis? Most Rasch software output includes a form of item–person map in which person ability and item difficulty relations are easily seen. However, representing all the Rasch concepts on one variable map as we have in Fig. 3.1 can be very difficult, so estimates for fit and error usually are included in tables along with ability and difficulty estimates, as shown in Table 3.1.

Item difficulty estimates are expressed in logits, in which a logit value of 0 is arbitrarily set as the average, or mean, of the item difficulty estimates. Thus, item O is near the average on the scale; L and N are easier, having negative logit scores; whereas R, S, and T have positive logit estimates, meaning that they are progressively more difficult. Those who are put off a little by negative logit values could refer to estimates of temperature, in which values below 0 are routine, depending on the climate in which you live. Seven degrees below 0, $-7°C$, easily carries the message of just how cold it is.

Person ability is estimated in relation to the item difficulty estimates (e.g., the more negative the value, the lower the child's ability on this test). Bill's ability estimate of +2.3 makes him clearly "top of the class" on this test, even with the relatively imprecise nature of his estimate. Please take a few minutes to examine how each of the estimates in Tables 3.1 and 3.2 have been represented diagrammatically in Fig. 3.1. It is the item–person map representation of Rasch modeling that is very attractive to both new and experienced users. The values of the

TABLE 3.1
Ersatz Item Statistics for the Developmental Pathway in Fig. 3.1

Item Name	Difficulty Estimate	Error of Estimate	Fit Estimate as t
U	+3.0	0.60	−0.3
T	+1.9	0.43	+1.3
S	+1.6	0.33	−0.9
R	+1.2	0.28	+0.2
W	+0.9	0.43	−2.6
Q	+0.8	0.30	−0.6
P	+0.2	0.30	+0.4
O	−0.3	0.28	−0.4
V	−1.1	0.30	+2.4
N	−1.5	0.43	−0.2
M	−1.8	0.45	+0.6
L	−2.5	0.60	+1.0

TABLE 3.2
Ersatz Person Statistics for the Developmental Pathway in Fig. 3.1

Person Name	Ability Estimate	Error of Estimate	Fit Estimate as t
Bill	+2.3	0.45	−0.6
Betty	+1.2	0.36	+2.8
Bob	+0.8	0.36	+0.8
Jean	+0.2	0.30	−0.8
Jack	−0.7	0.30	+0.5
Jill	−1.0	0.36	−1.6
Mike	−2.4	0.50	−1.0

key attributes being measured can be meaningfully interpreted at a glance. A picture paints a thousand words.

IN SUMMARY

Figure 3.2 is included to clarify the principles that we will use to construct the developmental pathway variable maps, and that readers will need to understand to interpret these maps in chapters 3 through 7.

Estimation

Both items (as circles) and persons (as squares) are located on the same map.

The logit scale is an interval scale, in which all logit units have the same value.

The highest values are located at the top of the map, and the lowest values are located at the bottom.

Each item and person is located along the logit scale according to its estimated value: More positive (higher) persons are more able, and more positive (higher) items are more difficult.

The measurement error of the item and person estimates is indicated by the size of the symbol: Larger symbols indicate greater error (in logits).

Estimated values are read vertically on the logit scale for both estimates and errors.

Fit

Items and persons that fit the model's expectations are located in the white zone.

Items and persons that do not fit the model are located in the shaded zone.

Fit values are read horizontally on a standardized *t* scale. Acceptable values (white) fall between −2.0 and +2.0.

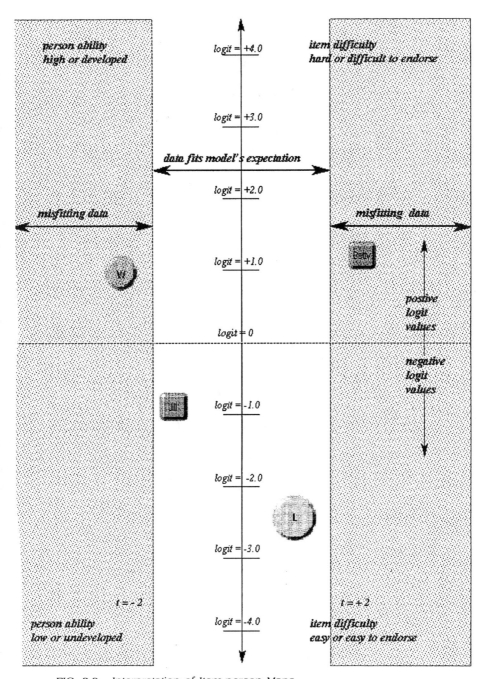

FIG. 3.2. Interpretation of Item-person Maps.

35

4

Building a Set of Items
for Measurement

It would be a useful reference point to consider that there exists a family of Rasch models for measurement (Andrich, 1988; Masters & Wright, 1984). In this chapter we look at the use of the simplest model, the model for analyzing dichotomous data. This was, in fact, the model on which Georg Rasch did his initial work. Since then, the procedures for performing dichotomous Rasch analysis have been developed further by a number of researchers (foremost among them, Ben Wright from Chicago; Wright & Stone, 1979), whereas others have extended the basic Rasch model to include analysis of Likert-type rating scales (David Andrich, Perth, Australia, 1978a, 1978b, 1978c), responses that could be given partial credit (Geoff Masters, Melbourne, Australia, 1982), and testing situations in which many facets other than just person and item needed to be measured (Mike Linacre, Chicago, 1989). In each case, many researchers could claim that they contributed to the development of the Rasch-family models. However, the researchers that have been cited certainly are the most energetic proponents of these particular models. Each of these models from the Rasch family is more complex than the preceding one, but has the basic dichotomous model at its core. Therefore, if the researcher chooses not to use an added feature of any more complex model, it just collapses to the preceding, simpler model.

At the basis of all Rasch modeling is the model developed first: the model for analyzing dichotomous data, which are data that have simply two values, usually 0 and 1. It is easy to mistake this level of data as being "nominal," the sort of data we get when we categorize hair color as being brunette or blonde, or when we categorize a subject's sex as male or female. However, there is an important distinction concerning the data that is appropriate for analysis with the Rasch dichotomous model: The value of 1 is meaningfully greater than the value of 0, not merely different from 0. This might sound pedantic, but it is a very important point. If we allocate the code of 0 for the females in a sample, and 1 for the males, we intend just to differentiate them in terms of sex, showing that the sex of one group of respondents is different from that of the other group. However, when we use the code 1 to indicate the correct answer to a math problem and 0 as the code for the incorrect answer, we are saying something very different: Not only is the correct answer different from the incorrect answer; it also is better than the incorrect answer in a fundamentally important way. We regard the correct answer as superior to the incorrect answer, and we routinely regard children who get the correct answer as showing more ability than those who do not. Note then that Rasch modeling is appropriate only when we can impute some order in the allocation of scores such that 1 is better than 0 (as is a correct response versus an incorrect response). Order does not apply to the case in which 1 (e.g., male) is merely different from 0 (e.g., female), but certainly not better.

Two important points should be mentioned here. The first point is that the codes 1 and 0 merely record our observation of what the child actually did or did not do in response to the test prompt, not what the child could or could not do. Although we all might try to make measures out of the performances that we actually observe and record, and we might do this just so we can make decisions about the people who make the performances, we do not have any magic insight into how competent each person really is. All we have recorded is what the child did or did not do in response to the test prompt, not what the child could or could not do if given another response opportunity.

The second point is that researchers can save themselves a bit of hair tearing in the future by remembering always to use the code of 0 to record the lowest level of performance on any test item. Although this is obvious in the 0 = wrong and 1 = right format, it is not as obvious in coding a rating scale or awarding part marks. With Rasch analysis, it is a convenient and common practice to allocate 0 to indicate the lowest level of response and 1 the next level above that and so on. One routinely used format for the collection of dichotomous data is the multiple-choice test. Such a test would have only one "completely correct" or "best" answer that would receive the score of 1 for that item, with all the other distractors or alternative answers receiving the score of 0, although a partial-credit scoring and model might also be arranged from multiple-choice data (see chapter 7).

ANALYZING DICHOTOMOUS DATA:
THE BLOT

In keeping with an important premise of this volume, that the key worked examples will be derived from the research of developmentalists, educators, and others trying to solve actual measurement problems, the dichotomous data discussed in this chapter come from a test of cognitive development for adolescents: Bond's Logical Operations Test (BLOT; Bond, 1976/1995). The BLOT was developed to provide a test suitable for administration to whole-class groups at a time, as a partial replacement for the individual interview technique developed and used by Jean Piaget and his colleagues in Geneva. The idea was to develop a multiple-choice test with response sheets that could be computer scored, so that a child's cognitive development could be categorized as more or less developed according to the total number of test items the child answered correctly. Of course, this general principle applies to most educational and psychological tests, so the principles outlined in the following discussion have far wider application than just to those interested in Piaget's idea of formal operational thinking.

One theme reiterated throughout this volume is that good tests have, as their basis, a very clear and explicit understanding concerning the line of inquiry the test is trying to put into practice—what was once termed "construct validity." Of course, this understanding might be revealed in a number of different ways. It could be part of a general psychological theory explained in one or more textbooks by some renowned guru, or part of a treatise on the exact sequence of development during a certain period of life. It might derive from a set of curriculum statements in a particular subject area at the grade school or high school level, or it might just as easily be taken from detailed theoretical or conceptual analysis of a field of knowledge being tested (e.g., math or spelling). In medical settings, it might be the understandings of rehabilitation progress after stroke, gleaned by medical professionals who reflect on the effects of their practice.

In the case of the BLOT, the specifications for the items were taken one by one from chapter 17 of the textbook entitled *The Growth of Logical Thinking* (Inhelder & Piaget, 1958). In this chapter Piaget spelled out in detail each of the logical operations that he thought were central to mature thought. The test developer's task then was to represent each of these logical specifications as accurately as possible in multiple-choice test items that would make sense to preadolescents and adolescents without requiring any specific background knowledge. As can be imagined, some items were rewritten a number of times as a result of trial runs with high school students.

Here, the key role of the test developer in putting the substantive theory into measurement practice is clear. In this case, it might have been handy to have Professor Piaget write the items, but then he was not interested in this aspect of group assessment at all. In all test development, the success of the enterprise will be determined largely by how well the intentions of the theory writer, the classroom teacher, or the medical specialist have been converted into items, not merely any items, but items such that the performances of the target audience will reveal exactly those intentions and not some other sort of ability. Clearly then, the test developer needs some detailed understanding of the substantive area of inquiry as well as a great deal of commitment to the implementing of that understanding into measurement practice.

The BLOT is a 35-item multiple-choice test that operationalizes item-by-item each of the schemas of the formal operational stage identified by Inhelder and

Piaget (1958). Each item comprises an item stem of two to four short sentences followed by a set of four or five alternative responses. The students' responses are collected on computer scan sheets and computer scored. The following interpretation shows us the sense that Rasch modeling can make of the BLOT and allows us to determine how much faith we can place in the idea that adolescents' cognitive development can be represented by the total raw score on the BLOT.

When using the BLOT, we generate a data file that looks like the following sample:

```
11111111110110101101011111111011111
11111111111111111111111111101111111
11010111111111011111011111101011111
11111111111111111111101111111111111
11111111111101111111011111111111111
11111111111110111101011111111111111
11111111111110111111011111111111111
11111111111111111111111111101011111
11111111111111111111111101111111111
11011111011111011111011111000110111
11111110111111111111011011111101111
11111110111111111111111111101001111
11111111111111011111010111101111111
11111111111110111110111111111111111
11111111111110111110111111111111111
11111111111110111111011111101110111
etc.
```

Each row represents the performances of one student on the 35 BLOT items. Given the principle of dichotomous scoring, the 1's represent the correct answers and the 0's represent the incorrect answers: The score for item 1 is in column 1, for item 2 in column 2, and so on up to item 35 in column 35. With this example, there is no student ID. The file is set up in the input order of the students' results. Although the BLOT can be computer scored, this file was typed in as a Word (text-only) file by the investigator.

ITEM DIFFICULTY LOCATIONS
AND ERRORS

For the first part of the interpretation, we have included the results of the item analysis only, as Fig. 4.1. This is in exactly the same format as that described for the developmental pathway analogy introduced in chapter 3: easy items at the bottom and difficult items at the top. The error of the item difficulty estimate is shown by the comparative size of the item circle, whereas items that fit the Rasch model are located between the parallel dotted lines.

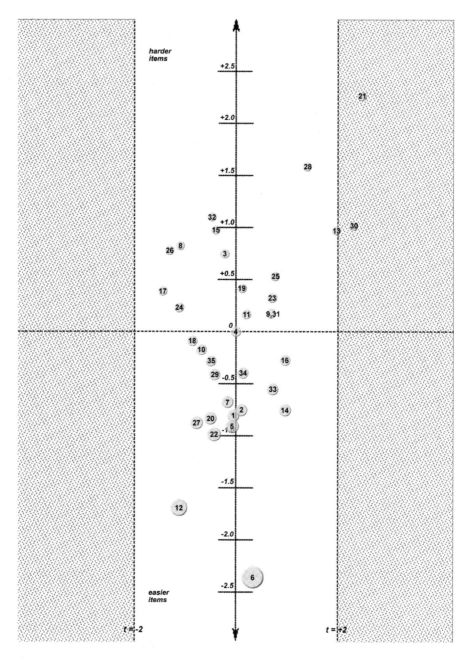

FIG. 4.1. BLOT item pathway.

A number of things can be immediately appreciated as a result of trying to find meaning in Fig. 4.1. First, it seems to represent some sort of developmental acquisition of ability: There are easy items, not-so-easy items, more difficult items, and even more difficult items. For example, items 6 and 12 are the very easiest BLOT items, and items 21 and 28 are extremely difficult in comparison with the others, whereas item 4 sits exactly at the midpoint (0) on the item difficulty scale. Given the range of varying difficulties of BLOT items, we might reasonably expect that a group of suitable students would show a range of developmental abilities on this test. It is worth noting that the extremely easy items (6 and 12) have the least precise estimates, whereas the error estimates for the remaining 33 items are comparatively quite small.

A glance at the dotted lines reveals that the fit of the BLOT to the Rasch model's expectations is pretty good. Locations for just two of the items (i.e., items 21 and 30) do not seem to fit satisfactorily to the same developmental pathway as do the remaining items. Items 21 and 30, therefore, should be candidates for closer inspection before they are included routinely in students' BLOT scores in the future. This is good evidence for reasonably inferring that the ability underlying the BLOT items follows a single line of inquiry. The Piagetian conception of cognitive development seems to be a reasonable description of that line of inquiry, given its explicit use in the BLOT development phase.

Although the item difficulties span five complete units on the logit scale, Fig. 4.1 shows that more than two logits of that development are represented by merely four items: 6 and 12 at the bottom of the scale and 21 and 28 at the top. However, from below −1 logits to above +1 logits, we have approximately 30 closely packed and overlapping items. The consequence of this is that we would find it very hard to locate persons precisely at the extreme ends of the scale represented by the BLOT items, but we could have a great deal of confidence if we had to make important decisions relating to students who perform in the −1 to +1 logits zone.

Although it is rather artificial to consider item performance separately from person performance, the purpose of this chapter is to demonstrate the development of a dichotomous test. At this point, suffice it to say that the distribution of person abilities among children who have been given the BLOT follows the same general pattern as that for items. The vast majority of person performances fit the Rasch model, whereas the distribution of persons along the ability scale is not as clumped as for items. This latter observation can be confirmed by referring to Fig. 4.2: the item–person map for the BLOT analysis.

ITEM FIT

Table 4.1 includes the item statistics from a Rasch analysis of dichotomous BLOT data. For each item number, the estimate of item difficulty and its accompanying error estimate in logits are given. These should correspond in a one-to-

```
-----------------------------------------------------------------------------
BLOT Person Ability Estimates        BLOT Item Difficulty Estimates
-----------------------------------------------------------------------------
  4.0
                  XXXXXXXXXXXXXXX


                  XXXXXXXX
  3.0
                  XXXXXXX

          XXXXXXXXXXXXXXXXXXX            21
                  XXXXX
  2.0
                  XXXXXXX
                  XXXXX                  28
                XXXXXXXXX
                XXXXXXXXXXXX             32
                XXXXXXXXXX               30
  1.0             XXXXX                  13       15
                XXXXXXXX                  8       26
                                          3
                   XXX                   25
                   XXX                   17       19
                XXXXXXXX                 23
                  XXXXX                    9       11      24      31
   .0                XX                    4
                     XX                   18
                      X                   10
                      X                   16       35
                      X                   29       34
                      X                    7       33
                    XXX                    1        2      14
                                          20
 -1.0                 X                    5       27
                      X                   22


                      X

                                          12
 -2.0
                      X

                                           6



 -3.0
-----------------------------------------------------------------------------
Each X represents    1 student
```

FIG. 4.2. Item–person map for the BLOT analysis (QUEST).

42

one way with the pictorial representation in the earlier figure, although only some of the BLOT items are numbered: the higher the difficulty estimate, the further up the pathway, and the larger the error estimate, the larger the item stepping-stone. However, the columns that contain the fit statistics are not so easily interpreted.

Generally speaking, fit statistics focus on two aspects of fit, each of which is routinely reported in both an unstandardized and a standardized form. In Table 4.1 the two aspects of fit reported are item infit and outfit. The unstandardized form is reported as mean squares, and the standardized form is reported as a t statistic, in which acceptable values are those routinely accepted for t (i.e., -2 to $+2$). The mean square is the unstandardized form of the fit statistic and merely the mean, or average value, of the squared residuals for that item. The residual values represent the differences between the Rasch model's theoretical expectation of item performance and the performance actually encountered for that item in the data matrix. Larger residuals mean an item with larger differences between how the item should have performed (i.e., Rasch model expectations) and how it actually performed. Residuals are squared, following the usual statistical convention, to make all "actual minus expected" differences positive so they can be added to give a sum of differences. The concept of fit is the subject of chapter 12.

In the standardized versions of fit statistics, the mean square value is transformed, with the sample size kept in mind, to produce a statistic with a distribution just like t. The "fit" issue will be raised again and again in this volume and everywhere that Rasch analysts gather to chat (e.g., see Smith, 2000).

The infit and outfit statistics adopt slightly different techniques for assessing an item's fit to the Rasch model. The infit statistic gives relatively more weight to the performances of persons closer to the item value. The argument is that persons whose ability is close to the item's difficulty should give a more sensitive insight into that item's performance. The outfit statistic is not weighted, and therefore is more sensitive to the influence of outlying scores. It is for this reason that users of the Rasch model routinely pay more attention to infit scores than to outfit scores. Aberrant infit scores usually cause more concern than large outfit statistics. Of course, outfit statistics do have meaning, and we return to the issues involved in interpreting infit and outfit statistics in chapter 12.

INTERPRETING RASCH ANALYSIS OUTPUT

To make this analysis work, you would need to tell your Rasch software:

The name of the data file and where it is located.

The format of the data: easy in this case, 35 items (one item per column usually is the default).

TABLE 4.1
BLOT Item Difficulty Estimates With
Associated Error Estimates for Each Item

Item	Difficulty Estimate	Error Estimate	Infit Mean Square	Outfit Mean Square	Infit t	Outfit t
1	−0.77	0.26	0.98	0.69	0.0	−0.8
2	−0.70	0.26	1.01	0.75	0.1	−0.6
3	0.74	0.2	0.98	0.9	−0.2	−0.5
4	0.00	0.22	1.00	0.88	0.0	−0.4
5	−0.98	0.28	0.98	0.76	−0.1	−0.5
6	−2.42	0.47	1.06	0.83	0.3	0.1
7	−0.64	0.25	0.97	0.65	−0.1	−1.0
8	0.85	0.19	0.91	1.00	−1.1	0.1
9	0.18	0.21	1.07	0.97	0.7	0.0
10	−0.19	0.23	0.92	0.68	−0.7	−1.1
11	0.18	0.21	1.02	0.96	0.2	−0.1
12	−1.76	0.36	0.69	0.24	−1.1	−1.5
13	1.00	0.19	1.16	1.32	2.0	1.8
14	−0.70	0.26	1.15	1.32	1.0	0.9
15	1.00	0.19	0.96	0.84	−0.4	−0.9
16	−0.30	0.23	1.13	1.03	1.0	0.2
17	0.39	0.2	0.87	0.75	−1.4	−1.2
18	−0.05	0.22	0.9	0.74	−0.9	−1.0
19	0.47	0.2	1.01	1.05	0.1	0.3
20	−0.84	0.27	0.91	0.81	−0.5	−0.4
21	2.33	0.2	1.27	1.75	2.6	3.4
22	−1.06	0.29	0.91	1.69	−0.4	1.4
23	0.35	0.21	1.06	0.92	0.7	−0.3
24	0.22	0.21	0.89	1.03	−1.1	0.2
25	0.51	0.2	1.07	1.26	0.8	1.2
26	0.78	0.2	0.89	0.75	−1.3	−1.4
27	−0.91	0.27	0.85	0.62	−0.8	−0.9
28	1.63	0.19	1.12	1.23	1.4	1.4
29	−0.46	0.24	0.94	0.71	−0.4	−0.8
30	1.07	0.19	1.19	1.15	2.3	0.9
31	0.18	0.21	1.07	1.55	0.7	2.0
32	1.14	0.19	0.96	0.85	−0.5	−0.9
33	−0.52	0.25	1.1	0.93	0.7	−0.1
34	−0.41	0.24	1	0.79	0.1	−0.6
35	−0.30	0.23	0.93	0.73	−0.5	−0.9

Note.   Fit statistics are shown in their natural (mean square) and standardized forms (standardized as *t*).

The type of analysis: easy again, dichotomous is the usual default.

The name and location for the output file.

Most versions of Rasch analysis software produce some form of the item–person map shown as Fig. 4.2, in which the items are indicated by the item number, and each individual person's performance is represented by an "X." The delightful thing about this Rasch representation of data analysis is that many of the person and item relations are shown in meaningful pictorial, or "map," form.

The logit scale, which is the measurement unit common to both person ability and item difficulty, is displayed down the middle of the map in Fig. 4.2. Because the logit scale is an interval scale, the equal distances anywhere up and down that scale have equal value. Therefore, item 15 is as much more difficult than item 4 as item 4 is more difficult than item 5. The distances between are equal (1 logit). Of course, the same equal-value principle applies to differences in person locations as well. Persons and items are located on the map according to their ability and difficulty estimates, respectively.

As a convenient starting point for the mapping process, the mean of the item difficulties is adopted by default as the 0 point. In this case, ignoring the error of measurement for a moment, item 4 is calculated as having that exact difficulty estimate (0 logits), so it is located at the 0 point on the item–person map. Person locations are plotted so that any person has a 50% probability of succeeding with an item located at the same point on the logit scale. For example, a person with an ability estimate of 0 logits has a 50% probability of succeeding on item 4. That same person would have a greater than 50% chance of succeeding on items less difficult than item 4 (say, items 18, 29, and 5) and a less than 50% probability of succeeding on items more difficult than item 4 (say, items 17, 25, and 26). The 50% *limen*, or threshold, is adopted routinely by Rasch analysis, although some Rasch software allows for variations from this value to be specified. For example, those committed to the concept of mastery learning might want to use the 80% threshold that is used routinely to assess mastery.

With those basic principles in mind, we now can tell immediately from the item–person map in Fig. 4.2 that the BLOT is too easy for a sample like this one. Just look where the persons are located in comparison with the items. First, the person distribution is top-heavy in comparison with the item distribution. Second, the top 50 BLOT performers (one third of this sample) are targeted by only two questions: items 21 and 28. The Rasch output tells us as well that three candidates topped out on the BLOT with a perfect score of 35 of 35. From a general test-development perspective, this would be regarded as a serious inadequacy in a test. If this is the usual sort of target group for this test, then the test needs some more questions of a difficulty like that of 21 and 28 so the abilities of the high-fliers can be more precisely estimated. Also, we would need some even more difficult questions to raise the "ceiling" of the test.

A key point to remember, however, is that Rasch analysis item–person maps usually report the relations between the two key variables only: item difficulty estimates and person ability estimates. Other key parts of the analysis—the precision of those estimates (error), the fit of the items, the fit of the persons, the reliabilities of the person and item estimates—are reported in detail in the output tables.

For items we have the following information that is useful:

```
Summary of Item Estimates
-------------------------
Mean                              0.00
SD                                0.95
SD (adjusted)                     0.92
Reliability of estimate           0.94


Fit Statistics
--------------
Infit Mean Square              Outfit Mean Square
   Mean          1.00             Mean    0.95
   SD            0.11             SD      0.31

        Infit t                     Outfit t
   Mean          0.09             Mean   -0.05
   SD            0.98             SD      1.10

0 items with zero scores
0 items with perfect scores
```

We already know that the mean of item estimates is located at 0 (by default), and that the standard deviation for item estimates is nearly 1. We can confirm the latter by referring to the item–person map: The vast majority of items are located in the narrow band between +1 and −1 logits. The reliability of the item difficulty estimates is a very high .94 on a 0 to 1 scale. Item reliability can be interpreted on this 0 to 1 scale, much in the same way as Cronbach's alpha is interpreted, or it can be transformed to an item separation index, wherein the reliability is calculated as the number of standard errors of spread among the items (see Fox & Jones, 1998, or Wright & Masters, 1982, for an explanation). Item reliability and item separation refer to the ability of the test to define a distinction hierarchy of items along the measured variable. The higher the number, the more confidence we can place in the replicability of item placement across other samples. Therefore, the item reliability index of .94 means that we can quite readily rely on this order of item estimates to be replicated when we give the BLOT to other samples for whom it is suitable.

The summary of fit statistics also can be informative. Unstandardized fit estimates (i.e., mean squares) are modeled by the Rasch algorithm to have a mean of 1. The actual unstandardized item fit statistics for the BLOT have their means very close to the expected 1, with the infit mean squares showing little spread from that ideal and the outfit mean squares much greater variation.

In the standardization of fit scores, the mean square values are transformed so they are distributed like t, with a mean of 0 and a standard deviation of 1. Therefore, we should not be surprised to see the preceding raw item mean squares transformed into near-0 values. But for how many of the BLOT items is this information applicable? The little note at the bottom of the output reminds us that all the BLOT items were useful for this sample. An item would not be useful for discriminating ability among members of this group if everyone was successful with it (item too easy) or everyone got it wrong (item too hard).

COMPARING PERSONS AND ITEMS

When we turn our focus toward the summary of person performances, we find that Rasch modeling has the distinct advantage of applying the same analytical logic, and therefore the same logic of interpretation, to persons as it does to items.

```
Summary of Case Estimates
--------------------------------
Mean                          1.56
SD                            1.30
SD (adjusted)                 1.17
Reliability of estimate       0.81


Fit Statistics
---------------
Infit Mean Square          Outfit Mean Square
  Mean       0.99            Mean      0.95
  SD         0.13            SD        0.46

      Infit t                  Outfit t
  Mean       0.13            Mean      0.10
  SD         0.58            SD        0.63

0 cases with zero scores
3 cases with perfect scores
```

The person ability estimate mean of +1.56 is the first indicator that this sample finds this test comparatively easy. Figure 4.3 shows three possible relations between item difficulty and person ability. The mean person estimate (i.e., the group average) would be closer to 0 for a well-matched test (Fig. 4.3b). A tough test would yield a mean person estimate with a large negative value (Fig. 4.3c). The standard deviation of 1.30 for person estimates indicates greater spread of person measures or variation in those measures than with item measures. The reliability of the person ability estimates is high at .81, which is not as reliable as the item separations, but more than acceptable nonetheless.

This corroborates the targeting problem we identified from the item–person map. Although we can rely on this order of person estimates to be replicated when we give these persons another test like the BLOT, in the current analysis we have better information about the items than we do about the persons, so the item estimates are more reliable. In other words, the performances of 150 persons give us more good information about the 35 BLOT items than the 35 BLOT items give about the 150 persons. From consideration of the three distributions in the item–person maps of Fig. 4.3, we could expect the best person separability index in case b, where the match between items and persons is the best. In case c, the difficult test, both item and person reliability would be lower: The least able persons have no items to distinguish between them, whereas the toughest questions have no persons sufficiently able to provide good information about them.

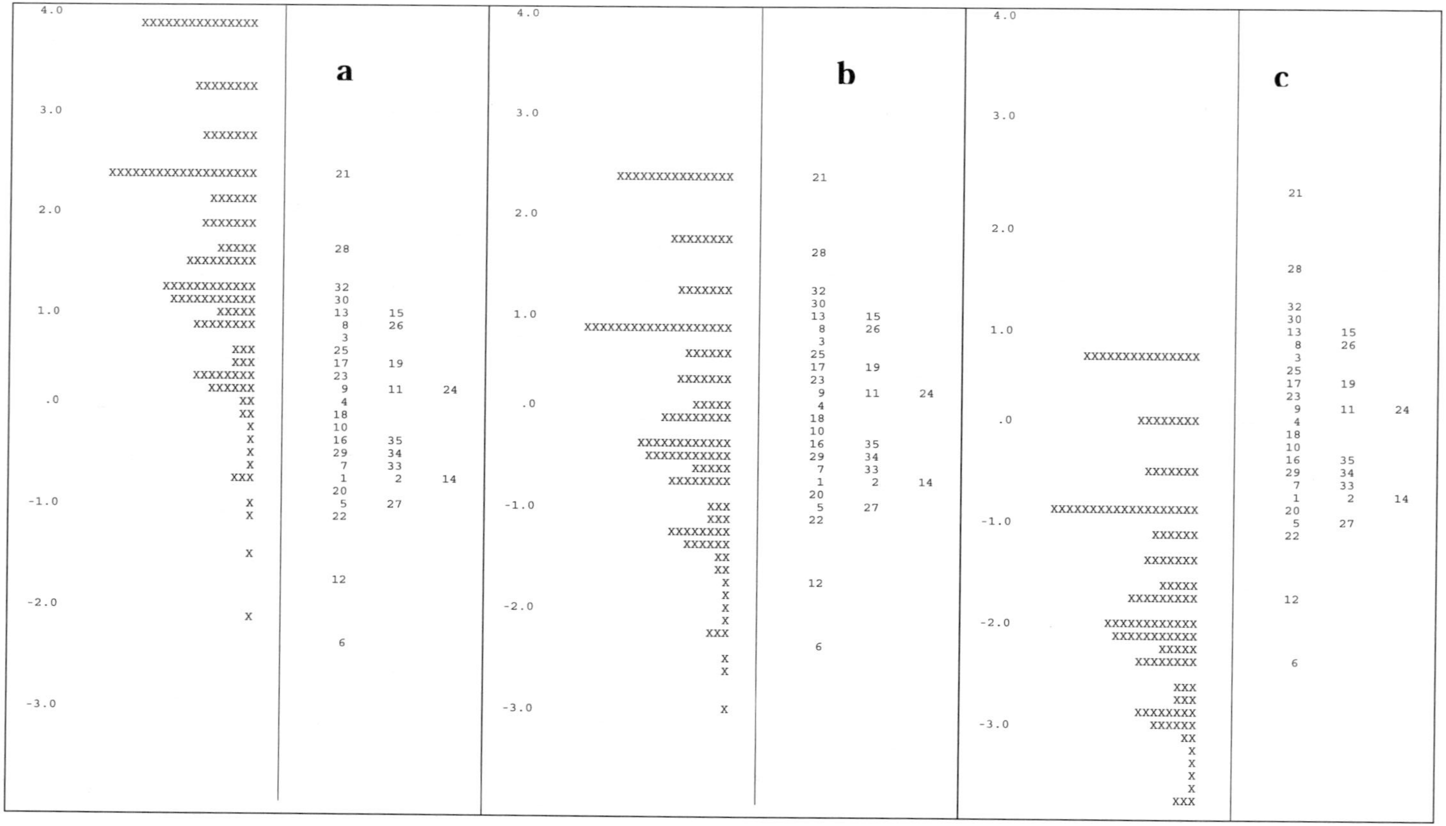

FIG. 4.3. Item-person maps showing the test as (a) relatively easy for the sample, (b) well-matched to the sample, and (c) relatively difficult for the sample.

Again, the person fit summary statistics are equally good. The mean of the infit mean squares at 0.99 and the outfit mean squares at 0.95 are very close to the Rasch-modeled expectations of 1. Consequently, they produce standardized fit t values just greater than 0. The spread in, or variation of, modeled fit scores for persons (infit t $SD = 0.58$ and outfit t $SD = 0.63$) suggests that the vast majority of person ability estimates will have error estimates well inside the conventionally acceptable range of −2 to +2.

THE THEORY–PRACTICE DIALOGUE

Of course, every test developer and user should try to discern what the results from the performance of the items and persons in practice have to say about the substantive theory being investigated, and should try to decide what the theory tells about the persons and items under investigation. This should always be seen as an ongoing dialectical process. We have included a little of it here to indicate the sort of meanings that might be attributed to the results of the analysis shown earlier.

The analysis provides pretty good evidence that the items work well together to represent one underlying path of inquiry or ability. Given that the specifications for the logical structure of each and every item were lifted directly from the Inhelder and Piaget (1958) text, this could be seen to confirm the idea that Piaget's model for adolescent intelligence is coherent in itself. At least psychometric evidence points to "something" and not "many things" as the object of inquiry. Moreover, whatever this ability is, it also is evident in the BLOT-answering behavior of a bunch of suitable subjects: 150 adolescent schoolchildren.

Because both the items and the persons were shown to behave in sufficiently lawful and predictable ways, it is reasonable to conclude that this part of Piaget's theory and the BLOT interpretation of it are certainly worth the effort of continued refinement and investigation.

The ceiling effect on the BLOT continues to be an ongoing problem: The most cognitively developed kids top out on the test. Although that amounts to only 3 of the 150 tested for this chapter (at age 15), we could reasonably expect that more and more of these students would "hit the ceiling" as we tracked their development over time. This is further complicated to the extent that some Rasch analysis software routinely imputes an ability estimate for those who get a perfect score, whereas other software packages ignore the perfect scorers because they do not have enough information to provide an accurate estimate. Clearly, the BLOT needs more difficult items based on Piaget's specifications if we intend to use it to estimate accurately the cognitive development of our more intellectually able teenagers.

The spread of items, or the lack of spread, on the item–person map suggests that some of the BLOT items are redundant: The area from 0 to −1 logits is saturated with items. It seems that a number of the particular intellectual skills incorporated into BLOT items are very much like other skills/items, and that it would not be necessary to include them all in a parsimonious test. Indeed, dropping some of the psychometrically redundant items in favor of more difficult items would remedy two of the apparent deficiencies of the BLOT.

Of course, psychometrically redundant and theoretically redundant are two different but related perspectives on the theory–practice nexus: In the first round, the practice tells us that the conceptualization of the theory has a lot going for it, but that a more useful test could be developed by going back to the theory to find specifications for further item development and rationalization.

Software control files for this analysis and their explanations appear as follows:

QUEST:

```
title BLOT for Chapter Four
data bond87.txt
format items 5-39
est
show>>BLOT.out
show items>>Blot.items
quit
```

Line 1 gives a name to the output.

Line 2 tells QUEST which file has the data.

Line 3 that indicates that the BLOT responses are in columns 5 to 35.

Line 4 commands QUEST to perform a Rasch *est*imation.

Line 5 directs the general output to a file called BLOT.out.

Line 6 directs the item statistics output to a file called Blot.items.

WINSTEPS:

```
&INST
TITLE='BLOT for Chapter Four'
NI=35
ITEM1=5
NAME1=1
IFILE=BLOT.IF
&END
Item 1
Item 2
Item 35
END NAMES
111111111101101011010111111111011111
111111111111111111111111111101111111
```

```
1101011111111101111101111101011111
etc.
```

Line 1 contains a command that must begin every WINSTEPS file.

Line 2 provides a title for the output.

Line 3 indicates the number of items in the test.

Line 4 identifies the starting column for the data.

Line 5 identifies the starting column for the person identification number.

Line 6 directs the item statistics output to a file called Blot.if.

Line 7 indicates the end of the commands and the beginning of the item names.

Lines 8 to 10 give a line-per-item name. Only the first two and the last BLOT items are named here.

Line 11 indicates an end to the names.

Line 12 etc. ASCII data file, like the 0's and 1's shown earlier in the chapter, follows immediately after this line.

5

Test Equating:
Can Two Tests Measure
the Same Ability?

We have already raised the idea that central to the concept of measurement is the view that we must attempt to measure one single construct at a time. In chapter 4, we gave an example of how this might be achieved in practice. A detailed theoretical description was taken at the starting point, and we used Rasch methodology as the technique to show us how successful our attempt had been to implement that construct into measurement practice.

One of the questions continually addressed in psychological and other human sciences research is, "Does this test measure the same construct as this other test?" This is one important technique in establishing the validity of a test. Although the central validity issue in test development revolves around the crucial question of construct validity, test developers legitimately appeal to the psychometric parallels between a new test and an established and recognized test to claim that the new test has concurrent validity. It is, indeed, unfortunate that a combination of concurrent and face or content validity often is held as the sufficient prerequisite for test development. Almost total reliance on the results of empirical data analysis techniques to resolve issues of validity have obscured the central role of construct validity in the human sciences. We return to this important issue in the closing chapter. Suffice it to say, here, that the researcher must be satisfied by an elaboration of the theoretical construct under examination in a pair of tests that they purport to measure the same construct. Of course, the answer to the question "Do two tests measure the same construct?" involves another issue, "How could we tell if test A measures the same construct as test B?"

One purpose of a test A versus test B comparison might be to develop parallel forms of the same test so that we can validly use them as equally useful alternatives in a test–retest format. Why else would we want to develop a test that measures the same construct as an already existing test? Of course, there are a number of very pragmatic reasons. The new test might be shorter, offer a new format, or allow greater ease of administration, scoring, or interpretation. It might be more suitable to a particular target population or a particular testing context. It might provide greater precision around important high-stakes decision points, or it might help to prevent cheating, or to avoid the learning effect when tests are used more than once. On the other hand, it might just provide a useful, low-cost, quick-to-use, screening device when the high cost of high-power testing of all potential research subjects is not warranted. Inherent in all these possibilities is the theory–practice dialogue that is the important focus of all good measurement. Tests apparently quite dissimilar in format that measure the same construct will inform us about the theoretical construct we are investigating, as will apparently similar tests that cannot be accepted as measuring the same underlying trait.

In this chapter we investigate the properties of a classroom test of formal operational thinking developed in the United Kingdom. Then we use Rasch modeling to see whether this test can be judged to be measuring the same construct as that shown in the results of the Bond's Logical Operations Test (BLOT) analysis in the previous chapter.

THE PRTIII–PENDULUM

The Piagetian Reasoning Task (PRTIII–Pendulum) was developed in the United Kingdom (Shayer, Küchemann, & Wylam, 1976) to allow Piagetian reasoning tasks to be administered to whole-class groups. Using the PRTIII, the teacher demonstrates a number of experiments in front of the class and, from time to time, the children make written responses to the questions posed on individual answer sheets. The teacher later codes each written answer from the child (a few words, sometimes a sentence or two) as 1 (correct) or 0 (incorrect) according to a set of scoring criteria (derived from chapter 4 of Inhelder & Piaget, 1958), thereby producing the same sort of dichotomous data string for each child as that produced by the computer-scored BLOT results in the previous chapter. Any number of teacher-made tests adopt that general format of a written short-answer test given to a whole class at a time, with the teacher marking the answers right or wrong at a later time and reporting the total score as the test result, and any number of testing opportunities in the human sciences could profitably adopt the same approach.

The PRTIII contains 13 items, which are scored dichotomously. The data we have for analysis in this chapter came from the very same 150 children who completed the BLOT in chapter 4. Of course, we took the usual testing precaution of ensuring that half of the children completed the BLOT first, with the other half completing the PRTIII before the BLOT, to neutralize any order effect.

The dispersal of the PRTIII items in terms of their difficulty locations, the error of those difficulty estimates, and the fit of those estimates to the Rasch model are illustrated using the pathway principle in Fig. 5.1. The details of the item statistics for the PRTIII results from these 150 children are reported in Table 5.1. Item difficulties span a range from −3.17 logits for the easiest item (item 1) to +3.40 logits for the most difficult of the PRTIII items (item 2). All of the PRTIII items fit within the conventional limits for the infit t statistic, in this case ranging from +1.5 to −1.4. At this point, we should recall that Rasch analysis routinely adopts an arbitrary 0 point for each scale, usually the mean of the test's item difficulties.

TEST SCORE EQUATING

Central to the demonstration that we need to use here is the notion that one sample of children has been the subject of two test administrations, each test of which is held to measure the same underlying construct. One very simple procedure could be adopted. We could reasonably regard all these items as attempts to measure the same underlying construct and just analyze the BLOT and PRTIII items together as one test. Such an analysis might easily be regarded as sufficient for the basic purpose of establishing whether two sets of items adhere to Rasch principles sufficiently to be regarded as measuring the same construct. If the principles espoused in chapter 4 allow us to regard the 35 BLOT items as measuring just one construct, then we could draw the same conclusion about the 48 BLOT and PRTIII items if they were Rasch-analyzed as one test. However, a possible problem with this technique is raised in chapter 12, whereas the procedures we demonstrate in this chapter are much more informative, introducing ideas that have a wide range of measurement applications.

The key issue is whether the performances of students across both tests are similar enough to sustain the argument that the one dimension being assessed on each test is the same dimension for both tests. The simple first step then is to plot each pair of test results for each student onto a simple scatter plot, using the Rasch-modeled ability estimate measures (in logits) for each person rather than just raw scores. Although the Rasch measures are based exactly on the raw scores for each of the tests, these modeled ability estimates contain much more information about the interval scale and the measurement errors associated with each of the measures. Those working in the application of fundamental measurement principles usually take care to distinguish between raw scores, which usually are regarded as counts, and Rasch-modeled ability estimates, which satisfy the requirements necessary to be regarded and used as measures. The ability es-

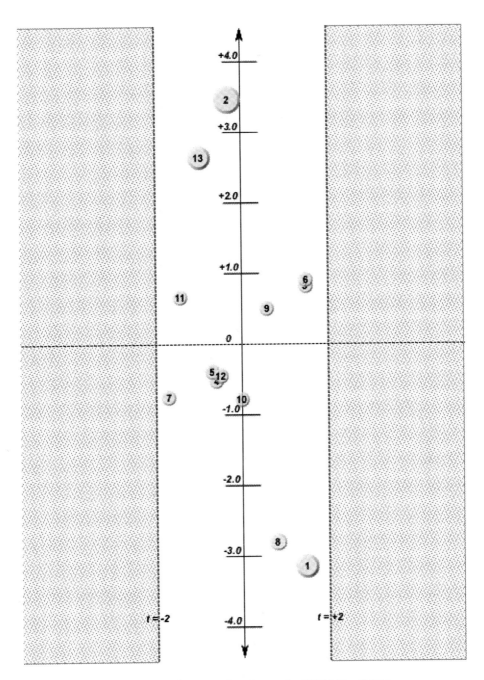

FIG. 5.1. Developmental pathway for PRTIII–Pendulum.

55

TABLE 5.1
Item Statistics for PRTIII–Pendulum

PRTIII Item No.	Difficulty Estimate	Error Estimate	Infit Mean Square	Outfit Mean Square	Infit t	Outfit t
1	−3.17	0.30	1.26	1.08	1.4	0.3
2	3.40	0.44	0.91	0.64	−0.2	0.1
3	0.8	0.22	1.17	1.09	1.5	0.4
4	−0.61	0.21	0.94	0.98	−0.6	0.0
5	−0.37	0.21	0.93	0.90	−0.7	−0.4
6	0.94	0.23	1.17	1.30	1.5	1.0
7	−0.77	0.21	0.82	0.75	−1.8	−1.3
8	−2.81	0.27	1.10	3.01	0.7	2.6
9	0.53	0.22	1.04	1.30	0.4	1.2
10	−0.81	0.21	1.00	0.86	0.0	−0.6
11	0.67	0.22	0.85	0.72	−1.4	−1.0
12	−0.41	0.21	0.97	0.83	−0.3	−0.9
13	2.60	0.33	0.79	0.67	−1.0	−0.2

timates of students taking both the BLOT and the PRTIII are plotted on the corresponding x and y axes in Fig. 5.2.

The only difference between the BLOT ability scale and the PRTIII ability
scale is the difference in the arbitrary 0 points allotted to each scale during the
Rasch analyses. First, take the mean ability score for the BLOT (B.x: ability estimate on test x) and for the PRTIII (B.y: ability estimate on test y) and plot that

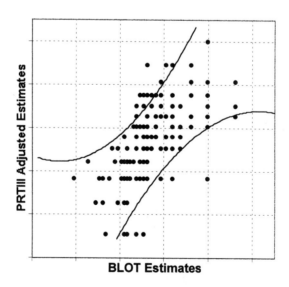

FIG. 5.2. Common person equating BLOT and PRTIII.

point on the graph. If we draw a diagonal line (45° or slope = 1) through the point representing the group means of B.x and B.y, we would construct a line that represented the exact modeled relation between the two tests if they measured the same ability under perfect (i.e., error-free) measurement conditions. In this situation (unachievable in practice), all the points (i.e., the B.x and B.y location for each person) would lie along this diagonal line. Usefully, Rasch modeling provides us with error estimates for each and every ability estimate, and we can use these to construct control lines (shown in Fig. 5.2) to see whether the distribution of the plotted ability points is close enough to the modeled relationship diagonal line for the measures to be regarded as sufficiently identical (i.e., identical within the limits of measurement error).

The formula for constructing the control lines for a 95% confidence band around the diagonal through the mean ability estimates, derived originally from Wright and Stone (1979, pp. 94–95), is given as an Excel spreadsheet at the end of this chapter. Whereas some Rasch analysis software (e.g., Quest) will produce a graph of such comparisons on demand, anyone familiar with the graphing procedures in a spreadsheet can develop a worksheet that will import Rasch analysis output and use the pairs of person ability estimates to plot the locations, and the associated pairs of error estimates to plot the control lines. Simple visual inspection will reveal whether enough of the points (i.e., 95% or more of them) lie within the control band. Under these conditions, it seems reasonable to argue that the tests may be regarded as measuring the same underlying trait.

The next point of interest in this comparison is the relative difficulty of the two tests being analyzed. Recall that each of the analyses we have used for this exercise was conducted separately. The origin of the scale developed for the BLOT (0 logits) was the mean of the BLOT item difficulty estimates, and the origin of the scale developed for the PRTIII (0 logits) was the mean of the PRTIII item difficulty estimates. If the tests are of the same difficulty for these students, the BLOT 0 and the PRTIII 0 will be identical. In that case, the mean ability on the BLOT and the mean ability on the PRTIII also will be identical (within error). Then the intercept of the diagonal line on the x axis is the adjustment that must be made to the BLOT estimates to bring them to the scale of the PRTIII estimates. In this case, the BLOT estimates require an adjustment of –2 logits to align them with the PRTIII scale (i.e., the PRTIII is 2.28 logits more difficult for this sample than the BLOT). We already had some hint of that in the individual analyses. Whereas three students "topped out" on the BLOT with perfect scores, only one of them did so on the PRTIII. Conversely, six students scored 0 on the PRTIII, whereas the lowest BLOT score was 5/35. All prima facie evidence suggests that the students found the PRTIII tougher than the BLOT. If the two tests were both measuring the same ability *and* were of the same difficulty, at least 95% of the plotted points would lie within the control lines, and the diagonal line representing the modeled relations between the performances would pass through the origin point of the graph.

How much variation can be expected depends on the size of the error estimates for each of the person ability locations. The error sizes depend on the
amount of good information we have about person abilities. More items in a test
produce smaller measurement errors for persons taking the test. Equally, test
items that are appropriately difficult for the sample produce tighter error estimates than poorly targeted items. Moreover, in Rasch modeling, the converse is
true: More persons produce less measurement error for items, and samples that
are well chosen for the test yield better item difficulty error estimates.

A quick look at the item error estimates for the BLOT (Table 4.1) will show
that they are approximately the same magnitude as the item error estimates for
the PRTIII (Table 5.1), mostly about 0.20 logits. This is largely because we have
150 well-targeted persons to provide information about both the BLOT items
and the PRTIII items. For PRTIII item 2, however, the targeting of persons is
not so good: The item is very difficult for these year 9 students, and the error estimate "blows out" to 0.44 logits as a consequence. Now, let us apply the same
logic to the person error estimates in Table 5.2. This table contains a slice of the

TABLE 5.2
Raw Scores and Ability Estimates With Errors
on the PRTIII and BLOT for a Subsample of Students

Student ID No.	PRTIII Score (/13)	Ability Estimate	Error Estimate	BLOT Score (/35)	Ability Estimate	Error Estimate
58	8	0.69	0.70	29	1.83	0.48
59	9	1.20	0.74	34	3.93	1.03
60	7	0.22	0.68	28	1.62	0.45
61	3	−1.80	0.81	26	1.24	0.41
62	9	1.20	0.74	26	1.24	0.41
63	2	−2.54	0.92	29	1.83	0.48
64	9	1.20	0.74	31	2.36	0.56
65	8	0.69	0.70	31	2.36	0.56
66	7	0.22	0.68	31	2.36	0.56
67	0	Case has zero score		25	1.08	0.40
68	2	−2.54	0.92	26	1.24	0.41
70	3	−1.80	0.81	22	0.62	0.38
72	9	1.20	0.74	28	1.62	0.45
73	4	−1.21	0.74	27	1.42	0.43
74	9	1.20	0.74	31	2.36	0.56
75	2	−2.54	0.92	24	0.92	0.39
76	11	2.55	0.93	26	1.24	0.41
77	4	−1.21	0.74	30	2.07	0.51
78	7	0.22	0.68	23	0.77	0.38
79	3	−1.80	0.81	26	1.24	0.41
80	6	−0.24	0.68	26	1.24	0.41
81	8	0.69	0.70	32	2.71	0.63
82	7	0.22	0.68	33	3.17	0.75

person results from the analyses of the BLOT and PRTIII. Here we have results for 23 persons. Although 150 persons provided information about the test items, we have only 35 BLOT items providing information about the persons and a mere 13 PRTIII items, one of which is arguably not targeted on most of the sample. The person error estimates yielded by the BLOT are approximately 0.50 logits, whereas the PRTIII yields person error estimates approximating the 0.70 mark, confirming the claim that more good items provide more precise estimates of person ability than do fewer good items. The near extreme BLOT score of 34 for person 59 produces a high ability estimate (+3.93 logits), but with low precision (error = 1.03 logits).

The statistics often used in human sciences research usually do not provide individual error estimates for each person and each item. Any dispersion of scores from the perfect diagonal is regarded as unmodeled or residual variance. Consequently, test development approaches based on the inspection of correlations generally are less than adequate. Precision in measurement derives from the amount of good information we have on which to model the measures. Measurement error must be taken into account when correlation statistics are interpreted: The more information, the smaller the error and the higher the correlation must be. Conversely, a small circle of plotted points well within the control lines of Fig. 5.2 could help to justify the assertion that two tests were measuring the same variable even though the correlation coefficient was "disastrously" low (Masters & Beswick, 1986).

Therefore, although plotting raw test scores, or counts, against each other might be more or less informative, the plotting of Rasch-modeled estimates of person ability, or item difficulty, can be far more useful when interpreted in the context of the precision (i.e., measurement error) of these estimates. The relative invariance of person ability, whether measured by the BLOT or the PRTIII, is good evidence to suggest that these tests can be used interchangeably. Invariance of person estimates and item estimates within the modeled expectations of measurement error over time, across measurement contexts, and so on is a key Rasch measurement strategy. Disturbances to expected invariance beyond the bounds imposed by modeled error in these situations can be deduced as evidence that our measurement expectations have not been sustained in practice: that parallel versions of a test are not parallel, that some test items are biased, that some test formats discriminate against some persons or group of persons, that some items are context dependent, and so on.

The principles we have described are more often used in testing situations to compare the abilities of two groups of subjects who are given the same test. Rasch modeling allows us to determine the relationships between two different groups of people who share performance on a common test. This is called common test equating. In the case of equating BLOT and PRTIII, however, the position was reversed: We had two groups of items (different tests) that had been given to the same sample (a single group of subjects). In this example, Rasch

modeling was used to investigate the relations between the two tests. This benefit of Rasch modeling comes about exactly because the computational logic applied to persons in relation to items is exactly the same as the logic applied to
items in relation to persons. With experience in using Rasch analysis, the grow-
ing realization that these principles are exactly the same for items and for persons (e.g., estimates, errors, and fit are expressed in exactly the same units on a
single scale for both) allows for considerable power and flexibility in addressing
a range of problems that we must address when we try to solve practical measurement questions in the human sciences.

THE THEORY–PRACTICE DIALOGUE

How could two tests be so apparently different and still measure the same underlying ability trait? The PRTIII requires a teacher demonstration of pendulum experiments while students write their answers in sentences, which the teacher
later carefully assesses with the use of a detailed marking key. The BLOT is ma-
chine-marked, multiple-choice testing in its plainest form, untouched by human
hands. Although the PRTIII is obviously, and now measurably, more difficult
than the BLOT, they both can be seen as two practical instantiations of the theoretical ideas expounded by Inhelder and Piaget (1958). Both tests aim to be
classroom measures of mature adolescent thinking that teachers could use to inform themselves about the relevance and suitability of particular learning experiences for their high school students.

Given that Piaget's conception of formal operational thought is regarded
by some as passé or even fatally flawed, the equivalence of the PRTIII and the
BLOT, despite their distinct differences, suggests that there might be more to the
underlying theory than meets the critic's eye. It is clear that selecting the correct
operational answer from many distractors (BLOT) is much easier than constructing the correct written answer in the particular context of a high school
physics experiment (PRTIII). The BLOT will provide a fine-grained analysis of
the development of formal operational thinking, whereas the PRTIII will show
just how developed that thinking can be. Test users who do not have the skills
necessary to administer and grade the PRTIII can use the BLOT, but at the cost of
the "ceiling effect" for the most able test takers. As would be expected, both tests
have strong relations with high school achievement, especially in the area of science, in which most of the research has been carried out.

The following software control files are used in the analysis to yield PRTIII
person estimates:

QUEST:

```
title PRTIII for Chapter Five
data bond87.txt
```

```
format name 1-3 items 41-53
est
show>>PRTIII.out
show cases>>PRTIII.cases
quit
```

Line 1 gives a name to the output.

Line 2 tells QUEST which file has the data.

Line 3 indicates that the PRTIII responses are in columns 41 to 53.

Line 4 commands QUEST to perform a Rasch *est*imation.

Line 5 directs the general output to a file called PRTIII.out.

Line 6 directs the person statistics output to a file called PRTIII.cases.

The inclusion of the following line before the "quit" command in the chapter 4 QUEST control file will produce BLOT person estimates for the common person equating plot: `show cases>>BLOT.cases`.

WINSTEPS:

```
&INST
TITLE='PRTIII for Chapter Five'
NI=13
ITEM1=41
NAME1=1
IFILE=BLOT.IF
&END
Item 1
Item 2

Item 13
END NAMES
etc.
```

Line 1 contains a command that must begin every WINSTEPS file.

Line 2 provides a title for the output.

Line 3 indicates the number of items in the test.

Line 4 identifies the starting column for the data.

Line 5 identifies the starting column for the person identification number.

Line 6 directs the item statistics output to a file called Blot.if.

Line 7 indicates the end of the commands and beginning of the item names.

Lines 8 and 9 give a line-per-item name. Only the first two and the last BLOT items are named here.

Line 10 indicates an end to the names.

Line 11 etc. ASCII data file, like the 0's and 1's shown earlier in the chapter, follows immediately after this line.

PROCEDURE FOR COMMON PERSON EQUATING PRTIII AND BLOT USING EXCEL

1. Run PRTIII analysis in WINSTEPS or QUEST and obtain person ability estimates and error estimates. Import these measures, including the ID number, into an Excel spreadsheet. Do the same for BLOT.
2. Merge the two files by ID (column A) and obtain the file shown in Fig. 5.3.
3. Compute the average of ability estimates for BLOT (column D) and PRTIII (column E) and obtain the file demonstrated in Fig. 5.4.

   Average measure for BLOT = 1.6461

   `D152=AVERAGE(D2:D151)`

   Average measure for PRTIII = –0.6323

   `E152=AVERAGE(E2:E151)`

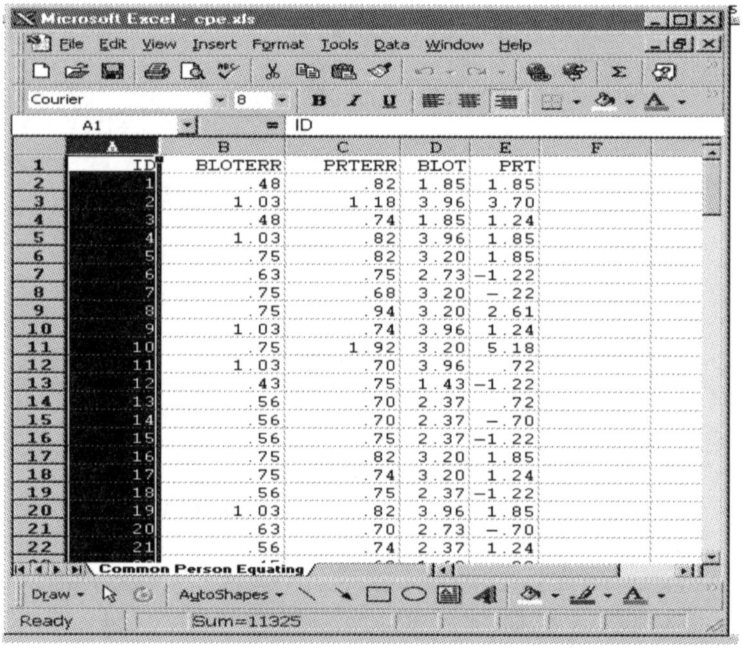

ID	BLOTERR	PRTERR	BLOT	PRT
1	.48	.82	1.85	1.85
2	1.03	1.18	3.96	3.70
3	.48	.74	1.85	1.24
4	1.03	.82	3.96	1.85
5	.75	.82	3.20	1.85
6	.63	.75	2.73	−1.22
7	.75	.68	3.20	−.22
8	.75	.94	3.20	2.61
9	1.03	.74	3.96	1.24
10	.75	1.92	3.20	5.18
11	1.03	.70	3.96	.72
12	.43	.75	1.43	−1.22
13	.56	.70	2.37	.72
14	.56	.70	2.37	−.70
15	.56	.75	2.37	−1.22
16	.75	.82	3.20	1.85
17	.75	.74	3.20	1.24
18	.56	.75	2.37	−1.22
19	1.03	.82	3.96	1.85
20	.63	.70	2.73	−.70
21	.56	.74	2.37	1.24

FIG. 5.3. The merged file from PRTIII and BLOT estimates.

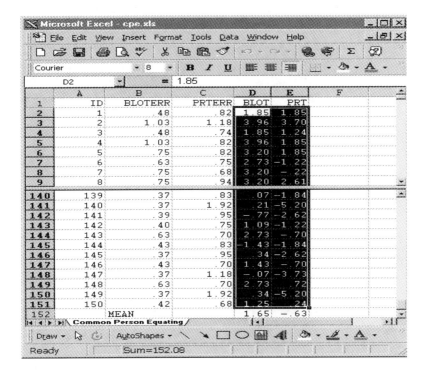

FIG. 5.4. Calculating the means of PRTIII and BLOT estimates.

4. Calculate the difference between the two means:

   Difference = 1.6461 − (−.6323) = 2.2784 = 2.28
   `=(D152-E152)`

5. Adjust the PRTIII person measures by incorporating the mean difference, as shown in Fig. 5.5:

   Person ability estimates of PRTIII adjusted for BLOT
   = person ability estimates of PRTIII + 2.28
   PRTADJ:
   `F2=(E2+2.28)` then 'Fill Down'.

6. Compute the paired 95% quality control lines:

   D-2*EBLOT:
   `G2=((D2+F2)/2-SQRT(B2*B2+C2*C2))`
   D+2*EPRT:
   `H2=((D2+F2)/2+SQRT(B2*B2+C2*C2))`
   D+2*EBLOT:
   `I2=((D2+F2)/2+SQRT(B2*B2+C2*C2))`

	ID	BLOTERR	PRTERR	BLOT	PRT	PRTADJ
2	1	.48	.82	1.85	1.85	4.13
3	2	1.03	1.18	3.96	3.70	5.98
4	3	.48	.74	1.85	1.24	3.52
5	4	1.03	.82	3.96	1.85	4.13
6	5	.75	.82	3.20	1.85	4.13
7	6	.63	.75	2.73	−1.22	1.06
8	7	.75	.68	3.20	−.22	2.06
9	8	.75	.94	3.20	2.61	4.89
10	9	1.03	.74	3.96	1.24	3.52
11	10	.75	1.92	3.20	5.18	7.46
12	11	1.03	.70	3.96	.72	3.00
13	12	.43	.75	1.43	−1.22	1.06
14	13	.56	.70	2.37	.72	3.00
15	14	.56	.70	2.37	−.70	1.58
16	15	.56	.75	2.37	−1.22	1.06
17	16	.75	.82	3.20	1.85	4.13
18	17	.75	.74	3.20	1.24	3.52
19	18	.56	.75	2.37	−1.22	1.06
20	19	1.03	.82	3.96	1.85	4.13
21	20	.63	.70	2.73	−.70	1.58
22	21	.56	.74	2.37	1.24	3.52
23	22	.45	.68	1.63	−.22	2.06
24	23	1.84	.82	5.21	1.85	4.13
25	24	1.03	.95	3.96	−2.62	−.34
26	25	1.03	.82	3.96	1.85	4.13
27	26	.48	.68	1.85	.24	2.52
28	27	1.84	.70	5.21	.72	3.00
29	28	.51	.94	2.09	2.61	4.89

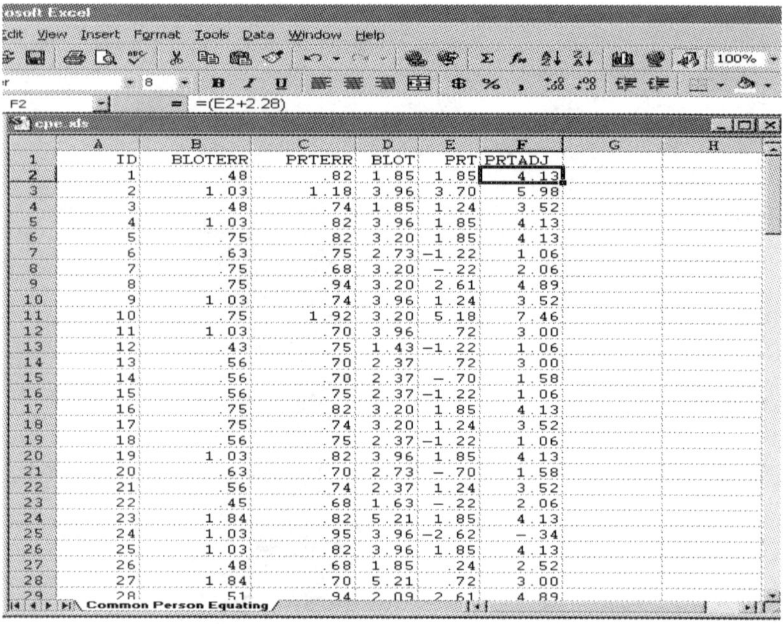

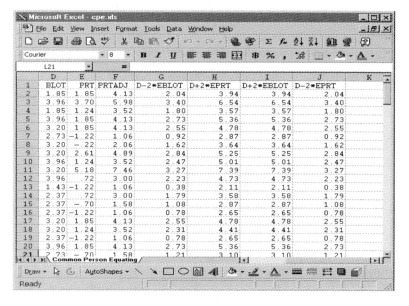

FIG. 5.5. Adjusting PRTIII measures by incorporating the mean difference.

	BLOT	PRT	PRTADJ	D−2*EBLOT	D+2*EPRT	D+2*EBLOT	D−2*EPRT
2	1.85	1.85	4.13	2.04	3.94	3.94	2.04
3	3.96	3.70	5.98	3.40	6.54	6.54	3.40
4	1.85	1.24	3.52	1.80	3.57	3.57	1.80
5	3.96	1.85	4.13	2.73	5.36	5.36	2.73
6	3.20	1.85	4.13	2.55	4.78	4.78	2.55
7	2.73	−1.22	1.06	0.92	2.87	2.87	0.92
8	3.20	−.22	2.06	1.62	3.64	3.64	1.62
9	3.20	2.61	4.89	2.84	5.25	5.25	2.84
10	3.96	1.24	3.52	2.47	5.01	5.01	2.47
11	3.20	5.18	7.46	3.27	7.39	7.39	3.27
12	3.96	.72	3.00	2.23	4.73	4.73	2.23
13	1.43	−1.22	1.06	0.38	2.11	2.11	0.38
14	2.37	.72	3.00	1.79	3.58	3.58	1.79
15	2.37	−.70	1.58	1.08	2.87	2.87	1.08
16	2.37	−1.22	1.06	0.78	2.65	2.65	0.78
17	3.20	1.85	4.13	2.55	4.78	4.78	2.55
18	3.20	1.24	3.52	2.31	4.41	4.41	2.31
19	2.37	−1.22	1.06	0.78	2.65	2.65	0.78
20	3.96	1.85	4.13	2.73	5.36	5.36	2.73
21	2.73	−.70	1.58	1.21	3.10	3.10	1.21

FIG. 5.6. The complete working file.

D-2*EPRT

```
J2=((D2+F2)/2-SQRT(B2*B2+C2*C2))
```

By now, the working file should have the following variables added: PRTIII adjusted ability estimates, and a1 (D-2*EBLOT), b1 (D+2*EPRT), a2 (D+2*EBLOT), b2 (D-2*EPRT), as demonstrated in Fig. 5.6.

7. Plot the obtained results in EXCEL using scatterplot. There are three series to be plotted:

   Series 1 contains BLOT ability estimates on the x axis and PRTIII ability estimates on the y axis.

   Series 2 contains a1 on the x axis and b1 on the y axis.

   Series 3 contains a2 on the x axis and b2 on the y axis.

   The resulting graph is shown in Fig. 5.2.

   (Note: Values for a1 are in column G, b1 values are in H, a2 values are in I and values for b2 are in column J.)

6

Measurement Using
Likert Scales

The previous chapters have demonstrated how the basic features of Rasch modeling can be used to deal with simple right–wrong, or dichotomous, data. An extension of these principles allows us to extend the idea of Rasch modeling to polytomous (previously called polychotomous) data. One form of this approach to collecting data that has been around for a long time is the principle of the Likert scale, which usually is used to collect attitude data. Likert scales share a number of common features, regardless of which attitudes they assess, and usually are expressed in the following format. This particular Likert scale offers SD (strongly disagree), D (disagree), N (neutral), A (agree), and SA (strongly agree) as the possible responses:

19. I am afraid that I will make mistakes when I use my computer.   SD D N A SA

Similarly, each Likert scale item is provided with a stem (or statement of attitude) and a three-, five-, or seven-position scale, in which the respondent is required to mark a response on the disagree–agree continuum, indicating the extent to which the statement in the stem is endorsed.

Interestingly, Likert scales usually are regarded by psychologists as a softer form of data collection, in which the researcher clearly acknowledges that the questions are requiring merely expressed opinions. This at least recognizes the inherent subjectivity involved in collecting information about any human condition (Hales, 1986). However, the standard methods for analyzing Likert scales then disregard the subjective nature of the data by making unwarranted assumptions about their meaning. These assumptions are made in order to find a quick and easy way of producing some sort of overall score in terms of, say, computer anxiety, attitudes toward study, or endorsement of particular medical practices. We can easily show how it is both counterintuitive and mathematically inappropriate to analyze Likert data in the traditional way.

A standard display of Likert response options might take this form:

SD	D	N	A	SA
SD	D	N	A	SA
SD	D	N	A	SA
SD	D	N	A	SA
SD	D	N	A	SA

The coding for responses then would be treated in the following way:

1	2	3	4	5
1	2	3	4	5
1	2	3	4	5
1	2	3	4	5
1	2	3	4	5

where the higher number indicates a higher degree of agreement with the statement being evaluated. Five endorsements of the SA code by a respondent results in a satisfaction score of 25, five times the amount of satisfaction indicated by the respondent who endorses the five SD categories ($5 \times 1 = 5$), or almost exactly twice the satisfaction of someone who endorses two N's and three SD's ($2 \times 3 + 3 \times 2 = 12$).

Whenever scores are added in this manner, the ratio, or at least the interval nature of the data, is being presumed. That is, the relative value of each response category across all items is treated as being the same, and the unit increases across the rating scale are given equal value. These assumptions are conveyed when the data analysis treats $SA = 5$ as having a value five times greater than that of $SD = 1$, and does so for each and every item on the scale. On the one hand, the subjectivity of attitude data is acknowledged each time the data are collected. Yet on the other hand, the data are subsequently analyzed in a rigidly prescriptive and inappropriate statistical way (i.e., by failure to incorporate that subjectivity into the data analysis).

It is more than likely that the stem

20. I am so afraid of computers I avoid using them.   SD D N A SA

indicates much higher levels of computer anxiety in educational situations than does the stem

19. I am afraid that I will make mistakes when I use my computer.   SD D N A SA

Indeed, the children who respond SA on the "mistakes" stem might routinely endorse N on the "avoid using" stem, yet traditional analyses of the SA responses to each of the stems will contribute exactly five points to the overall computer anxiety score. A more realistic representation of the way that a sample of grade school children might actually use these two stems could be something like this:

	Less Anxious	More Anxious
20. Avoid using	SD D N A SA	
19. Mistakes	SD D N A SA	

where any move to the right indicates more anxiety overall.

From this example, we can see that endorsing SA on "avoid using" should carry more importance on the overall computer anxiety scale. This makes intuitive sense: Students who "strongly agree" with avoidance of computers because of fear seem to show a much higher level of the "computer anxiety" construct than those who "strongly agree" with a fear of making mistakes.

Already, the parallels can be seen between the Rasch approach to Likert scale data and what we have detailed in the previous chapters. In particular, the Rasch model allows the item difficulty of each stem or question to be based on the way in which an appropriate group of subjects actually responded to that stem in practice. Given that the subject might possibly endorse one of many response categories on a Likert scale, rather than make just the right/wrong distinction possible under the dichotomous model, the application of the Rasch model to these polytomous data will be a little more complex. In a manner similar to that used for dichotomous data, the Rasch model establishes the relative difficulty of each item stem in recording the development of computer anxiety from the lowest to the highest levels the instrument is able to record. Therefore, each item will be accorded a difficulty estimate. Rasch modeling also will establish the pattern in the use of the Likert scale categories to yield a rating scale structure shared by all the items on the scale.

In Fig. 6.1, we have represented the locations of five Likert stems and five respondents drawn from a much larger number of stems and respondents on a make-believe anxiety scale. Of course, we have used the developmental pathway analogy introduced earlier, so the principles of Rasch analysis interpretation will remain the same as before. In fact, before reading any further, the reader should take a few minutes to try interpreting the key attributes of the items and the persons in Fig. 6.1: 1.1 = item 1, threshold 1; 1.2 = item 1, threshold 2; and so on.

The locations of the persons, as indications of how much anxiety they revealed in their responses, are indicated by the squares as previously. The location of the square indicates the person estimate (in this case, the amount of anxiety), and the size of the square shows the error estimate for that location. It will be easy to recognize Tess as the most anxious person because she has the highest location on the logit scale. Ziggy is shown as the least anxious of all. Although the locations for Vicki and Wayne would be different in terms of the person estimates alone, the size of the associated error estimates means that no

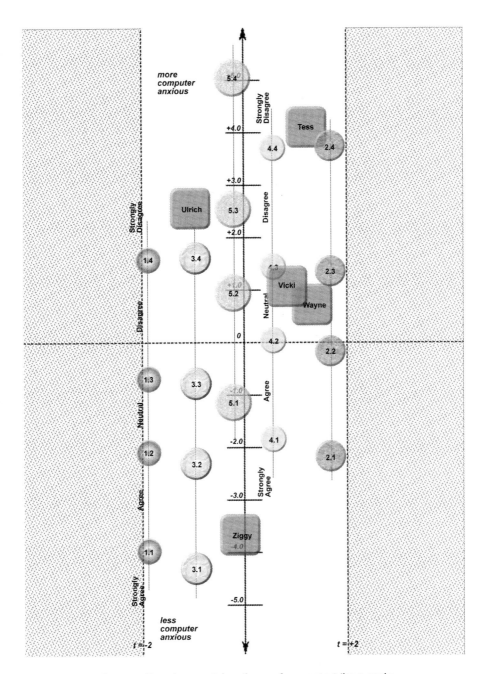

FIG. 6.1. Developmental pathway for ersatz Likert scale.

meaningful difference in the anxiety levels reported by these two persons may be inferred.

The items, however, indicate a rather more complicated representation than we are accustomed to observing with dichotomous data. For dichotomous data, each item was represented on the developmental pathway (and in the computer printout) as having a single item estimate, with an associated error estimate. For rating-scale data, not only does each item have a difficulty estimate, but the scale also has a series of thresholds. This is the level at which the likelihood of failure at a given response category (below the threshold) turns to the likelihood of success at that category (above the threshold). Although it might seem a little strange to talk about failure and success on Likert attitude scales, we can easily see the appropriateness of, say, failure to agree with, or even better, failure to endorse, any particular response category. Similarly, success can be interpreted as agreement with, or better still, endorsement of, a particular response category. For the polytomous data we have collected with our Likert scale, we will need a number of thresholds for the anxiety scale to show the progression:

$$SD \rightarrow D \rightarrow N \rightarrow A \rightarrow SA.$$

Therefore, what we represented in earlier chapters with dichotomous items as

one item threshold estimate

showed how the item difficulty estimate indicated the threshold between the two possible response categories on an item. With the rating scale model, this now is represented as

SA

Fourth threshold estimate

A

Third threshold estimate

N

Second threshold estimate

D

First threshold estimate

SD

because four thresholds are needed to separate the five possible response categories on the Likert scale. But more than just that, the Rasch rating scale model does not presume the size of the step necessary to move across each threshold. It detects the threshold structure of the Likert scale in the data set, and then estimates a single set of threshold values that apply to all of the item stems in the scale.

Going back to Fig. 6.1, it is obvious that the thresholds for any one item (e.g., 1.1, 1.2, 1.3) are not spread equidistantly. Some steps (say, from threshold 2 to threshold 3) require smaller increases in anxiety than other steps (say, from threshold 1 to threshold 2). However, the step structure (the pattern of the thresholds across items) is identical for every item in the Likert scale. We can see, as well, that the relative difficulty of the items also varies as it did for the dichotomous data examples. Item 1 is much easier to endorse than item 5, for example. We can see now that even a response of SA on item 3 indicates only a modest amount of anxiety on the overall pathway, whereas an A response for item 5 indicates more anxiety than can be detected on item 3 at all. The traditional statistical analysis of Likert scale data is based on the a priori arrangement of the response opportunities as a rectangular, ordered block, as shown on the questionnaire. However, the locations of the step thresholds in Fig. 6.1 do not corroborate this traditional presumption. First, the locations for those scale positions, as revealed in the reality of practice, show that the increase in anxiety implied by the move from SD to N is less than the increase required by the move from N to A. Second, it shows that the item stems themselves also vary in the level of anxiety that they can actually detect.

We can use the item–person map representation of the anxiety variable to show what sort of anxiety levels are likely to be reported by persons with overall high, medium, and low anxiety levels as reported by their use of this scale. Please take a moment to examine Fig. 6.1, trying to determine for high-anxious person Tess, mid-anxious person Vicki, and low-anxious person Ziggy what categories (SD D N A SA) each is likely to have endorsed for items 1 to 5, respectively. The Rasch model treatment of Likert scale data is intuitively more satisfactory and mathematically more justifiable than the traditional "allocate 1 2 3 4 5 and add them up" approach. The Rasch model explicitly recognizes the SD D N A SA and the subsequent coding 1 2 3 4 5 as ordered categories only, in which the value of each category is higher than that of the previous category, but by an unspecified amount. That is, the data are regarded as ordinal (not interval or ratio) data, and we use the Rasch model to transform the counts of the endorsements of these ordered Likert categories into interval scales based on the actual empirical evidence, rather than on some unfounded assumption made beforehand.

Therefore, in the Rasch rating-scale model, developed in the work of David Andrich (Andrich, 1978a, 1978b, 1978c) from Murdoch (Perth, Australia), the finer detail of the item structure is shown. The analyses provide both an item estimate for each Likert stem as well as a set of estimates for the four thresholds that mark the boundaries between the five Likert categories: SD D N A SA. By analyzing the data in this manner, we can see immediately that the items do not carry the same relative value in the construct under investigation. In Fig. 6.1, item 3 can differentiate between the lower levels of anxiety, whereas information from item 5 is useful in differentiating respondents who have moderate to high anxiety levels. Item 2 works in the midrange of this attitude construct, whereas item 4 works best from midrange to higher levels, and item 1 on this rating scale is a low- to mid-anxiety item. It can be seen, then, that a good Likert-style instrument in developmental or other psychological settings relies on the incorporation of item stems varying in degree of difficulty, just like a test composed of dichotomous items.

How the construction of step estimates for a Likert scale are conceptualized under the Rasch model might be seen easily in the ersatz data set given in Table 6.1.

The ersatz data in Table 6.1 summarize the responses of 40 persons to a 7-item Likert scale, in which the respondents were requested to indicate their degrees of agreement along a 5-point scale: SD, D, N, A, and SA. In the rows, the

TABLE 6.1
The Bases for the Estimation of Item Difficulties
and Thresholds for Ersatz Likert Scale Data

	SD (1)	D (2)	N (3)	A (4)	SA (5)	Item Counts	Possible (40 × 5)	%
Item 1	5	8	11	10	6	5×1+8×2+11×3+ 10×4+6×5= 124	200	62
Item 2	9	7	10	9	5	9×1+7×2+10×3+9 ×4+5×5= 114	200	57
Item 3	9	8	9	10	4	9×1+8×2+9×3+ 10×4+4×5= 112	200	56
Item 4	7	9	9	8	7	7×1+9×2+9×3+ 8×4+7×5= 119	200	59.5
Item 5	3	4	11	12	10	3×1+4×2+11×3+1 2×4+10×5= 142	200	71
Item 6	5	9	9	9	8	5×1+9×2+9×3+ 9×4+8×5= 126	200	63
Item 7	12	13	8	4	3	12×1+13×2+8×3+ 4×4+3×5= 93	200	46.5
Category counts	50	58	67	62	43			
Possible (7 × 40)	280	280	280	280	280			
%	17.9	20.7	23.9	22.1	15.4			

response information for each of the items has been recorded. The Item Counts column shows how the responses in each category were added to produce a count for each item. That information would used as the basis for the estimation of item difficulties. In the columns, the response information for each Likert response category has been recorded. The latter information would be used as the basis for the estimation of the thresholds, and the set of threshold values would be applied identically to all of the items on the scale. In other words, the thresholds are estimated once for all items. In the cases of both item difficulties and thresholds, the estimation is based on the proportion of the actual responses to the total possible responses. These proportions for items and response categories are shown as the percentage entries, which are the basis on which the transformation into log odd units or logits take place.

It is not merely the range of anxiety detected by the SD D N A SA categories that is important. To make a good instrument, it is necessary to use a collection of item stems that also tap into a range of anxiety levels. It is rather useless then to use a statistical procedure that treats all items as having the same value, and all SA's as worth 5 on the final score. In the hypothetical example of Fig. 6.1, responses of SA on items 4 and 5 should carry more importance than SA's on items 1 and 3. Although it is possible that the endorsement of SA for item 5 might really indicate five times the anxiety detected by the endorsement of SD on item 3, it is quite clear that SA on item 3 cannot be treated as indicating five times more anxiety than SD on item 4. There is a considerable anxiety scale increase between SD on item 3 and SA on item 5, but there is not nearly so large a gap between SD on item 4 and SA on item 3. We need to use Rasch modeling to help us construct a measure of our attitude construct, and then interpret each person estimate as our measure of the person's revelation of that latent trait as indicated on the assessment instrument.

PRACTICAL IMPLICATIONS

What then would we need to do to make a Rasch analysis of a rating scale work, given that we have used or developed a Likert-style instrument designed to investigate a single dimension of an attitude or opinion, and have administered that instrument to a suitable sample of appropriate persons?

First, we should note that moving from a dichotomous to a polytomous Rasch model should prompt us to reconsider what might constitute a suitable sample for a rating scale analysis. As always, we would need a sample varied enough in the presence of the underlying psychological construct that all the response options for all of the items will be used. However, given that a typical Likert scale has, say, five response opportunities (e.g., SD D N A SA) rather than just two (✓ or ✗), we will need proportionately more persons in our sample to achieve the same density of data for each response opportunity. It should be recalled that the quality (precision) of our estimates depends on the amount of good information we have. Whereas 40 persons might yield, say, 25 ✓ and 15 × responses on a dichotomous item, those same 40 persons might yield 6 SD's, 8 D's, 12 N's, 9 A's, and 5 SD's on a Likert-format item. The immediate consequence would be less measurement precision (i.e., larger error estimates) as a direct result of the thinner spread of the 40 responses across the five response categories. The problem would be further compounded if the full range of response opportunities was not used by the persons in the sample. The interpretation of a Likert data matrix containing empty cells in the data set (i.e., those with zero responses) is not unambiguous using the rating scale model. Such empty cells might be a result of not using a sample large enough to estimate effectively the difficulty for every category threshold, or it might be the result of using numbers or types of response categories that are inappropriate for the construct. These and other related issues are canvassed in chapter 11.

We then would indicate to the Rasch software the number of items we were attempting to analyze as well as the range of responses encountered in the data file. Whereas most simple statistical summations of Likert responses use the SD = 1, D = 2, N = 3, A = 4, and SA = 5 coding system, it is a good practice, at least in the beginning, to use a coding system that is a logical extension of that used for dichotomous data, thus starting with zero: SD = 0, D = 1, N = 2, A = 3, and SA = 4. In both instances, 0 is used to record the minimum level of the construct detected by the item, and 1 indicates the next detectable level. In both instances, 1 indicates detecting more of the underlying construct than 0 does.

With dichotomous data, we exhaust the response opportunities at that point. Even a mathematics professor will get the same code of 1 for a correct response to the item 3 + 4 = □ as does the little child in year 2 who responds correctly that 3 + 4 = 7. The item 3 + 4 = □ cannot differentiate the professor's mathematics ability from that of the child. With the Likert format, we have a larger, but still finite, number of ordered categories, to use in detecting gradual increases in the underlying attitude construct. Most importantly, the ordinal nature of the category relations SD < D < N < A < SA is conserved exactly in the use of the coding numerals 0 < 1 < 2 < 3 < 4.

Indeed, some Rasch software for rating scale analysis will require the use of 0 as the indicator of the lowest detectable category in the data set. In other software, the codes will be treated automatically as though 0 was used for the lowest category (i.e., by default). The possibilities for confusion and misunderstanding can be compounded further when other Rasch modeling techniques are used. It is possible to avoid being caught unaware by routinely using 0 for the lowest detectable category and 1 for the next higher detectable category, with 2, 3, and so on being used as appropriate. In passing, we should note also that 0 has a different meaning from "blank" in Rasch modeling: Whereas 0 is routinely used to indicate the presence of the lowest detectable category (e.g., wrong or SD, say), "blank" indicates the absence of a recorded response (i.e., missing data). Although it might be a reasonable inference to treat "blank" as 0 in dichotomous data (i.e., as × rather than ✓), there is a problem of how "blank" should be treated in a Likert data file. Should it be treated as the lowest detectable category, SD? Why? As this person's average score for the rest of the items? Why? As the person's modal response? Why? As the average or modal response for all other persons on this item? Why? These are the procedures routinely used in the traditional approaches to analyzing Likert scale data. Our assertion is that the best inference concludes that somehow the respondent did not respond to the item. It should be left blank. The Rasch model has no problem accommodating such missing data.

ANALYZING RATING SCALE DATA: THE COMPUTER ANXIETY INDEX

In this worked example based on King and Bond (1996), we have tried to determine the extent to which grade school children's Likert scale responses to the Computer Opinion Survey (Simonson, Maurer, Montag-Torardi, & Whitaker, 1987) could be used to construct a measure of computer anxiety. The Computer Opinion Survey consists of 26 positively or negatively worded Likert-type items developed from a larger number of items considered by its authors as indicative of a person's feelings of anxiety toward computers. As each stem has six response options (1 = strongly agree, 2 = agree, 3 = slightly agree, 4 = slightly disagree, 5 = disagree, 6 = strongly disagree), the possible range of the CAIN (Computer Anxiety INdex) scores extends from 26 (i.e., 26 answers each having a low anxiety value of 1) to 156 (i.e., 26 answers each having a high anxiety value of 6) for a complete response set. Following the principles set out in the Test Administrator's Manual (Montag, Simonson, & Maurer, 1984), negatively worded items are scored in the reverse direction (6-5-4-3-2-1), and the CAIN for each respondent is calculated by adding all the raw scores across the 26 items.

The authors of the Computer Opinion Survey claim that the CAIN scores have the usual high statistical estimates of reliability and concurrent validity for investigating computer anxiety (King & Bond, 1996; Montag et al., 1984; Simonson et al., 1987). The investigation of the CAIN (King & Bond, 1996) was prompted by the counterintuitive results from an earlier investigation (King, 1993), which showed by using conventional statistical procedures that a sample of 120 year 7 students made pre- to posttest gains in computer anxiety after being exposed to greater than usual numbers of microcomputers in normal classroom environments over a period of 9 months.

Figure 6.2 provides the item-map representation of responses that a large sample (*n* = 372) of year 7 students made to the Computer Opinion Survey. The display is in the format of the developmental pathway analogy introduced ear-

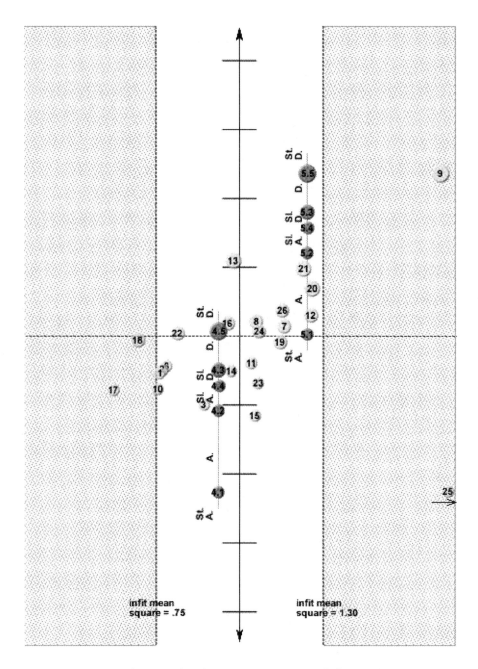

FIG. 6.2. Developmental pathway representation of all 26 CAIN items (some with associated threshold estimates).

lier. The figure is a little cramped given that it represents the item difficulties, error estimates, and item fit estimates for each of the 26 Computer Opinion Survey items while, for illustration purposes, it also represents the pattern of the five threshold locations for a number of items.

At this point in the chapter, we have provided a map of all 26 items to show the bases of the decision to include just some of these items in a subsequent analysis. A perusal of the details in Fig. 6.2 will lead to the inference that a number of the items do not appear to be revealing the same construct (computer anxiety) that the others seem to be tapping. Which items are they? What is the evidence of inadequate fit?

The map for the Computer Opinion Survey items also provides prima facie evidence for the claim made earlier in this chapter that as a general rule, Likert attitude or opinion items are likely to vary in terms of their difficulty, agreeability, or endorsability. Which are the easier Computer Opinion Survey items for these grade school students to endorse? With which items is it more difficult to agree? How does the plotting of the five-item threshold values for items 4 and 5 on the map provide evidence for varying item difficulty? The location of those threshold estimates reveals a basic problem with the Computer Opinion Survey for this sample. The thresholds between *slightly agree, slightly disagree,* and *disagree* (thresholds 3 and 4) are quite confused. Not only are the thresholds very close together, their locations do not increase according to the logical order principle required by the Rasch measurement model. Issues related to rating scale design are canvassed in chapter 11.

A section showing the output of the Rasch item estimates for the Computer Opinion Survey items is included as Table 6.2 so the detail of the map locations can be more easily confirmed. In this instance, the Rasch output was requested with the items listed in item difficulty order rather than the order in which the items appeared in the test (i.e., question 1 to question 26). This makes it possible

TABLE 6.2
Item and Threshold Estimates (With Fit Statistics)
for All 26 Computer Anxiety Index Items

Item No.	Difficulty Error	Taus					Infit Mean Square	Outfit Mean Square	Infit t	Outfit t
		1	*2*	*3*	*4*	*5*				
9	0.78	−0.67	−0.09	0.18	0.09	0.49	1.55	1.46	4.1	3.1
	0.07	0.03	0.03	0.03	0.04	0.08				
13	0.63	−0.67	−0.09	0.18	0.09	0.49	0.92	0.72	−0.7	−2.3
	0.06	0.03	0.03	0.03	0.04	0.08				
21	0.55	−0.67	−0.09	0.18	0.09	0.49	1.17	1.03	1.6	0.3
	0.06	0.03	0.03	0.03	0.04	0.08				
20	0.42	−0.67	−0.09	0.18	0.09	0.49	1.25	1.33	2.4	2.5
	0.06	0.03	0.03	0.03	0.04	0.08				

(Continued)

TABLE 6.2
(Continued)

Item No.	Difficulty Error	Taus					Infit Mean Square	Outfit Mean Square	Infit t	Outfit t
		1	2	3	4	5				
26	0.26	−0.67	−0.09	0.18	0.09	0.49	1.08	1.08	0.8	0.7
	0.05	0.03	0.03	0.03	0.04	0.08				
12	0.23	−0.67	−0.09	0.18	0.09	0.49	1.23	1.14	2.4	1.2
	0.05	0.03	0.03	0.03	0.04	0.08				
8	0.17	−0.67	−0.09	0.18	0.09	0.49	0.96	0.88	−0.5	−1.1
	0.05	0.03	0.03	0.03	0.04	0.08				
16	0.16	−0.67	−0.09	0.18	0.09	0.49	0.91	0.89	−1.1	−1.0
	0.05	0.03	0.03	0.03	0.04	0.08				
7	0.15	−0.67	−0.09	0.18	0.09	0.49	1.09	1.14	1.0	1.3
	0.05	0.03	0.03	0.03	0.04	0.08				
24	0.10	−0.67	−0.09	0.18	0.09	0.49	1.01	1.00	0.2	0.0
	0.05	0.03	0.03	0.03	0.04	0.08				
22	0.09	−0.67	−0.09	0.18	0.09	0.49	0.80	0.72	−2.6	−2.8
	0.05	0.03	0.03	0.03	0.04	0.08				
5	0.08	−0.67	−0.09	0.18	0.09	0.49	1.15	1.10	1.8	1.0
	0.05	0.03	0.03	0.03	0.04	0.08				
18	0.03	−0.67	−0.09	0.18	0.09	0.49	0.70	0.67	−4.2	−3.5
	0.05	0.03	0.03	0.03	0.04	0.08				
19	0.01	−0.67	−0.09	0.18	0.09	0.49	1.07	1.10	0.9	0.9
	0.05	0.03	0.03	0.03	0.04	0.08				
11	−0.08	−0.67	−0.09	0.18	0.09	0.49	0.95	1.02	−0.7	0.3
	0.04	0.03	0.03	0.03	0.04	0.08				
6	−0.11	−0.67	−0.09	0.18	0.09	0.49	0.78	0.80	−3.2	−2.1
	0.04	0.03	0.03	0.03	0.04	0.08				
2	−0.13	−0.67	−0.09	0.18	0.09	0.49	0.77	0.84	−3.3	−1.6
	0.04	0.03	0.03	0.03	0.04	0.08				
14	−0.14	−0.67	−0.09	0.18	0.09	0.49	0.92	0.91	−1.2	−0.9
	0.04	0.03	0.03	0.03	0.04	0.08				
1	−0.15	−0.67	−0.09	0.18	0.09	0.49	0.77	0.99	−3.5	−0.1
	0.04	0.03	0.03	0.03	0.04	0.08				
23	−0.24	−0.67	−0.09	0.18	0.09	0.49	1.01	1.10	0.1	1.1
	0.04	0.03	0.03	0.03	0.04	0.08				
10	−0.27	−0.67	−0.09	0.18	0.09	0.49	0.76	0.86	−3.8	−1.6
	0.04	0.03	0.03	0.03	0.04	0.08				
17	−0.28	−0.67	−0.09	0.18	0.09	0.49	0.63	0.64	−6.2	−4.4
	0.04	0.03	0.03	0.03	0.04	0.08				
4	−0.37	−0.67	−0.09	0.18	0.09	0.49	0.88	0.95	−1.8	−0.5
	0.04	0.03	0.03	0.03	0.04	0.08				
3	−0.39	−0.67	−0.09	0.18	0.09	0.49	0.85	1.02	−2.4	0.2
	0.04	0.03	0.03	0.03	0.04	0.08				
15	−0.49	−0.67	−0.09	0.18	0.09	0.49	1.00	1.00	0.1	0.0
	0.04	0.03	0.03	0.03	0.04	0.08				
25	−1.01	−0.67	−0.09	0.18	0.09	0.49	2.10	2.43	13.0	11.6
	0.04	0.03	0.03	0.03	0.04	0.08				
Mean	0.00						1.01	1.03	−0.3	0.1
SD	0.38						0.30	0.34	3.6	2.9

to start at the top of the table and at the bottom of the map to check the correspondences between the difficulty estimates and the item locations.

Items 1, 10, 17, and 18 fall to the left side of the satisfactory fit zone in Fig. 6.2, whereas items 9 and 25 fall to the right side "misfit" zone. In Fig. 6.2, the unstandardized infit mean square values, rather than the standardized infit t values, are plotted. Issues related to the interpretation of fit are canvassed in chapter 12. When King and Bond (1996) calculated Rasch computer anxiety person estimates for these data, they decided to eliminate the misfitting items and perform a second analysis using just the 20 fitting items, with the aim of getting more valid person computer anxiety measures from the Computer Opinion Survey responses. Although we take the idea that our test respondents are "sampled" from the total possible population of persons for granted, we tend not to view our tests, checklists, or Likert prompts as "sampled" from the total possible population of items. Given that the logic and techniques of modeling item responses in Rasch analysis are specifically and completely interchangeable with the logic and techniques of modeling person responses, it is useful to remember that our particular test items are selected from the total population of possible items in the same way that our particular test respondents are drawn from the total population of possible persons.

Figures 6.3 and 6.4 introduce complete person–item (or variable) maps for the computer anxiety analysis referred to earlier. It will be recalled that we introduced this representation of the data in chapter 4 when we looked at the idea of the sample of persons being properly targeted by the sample of items. Both figures show the distribution of person estimates along the logit scale for the variable on the left side. Figure 6.4 derives from WINSTEPS output and plots the item difficulty estimates for all 26 CAIN items (i.e., one difficulty estimate per item). Figure 6.3 derives from QUEST output and plots the threshold estimates for the 20 CAIN items included in the final analysis (i.e., five threshold estimates per item).

It is also worth noting that the versions of item–person maps routinely seen in Rasch analysis output from the regular analysis software programs (e.g., QUEST, WINSTEPS) focus on the relative distributions of item difficulty and person ability estimates only. These maps do not try to include item fit and person fit representations on the same map as we have with our developmental pathway analogy in which the dotted lines indicate sufficient fit.

In Fig. 6.3, we can discern that the targeting of this sample's computer anxiety levels has not been well accomplished by the current version of the Computer Opinion Survey. Three aspects of the graphic evidence help to demonstrate this. First, the "tail" of the distribution of persons (each X represents two persons here) hangs considerably below the lowest levels of item thresholds. In other words, some 60 of these school students have computer anxiety levels so low that they are barely detected at the extreme low range of the measure. The computer anxiety levels of these persons will be very imprecisely measured by

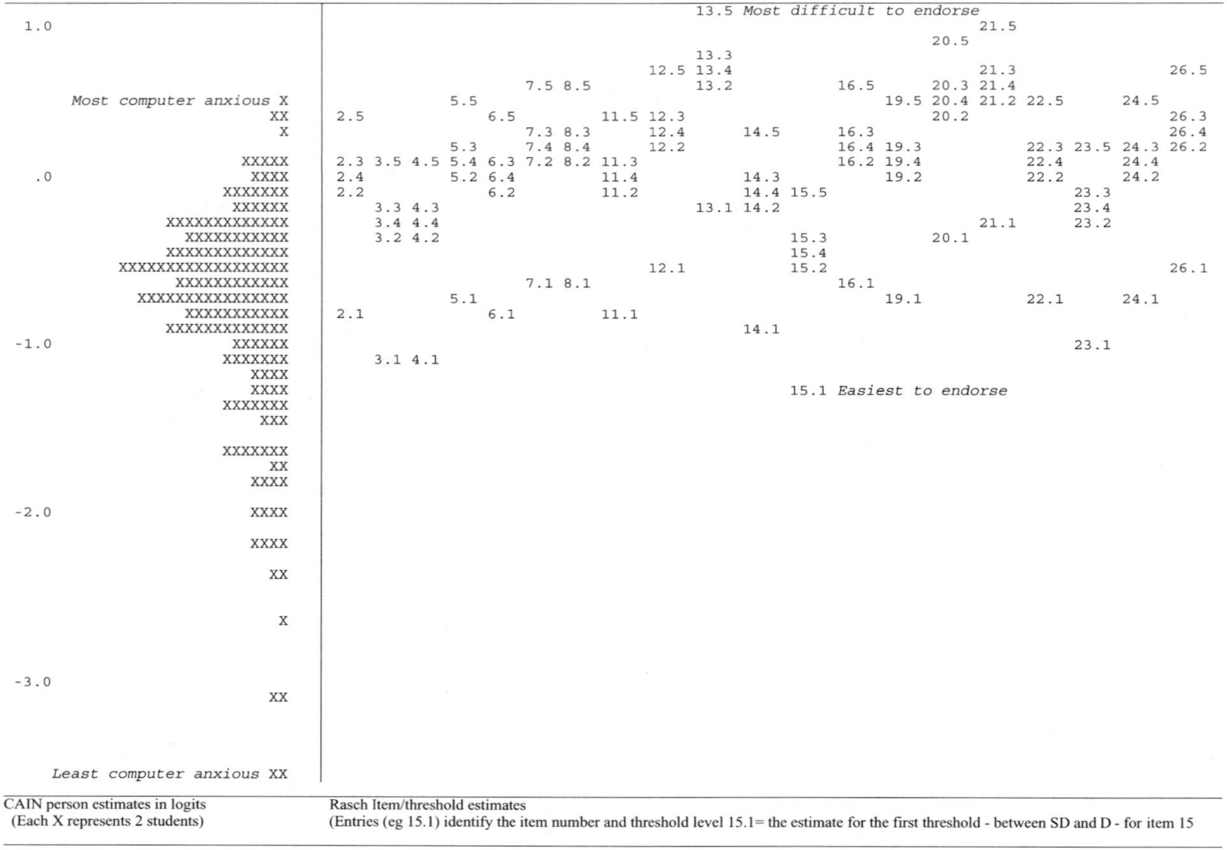

1.0

13.5 Most difficult to endorse

20.5   21.5

26.5

Most computer anxious X

21.3
21.4
16.5   19.5   20.3   21.2   22.5   24.5   26.3
XX   20.4   26.4
X   2.5   5.5   6.5   16.3   19.3   20.2   21.1   22.3   23.5   24.3   26.2

XXXXX   7.3   8.3   14.5   16.4   19.4   22.4   24.4
XXXX   2.3   3.5   4.5   5.3   6.3   7.4   8.4   11.5   12.3   16.2   19.2   22.2   24.2
XXXXXX 2.4   5.4   6.4   7.2   8.2   11.4   12.4   23.4
XXXXXXX 2.2   5.2   6.2   11.3   12.2   23.2
XXXXXXXXXX   3.3   4.3   11.2   13.1   14.4   15.5   23.3
XXXXXXXXXX   3.4   4.4   14.3
XXXXXXXXXXXXXXXX 3.2   4.2   13.3   15.3
XXXXXXXXXXXXXXXX   13.4   14.2   15.4
XXXXXXXXXXXXXX   13.2   15.2   20.1   21.1
XXXXXXXXXXXX   12.1   16.1   19.1   22.1   24.1   26.1
XXXXXX   2.1   5.1   6.1   7.1   8.1   11.1
XXXX
XX   3.1   4.1   14.1
XXXXXXX
XXXXX   15.1 Easiest to endorse   23.1

.0

-1.0

XXXX
XXXX

-2.0

XX

X

-3.0

XX

Least computer anxious XX

CAIN person estimates in logits
(Each X represents 2 students)

Rasch Item/threshold estimates
(Entries (eg 15.1) identify the item number and threshold level 15.1= the estimate for the first threshold - between SD and D - for item 15

FIG. 6.3.   Computer anxiety estimates for the large sample of 11/12 year olds and associated item thresholds for 20 CAIN items.

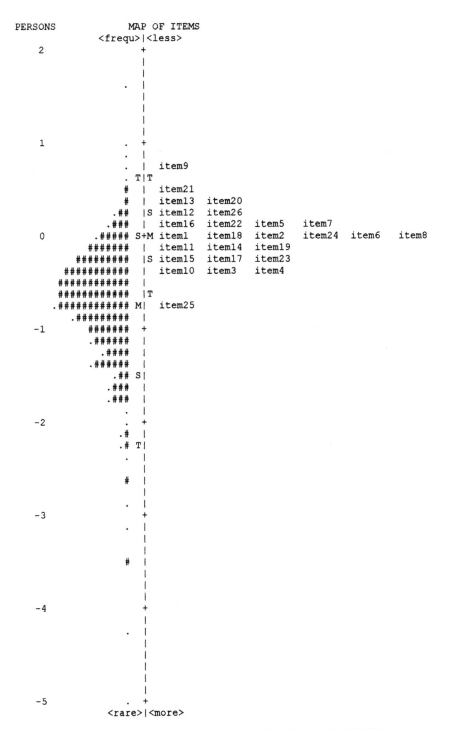

```
PERSONS            MAP OF ITEMS
                <frequ>|<less>
     2              +
                    |
                    |
                 .  |
                    |
                    |
                    |
                    |
     1           .  +
                 .  |
                 .  |  item9
               . T|T
                 #  |  item21
                 #  |  item13  item20
               .## |S item12  item26
               .### |  item16  item22  item5   item7
     0        .##### S+M item1  item18  item2   item24  item6   item8
             ######  |  item11  item14  item19
            ######## |S item15  item17  item23
           ########## |  item10  item3   item4
          ###########  |
          ########### |T
        .########### M|  item25
           .######### |
    -1      ######  +
           .###### |
            .#### |
           .##### |
             .## S|
            .### |
            .### |
              .  |
    -2        .  +
             .# |
             .# T|
              .  |
                 |
             #  |
                 |
              .  |
    -3        +
              .  |
                 |
                 |
             #  |
                 |
                 |
                 |
    -4        +
                 |
              .  |
                 |
                 |
                 |
                 |
    -5        .  +
                <rare>|<more>
```

FIG. 6.4.   Person–item map for all 26 CAIN items (WINSTEPS).

81

the Computer Opinion Survey. Second, and conversely, at least the A and SA categories of most items are located well above the locations of the most computer-anxious persons in this sample. We need a sample of respondents who are much more computer-anxious than this group if we want more than very imprecisely measured item difficulty estimates for the Computer Opinion Survey. Finally, the bulk of the persons are not located opposite the bulk of the items. The distribution of person anxiety estimates in Fig. 6.3 is centered around a mean value of −0.80 logits. Compared with the mean value of 0 logits routinely adopted for items, the anxiety levels of these persons are, on average, considerably lower than the anxiety levels of these items. Further administrations of the Computer Opinion Survey would be warranted with either persons who are more computer-anxious than these, with items that detect lower levels of computer anxiety, or preferably with both.

Figure 6.3 shows, and the values in Table 6.2 confirm, that items 3, 4, 14, 15, and 23 are the easier-to-endorse items. Not only are the SD categories (i.e., below the first thresholds) easier for the low-anxiety persons to endorse, but the SA categories for the same items (i.e., above the fifth thresholds) become endorsable at lower levels of computer anxiety than even the fourth threshold of other items such as 20 and 21. Indeed it is as easy to endorse item 15 at the highest anxiety (strongly agree) level (i.e., 15.5) as it is to respond "slightly disagree" to item 13 (i.e., 13.2).

The tabular output from the Rasch analysis for Likert-type items is necessarily more complicated than the tables for dichotomous items. Although we could expect to see a single difficulty estimate for each item, we also would expect to see values and errors for each of the response thresholds. In Table 6.2, we see that each of the 26 Computer Opinion Survey items has a single-item difficulty estimate as well as five threshold difficulty estimates (and error estimates) recorded. However, just one set of fit statistics is included for each item, just as we are used to having with dichotomous data. A little slice of the person statistics output (Table 6.3) shows that the person estimates, errors, and fit indices remain the same in the Rasch analysis for Likert-type data. In this example, each person has a single computer anxiety estimate expressed in logits (derived from the logarithmic transformation of the odds based on that person's total raw score on the 20 Computer Opinion Survey items), an error (or imprecision) estimate for that anxiety level, and both unstandardized and standardized fit estimates. The fit estimates warn us when the person estimate should not be regarded as a fair summary of that person's computer anxiety. The fit statistics for this section of the person output look very good, although we would want to be a bit circumspect about accepting the computer anxiety estimate of 0 logits for person 81 (infit $t =$ −2.79; outfit $t = -2.69$) at face value. The interpretation of fit is taken up more comprehensively in chapter 12.

The detailed threshold output is very helpful to our understanding of the variable under investigation, in terms of both the structure of the Likert-scale items

TABLE 6.3
Excerpt From Person Estimates on
20-Item Computer Anxiety Index

Name	Maximum Possible Score		Estimate	Error	Infit Mean Square	Outfit Mean Square	Infit t	Outfit t
81	48	100	0.00	0.16	0.44	0.44	−2.79	−2.69
82	7	100	−1.85	0.37	1.27	1.13	0.65	0.41
83	15	100	−1.13	0.25	0.67	0.70	−0.72	−0.63
84	25	100	−0.66	0.19	1.28	1.18	0.85	0.59
85	27	100	−0.59	0.19	1.28	1.20	0.90	0.65
86	5	100	−2.18	0.44	1.01	0.82	0.22	−0.14
87	19	100	−0.91	0.22	0.79	0.92	−0.45	−0.07
88	30	100	−0.49	0.18	0.51	0.60	−1.83	−1.33
89	35	100	−0.34	0.17	0.85	0.95	−0.47	−0.05
90	26	100	−0.62	0.19	1.14	1.31	0.50	0.91
91	16	100	−1.07	0.24	1.06	0.87	0.28	−0.16
92	46	100	−0.05	0.16	0.90	0.91	−0.30	−0.26
93	15	100	−1.13	0.25	0.71	0.95	−0.59	0.04
94	8	100	−1.72	0.35	1.13	0.95	0.41	0.08
95	18	100	−0.96	0.23	0.55	0.64	−1.19	−0.87
96	23	100	−0.73	0.20	0.70	0.93	−0.80	−0.08
97	20	100	−0.86	0.21	0.91	1.00	−0.11	0.15
98	27	100	−0.59	0.19	1.00	1.21	0.10	0.67
99	11	100	−1.42	0.29	0.96	0.91	0.07	−0.04
. . .								
Mean			−0.80		1.05	1.05	−0.12	−0.09
SD			0.69		0.63	0.66	1.64	1.61

and the direct interpretation of any person's most probable response to each item, given that person's location. However, for other purposes, such as using the test-equating procedures described in chapter 5 or comparing the response levels of two groups taking the same test, all that item information becomes unwieldy. What is needed is the single difficulty estimate and associated error for each rating scale test item. How could such a concept be interpreted in practice? If we go back to the depiction of the response categories that we used at the beginning of this chapter, we can introduce a necessarily naïve view of the Likert item difficulty/endorsability concept and then amplify it with what we have learned from the successful application of Rasch measurement principles to rating scale analysis.

The simplistic version has the response categories set up in the standard format with a little caret (^) to indicate the balance point for that item:

1.   SD   D   N   A   SA
                                 ^

The sample's responses to this first item are so regularly distributed across the five categories that the balance point for the item, its difficulty or endorsability, is in the N category. For the next item, many more respondents have endorsed the SD and D categories rather than the A and SA categories, so the balance point for that item is better represented thus:

2.   SD   D   N   A   SA
                                                     ^

Item 2 is more difficult for the sample to endorse. It takes all the N, A, and SA category responses together to balance the D and SD responses. Item 3 is evaluated rather differently by the sample:

3.   SD   D   N   A   SA
                                                          ^

Heavy use of the A and SA categories relative to the other three response items indicates that this item is much easier for this sample to endorse. The bulk of the sample "agrees" or "strongly agrees" with the statement in item 3.

When the response balance points for these items are aligned (after all, this is just one sample responding to all of these items), the comparative display of item difficulties relative to the one sample of persons has the following appearance:

1.   SD   D   N   A   SA
2.   SD   D   N   A   SA
3.   SD   D   N   A   SA
easy to endorse   ^   difficult to endorse

Item 1 is moderately difficult for this sample to endorse, and item 2 is more difficult to endorse, whereas item 3 shows as easier to endorse. The balance-point concept works a bit like a teeter-totter or seesaw. Both the number of persons endorsing the category and the distance of the category from the balance point will determine the effect of response distributions on item difficulty. Imagine the effect of the following possible variations in response distribution for the three preceding items. What would be the effect on the difficulty of item 3 if a few of the respondents were moved to N from A, or if the same number were moved to SD from D, or to SD from SA? Although we cannot definitively predict the effect of these category distribution changes in the absence of more complete information about sample size and distribution, the balance-point principle predicts that the last move (SD < SA) would cause the greatest increase in item difficulty, whereas the N < A move (closest to the fulcrum) would cause a minimal difficulty increase.

The Rasch measurement approach to rating scale analysis as it is applied to Likert-type items uses all the foregoing information in estimating overall item difficulty estimates. The reduction of apparent detail in summarizing four or five threshold points per item in just one item difficulty estimate and one error estimate per item is not performed by discarding information, but by modeling all the relevant information according to its location along the item scale.

Figure 6.4 provides a person–item map using the item estimates, rather than threshold estimates, from rating scale analysis. Each item estimate can be regarded as the balance point for the response distribution across that item's categories, and of course the variation of item difficulty estimates shows the difficulty of the items relative to each other and, in the case of the item–person map in Fig. 6.4, relative to the person distribution.

The tables of Rasch item outputs routinely contain two aspects that distinguish the output from that generated by the other members of the family of Rasch models: Every item has its overall estimate of item difficulty, whereas all items share a threshold structure that is common to all items. This is obvious in Table 6.2. The item difficulty estimates vary from item to item, but the threshold structure modeled by the Rasch analysis of the empirical data is common to all items. Figure 6.4 shows the overall item difficulties (the first column) from Table 6.2, whereas Fig. 6.3 combines that information with the threshold estimates (the taus for five thresholds) to show the item/threshold structure of the Computer Opinion Survey results. The reader can confirm that the item and threshold values displayed graphically in Figs. 6.2, 6.3, and 6.4 actually are those generated by the Rasch analysis as shown in Table 6.2. Of course, Figs. 6.3 and 6.4 do not display fit information.

The original developers of Likert scales such as the CAIN could easily complain that considerable injury has been done to their work when items are deleted from the analyses and levels of anxiety are reported by person estimates rather than raw scores. After all, the items were put there for very good reasons: content and face validity, and so on. But the very act of adding all the responses to get a total raw score presumes that the responses of all items contribute to the underlying construct, and that they contribute equally. This preliminary attempt to use the Rasch model to construct a measure of computer anxiety using the CAIN data suggests that such presumptions are not warranted in this case: Not all items contribute to the same latent trait, and of those items that do, they do not all contribute equally.

Of course, analyses of rating scales rarely remain at the uncomplicated level reported by King and Bond (1996) and discussed in this introductory chapter. Chapter 11 shows how quite sophisticated considerations of Likert response categories and Rasch-based analyses of rating scale data can be conceptualized. However, the continuing fundamental thrust of this volume is the prerequisite necessity: First of all, the researcher must construct a measure and understand the meaning of that measure in practice; then, go on to use all the usual statistical techniques after that.

Control file for QUEST:

```
Title CAIN Analysis ALL ITEMS
data CAIN.dat
codes 0123456
recode (123456) (012345)
recode (012345) (543210)  !5,7,9,11,12,14,18,19,20,21,22,23,24,25
format items 3-28
estimate rate
show!stat=tau>>CAINshow.doc
show items!stat=tau>>CAINitem.doc
show cases>>CAINcase.doc
quit
```

Title line gives a title "CAIN Analysis ALL ITEMS" to each output file.

Data names the data file as "CAIN.dat."

Codes indicates which codes in the file are valid.

First recode statement changes 1 to 0, 2 to 1, 3 to 2, and so forth for all items so each minimum response is a 0.

Second recode statement changes 0 to 5, 1 to 4, 2 to 3, and so forth for items 5, 7, 9, 11, 12, 14, 18, 19, 20, 21, 22, 23, 24, and 25 (the negatively worded items), so higher scores always represent more anxiety.

Format indicates the columns in the data file where the responses for the 26 CAIN items are located.

The "estimate" command is appended with "rate" to indicate the use of Andrich's rating scale model.

Show commands include the qualifier "!stat=tau" to request output according to Andrich's rating scale model, and to direct the output to files that will open with a word processor.

Control file for WINSTEPS:

```
; This file is Cain.CON
&INST
TITLE="RS analysis of CAIN data"
NI=26
NAME1=1
ITEM1=3
CODES=123456
Newscore=654321
RESCORE=00001010101101000111111110
TABLES='1111111111111100110000'
;IDELQU=Y
&END
```

```
item1
item2
item3
item4
item5
item6
item7
item8
item9
item10
item11
item12
item13
item14
item15
item16
item17
item18
item19
item20
item21
item22
item23
item24
item25
item26
end names
```

Codes indicates which codes in the file are valid.

Newscore statement changes 1 to 5, 2 to 4, 3 to 3, 4 to 2, and 5 to 1.

Rescore changes the coding in newscore for items 5, 7, 9, 11, 12, 14, 18, 19, 20, 21, 22, 23, 24, and 25 (the negatively worded items) so higher scores always represent more anxiety.

Note: In this WINSTEPS example, 1 not 0 is used to indicate the lowest response category.

7

The Partial Credit
Rasch Model

There can be no doubt that the extension of the Rasch model for simple dichotomous data into the rating scale model has had an enormous impact on Rasch
modeling (Anderson, 1977; Andrich, 1978b). The rating scale model is now
used routinely for the analysis of Likert scale data (chapter 6), but Andrich originally intended it for another purpose. It was first intended for use in the evaluation of written essays. It would assist the examination process by producing
measures from values applied to qualitative essay rating scales by examiners.
However, it also paved the way for all the Rasch models that involve data with
more than two values (0, 1).

The rating scale model requires that every item in a test have the same number of steps, as we have come to expect from Likert scales. The items can have
3, 4, 5, or even 6 response opportunities, but nevertheless, the number of steps
must be the same for every item on the test. That requirement suggests some unexpected difficulties that might occur even with Likert scales, especially in their
early use or development. Just because the response form provides, say, five response opportunities for each item, this does not ensure that all five response
categories actually will be used in practice by the chosen sample. In spite of the
researcher's intention to collect data for all five categories on all items, the data
set might reveal different numbers of actually used categories for some items.
We take up this and related problems in chapter 11. Moreover, we can easily en-
visage other testing situations in which it would be more useful not to be restricted to having the same number of steps for every item.

The most vigorous proponent of the partial credit Rasch model has been
Geoff Masters from Melbourne (Wright & Masters, 1982). The partial credit

model specifically incorporates the possibility of having differing numbers of steps for different items on the same test. Consider the possibility of tests in which one or more intermediate levels of success might exist between complete failure and complete success (i.e., partially correct answers). For this reason, the partial credit model is highly applicable in educational and other testing situations in which "part marks" are awarded for partial success. However, a very important Rasch principle must be observed in the awarding of part marks. Whereas school teachers might give two marks here, a half mark here, and one mark there, to give a total of 3.5 (part marks) out of a possible 5 for aspects of a partially correct solution to a math problem, Rasch modeling principles require that the part marks be awarded in an ordered way, so that each increasing value represents an increase in the underlying ability being tested.

For example, the ordered values 0, 1, and 2 might be applied to an item as follows: 0 = totally wrong, 1 = partially correct, and 2 = completely correct; values 0, 1, 2, and 3 might be used with another item thus: 0 = totally wrong, 1 = partially correct, 2 = almost completely correct, and 3 = completely correct. Well, is there a limit to the number of partial credit steps between complete failure and complete success on an item? Of course, we should recur to the guiding theory we are using. What does it tell us about the ordered steps between failure and success? Whereas this might be more straightforward for those who start with an explicit theoretical orientation, those with a more pragmatic bent will develop a "part marks" schedule by conceptual analysis, or by reflection on observation of candidates' performances. Eventually, in the application of that theory to an empirical situation such as a test, a marking key, or an observation schedule, we will be limited to the number of meaningful steps that are useful in discerning the display of the varying ability levels we find in our sample. An extreme case might be the use of visual analog scales (VAS) in psychophysical and medical research, such as requiring subjects to indicate along a 10-cm scale just how much pain they feel in arthritic joints. Although the score is routinely read from the scale in millimeters, there is no empirical evidence at all that respondents can meaningfully discriminate between the 101 response intervals on the scale.

AN EXAMPLE FROM
DEVELOPMENTAL THEORY

It is the application of the partial credit Rasch model to cognitive developmental data that has paved the way for original conceptions of how fundamental measurement principles might be meaningfully applied in unexpected settings. Let us take a well-known problem from Piaget's work, often called conservation of matter, an interview task often used with, say, 3- to 7-year-olds, and therefore quite unsuitable for a written task format. A child judges two balls of playdough to have the same amount. Then one of them is rolled out into a snake or sausage shape right in front of the child's eyes. The child then is asked to judge again. The question is something like, "Does the snake have more playdough than the ball; does the ball have more playdough than the snake; or do they have the same amount of playdough?" Anyone who has watched young kids share a cupcake, pour drinks for friends, or gladly swap little coins for bigger ones will know that whereas adults often do not "see the problem" here, it is only during the grade school years that children grow to understand that the amount of playdough, amount of juice, or number of sweets will remain invariant no matter how the objects are rearranged.

Piaget's approach was to claim that the child who consistently conserves shows qualitatively superior thinking to the child who does not, backing his claim with detailed logical analyses of the child's supposed thinking patterns. When we psychologists first tried to quantify our replications of this research, we adopted 0 = couldn't conserve, 1 = could conserve as the task performance summary, which hindsight has shown to be rather naïve. The extent of the trivialization that routinely went on can be imagined: Little Johnny gets interviewed for 15 min on three conservation tasks (amount of playdough, amount of juice, and number of sweets each suitably rearranged) and gets scored like this: 1, 1, 0 (conserves playdough and juice but misses number). Betty and the psychologist chat and play together for 20 min, and she gets scored 0, 1, 0; whereas Jane gets 1, 1, 1 after a mere 10 min of concentrated effort on her part. After an equally brief encounter, it seems Bill is enchanted with the magic that makes things more or less, just by moving them around (0, 0, 0). Then we would compound our errors by adding the scores up for each child: 2 for Johnny, 1 for Betty, and 3 for Jane, whereas Bill gets 0 however you look at it. Often we would take this even one step further and, claiming that 2/3 was enough to describe Johnny and Jane as "conservers" and Betty and Bill as "nonconservers." Consequently, if the purpose of the research was to relate cognitive development in kids to their mathematics scores, there was no meaningful result, which is not surprising!

Seen through the lens provided by the partial credit model, the opportunities for serious and sensitive measurement seem to multiply very productively. First, we could see that it would not be necessary to have just 0 and 1 scoring. We could also have 0, 1, 2 or 0, 1, 2, 3 if we found suitable criteria to score against. Not only could we have "items" with two or three steps (i.e., not the dichotomous model), but we also were not constrained to the same number of steps for each item (i.e., not the rating scale model). Even more, we could mix dichotomous and polytomous items in the one test. Moreover, instead of providing a single overall score for each task or complete interview, we could see each task addressing a number of key aspects, each of which could be scored. Thus, the playdough task could be broken down into the following subtasks: (a) judges initial equivalence: no = 0, yes = 1; (b) conserves after snake transformation: no = 0, yes = 1; (c) uses "longer" appropriately: never = 0, sometimes = 1, consistently = 2; (d) gives reasons based on perception = 0, by rolling the snake into a ball = 1, saying "You didn't add or take away anything" = 2, claiming "It's always the same no matter what you do" = 3.

Therefore, for the string of criteria or items a, b, c, d, for just the first test (playdough task), we could end up with Johnny's scores of 1, 1, 2, 2; Betty's 1, 1, 1, 1; Jane's perfect response string 1, 1, 2, 3; and Bill's 1, 0, 0, 0. It can be seen how we have now discriminated differences between Betty and Bill (both received 0 for playdough with dichotomous scoring), and between Jane and Johnny (both scored 1 in the dichotomous situation). Remember the ordered data matrix from chapter 2? We can do it again (see Table 7.1).

In Table 7.1, we see the same sort of evidence for developmental sequences that we saw in the sorted dichotomous data in Table 2.2. Being on guard about making unwarranted inferences from the data, we merely observe that we have recorded ordered increases in response levels (i.e., 0 < 1< 2 < 3, etc.). Of course, we also refrain from drawing unwarranted equivalences between the values of 1 for items a and b, between the scores of 2 for items c and d, and so forth. All we are entitled to say from these data categorizations is that for item a, 0 < 1, and for item b, 0 < 1. We may not claim that 1 (on a) = 1 (on b), or that 2 (on c) = 2 (on d). We would use Rasch modeling to estimate those relations, the intervals between those ordered values, during the analysis process.

The data used to demonstrate the use of the partial credit Rasch model in this chapter have been chosen for a number of important reasons. We could have chosen a routinely used written mathematics or science test, an essay scoring guide, or a medical rehabilitation example, as long as it offered the possibility of getting answers partly correct. Many scoring situations would do, as long as the grading principle represented by the following responses is implemented: "wrong–partly correct–right" or "fail–some progress towards mastery–more complete response–mastery." However, with the current example, we can learn something about the partial credit model while we open our eyes to the range of possibilities for quantifying what traditionally has been seen as qualitative data in the human sciences.

TABLE 7.1
Ordered Data Set for Four Children on Four Polytomous Items

Criteria	a	b	c	d
Bill	1	0	0	0
Betty	1	1	1	1
Johnny	1	1	2	2
Jane	1	1	2	3

Shayer, Küchemann, and Wylam (1976) from the University of London had a number of reasons for developing the Piagetian Reasoning Task (PRTIII–Pendulum) for classroom use. The PRTIII–Pendulum we used in chapter 5 was one of the demonstrated class tasks that they developed to replace administration using the traditional Piagetian interview technique. They wanted data collection devices that could be administered to whole classes at a time, whereas Piaget's technique was a one-on-one interview. They wanted tests that could be used by interested school science teachers, whereas Piaget claimed that his interviewers needed 1 year of daily practice to become competent. They wanted tests that could yield quantifiable data, whereas Piaget's work was notorious for its uncompromisingly qualitative approach. Well, the Rasch model cannot change the Piagetian requirements for superior interview skills or make it possible to interview 30 kids simultaneously, but it can make wonderfully quantitative what is regarded traditionally as qualitative data. It can construct interval scale measures on which a whole range of the usual statistical techniques can be meaningfully employed. Indeed, the following piece of research, first reported in Bond and Bunting (1995), was inspired exactly by the existence of the partial credit Rasch model (PCM).

CLINICAL INTERVIEW ANALYSIS: A RASCH-INSPIRED BREAKTHROUGH

Bond and Bunting (1995) reported in much more detail than necessary here the direct replication of the pendulum task using the Genevan interview technique as reported in chapter 4 of Inhelder and Piaget's (1958) *The Growth of Logical Thinking From Childhood to Adolescence*. The child is presented with a pendulum apparatus consisting of an adjustable string suspended from a fixed point and a series of weights: 40 g, 80 g, 100 g. When given a demonstration of the apparatus and provoked by an initial question such as, "Can you show me what causes the pendulum to swing more or fewer times in some short time interval?" the child experiments with the apparatus to determine which of the variables (weight, length, push, angle) affects the period of oscillation. The child is asked to "think out loud," and the interviewer asks prompting questions, seeks clarification, and challenges the child's conclusions as seems appropriate. No, this is not your usual standard test or even structured interview![1]

---

[1] The standard view of the Piagetian method can be summarized adequately by Wallace (1965): "Results obtained by such a flexible procedure as the *méthode clinique* do not lend themselves to statistical treatment" (p. 58). Indeed, even Piaget himself subscribed to that view. As a consequence, standardized individual interview procedures were developed, class tasks such as Shayer's (Shayer, Küchemann, & Wylam, 1976) were substituted, or pencil-and-paper tests such as Bond's (1976) were written to provide the sort of data amenable to statistical analyses.

What was original with Bond and Bunting (1995) in this work was the detailed scoring table (Table 7.2) developed exactly from chapter 4 of Inhelder and Piaget (1958). These performance criteria are far more comprehensive than any developed before, including those of Bond (1976), Shayer et al. (1976), and others, resulting directly from a detailed rereading of the key chapter with the possibilities opened up by partial credit Rasch modeling as the key stimulus. This probably sounds as though an excess of missionary zeal is sneaking in here, but the important claim is that when we see the old world of data through new eyes (in this case, Rasch modeling), whole new possibilities open up. We could have made a similar claim in the previous chapter for developing measures via the rating scale model, but the claim would not have been original. Many already have developed scores for Likert scales, even if they have made the "measurement" claim erroneously. Although the vast majority of standardized psychological and educational testing falls into the dichotomous tradition (of, say, IQ scores) or Likert scales (personality assessment) (Michell, 1986), the PCM allows for meaningful quantification in a virtually untouched category of human sciences research, in which the data are not dichotomous, nor do they have some fixed number of response categories.

Therefore, when seen through the eyes of PCM and not from the usual dichotomous/Likert viewpoint, the distinctive feature of the 15 tasks in Inhelder and Piaget (1958) is their careful construction of problems that are relevant and interesting to a wide sample of children. Because the focus of the work was to monitor the progress from the logical thinking of childhood to that of adolescence, kids do not get these tasks right or wrong. They get them, almost invariably, partially correct, and that whole domain of partially correct answers, whether it is in mathematics problem solving, essay writing, or medical rehabilitation, is the focus of the PCM.

SCORING INTERVIEW TRANSCRIPTS

Table 7.2 is a scoring guide that illustrates some important key features for those wishing to implement PCM in new testing situations. Across the top of the table, we can see the increasingly complex substages of thinking displayed: IIA (early concrete operational thought), IIB (mature concrete thought), IIIA (early formal operational thought), and, finally, IIIB (mature formal thought). The invariant *order* of stages is a critically distinctive feature of Piaget's work, just as order is the key requirement of Rasch measurement. Down the table, we have the 18 different aspects of solving the pendulum problem that Bunting found identified in the focus chapter. It is clear that lower level aspects of the problem (e.g., 1, 3, and 4) would be scored dichotomously: 1 for meeting the performance criterion and 0 for failing to meet it. Similarly, aspects 7, 8, and 9 have three identifiable levels of performance each and will yield ordered polytomous data: Criteria 7.0,

TABLE 7.2

Ordered Performance Criteria for 18 Aspects of the Pendulum Interview Task

	IIA *Early Concrete*	IIB *Mature Concrete*	IIIA *Early Formal*	IIIB *Mature Formal*
1	1.1 Able to accurately serially order lengths			
2	2.0 Unable to accurately serially order weights	2.1 Able to accurately serially order weights −2.4		
3	3.1 Able to accurately serially order push −2.4			
4	4.1 Establishes inverse relation between length and frequency of oscillation −2.4			
5	5.0 Unable to manipulate some variables −2.4	5.1 Able to vary all factors		
6	6.0 Does not make inferences. Limited to observations	6.1 Makes inferences based only on observed concrete correspondence −2.4	6.2 Makes inferences going beyond observations, without needing to test all possibilities +0.4	
7		7.0 To test for length, manipulates incorrect variable and in an unsystematic manner	7.1 Manipulates incorrect variable, but makes logical deductions by inference to results on earlier experiments — 1.0	7.2 Systematically manipulates lengths to test for their effects +0.9
8		8.0 Manipulates incorrect variable and is unsystematic in testing for weight	8.1 Manipulates incorrect variable, but makes logical deductions by inference to results on earlier experiments −0.7	8.2 Systematically manipulates weights to test for their effects −0.7

9	9.0 Manipulates incorrect variable and is unsystematic in test for push	9.1 Manipulates incorrect variable, but makes logical deductions by inference to results on earlier experiments −0.3	9.2 Systematically manipulates impetus to test for the effect of push +0.7	
10	10.0 Makes illogical deductions about the role of length (including illogical exclusion of length in favor of weight or impetus)	10.1 Excludes the effect of length (because of inaccurate observations) −1.2	10.2 Logically deduces positive relation of affirmation or implication for the role of length +1.1	10.3 Deduces equivalence of length and frequency of oscillation +3.1
12	12.0 Preoccupied with the role of impetus as the cause of variations in the frequency of oscillation. Illogical deduction of positive implication.	12.1 Testing results in the illogical exclusion of the role of push −0.1	12.2 Logically deduces a positive relation of affirmation or implication for push, based on inaccurate observations +1.7	12.3 Excludes the role of push +2.9
13	13.0 Does not produce combinations of length with other variables	13.1 Produces combinations of different lengths with different weights or pushes to test for effects −2.1	13.2 Produces sets of combinations of lengths with various weights and pushes to test for their effects +1.40	
14	14.0 Does not produce combinations of weights with other variables	14.1 Produces combinations of different weights with different lengths to test for their effects −1.6	14.2 Produces combinations of different weights with different pushes to test for the effects +1.1	14.3 Produces combinations weights with various lengths and pushes to test for their effects +1.1

(Continued)

TABLE 7.2
(Continued)

	IIA *Early Concrete*	*IIB* *Mature Concrete*	*IIIA* *Early Formal*	*IIIB* *Mature Formal*
15		15.0 Does not produce combinations of push with other variables	15.1 Produces combinations of different pushes with various lengths, to test for their effects $+1.0$ 15.2 Produces combinations of different pushes with different weights, to test for their effects $+1.2$	15.3 Produces combinations of various pushes with lengths and weights, to test for their effects $+2.14$
16			16.0 Unsystematic method	16.1 Systematically produces all combinations, using the method of varying a single factor, while holding all else constant $+1.4$
17			17.0 Unable to exclude the effect of weight	17.1 Logically excludes the effect of weight $+2.4$
18			18.0 Unable to exclude the effect of push	18.1 Logically excludes the effect of push $+3.1$

8.0, and 9.0 indicate the lowest observable levels of performance on these aspects and should be scored 0. Criteria 7.2, 8.2, and 9.2 indicate complete success on those aspects of the problem and will be scored 2. Because 7.1, 8.1, and 9.1 show partial success, they will attract the score of 1, somewhere on the ordered pathway between complete failure (0) and complete success (2).

Aspects 10 and 12 then have four ordered performance category levels and will be scored 0, 1, 2, and 3. Yet there is more: Although 16, 17, and 18 are to be scored dichotomously, successful performance on these aspects is supposed to reflect the highest level of mature thinking available to adolescents and adults. Clearly, the score of 1 here is meant to be of greater importance than the 1 scored for successful performances on aspects 1.1, 2.1, 3.1, and 4.1. The much-lauded and much-criticized flexibility in administration of the task is not a problem for Rasch modeling. Any aspects of the problem that are not actually encountered during the interview (omitted inadvertently or deliberately) are regarded as "missing data," and the data file has a blank recorded at that point. (The Rasch family of models will make do with less than complete data sets for either items or persons. It will provide estimates of ability and difficulty based on the available data. Of course, measurement precision declines as available information decreases.)

As a procedural point, all of the interviews ($n = 58$) of the high school students were video-recorded and transcribed. A matrix based on Table 7.2 was used for the recording of each child's performances, and the data string for each child recorded the score on each aspect of the problem (18 data points for each child), in which higher scores indicate more advanced performances. For example, the scores in column 14 (of the sample response strings that follow) indicate that student 21 satisfied criterion 14.1 from Table 7.2, whereas student 65 performed to the requirements in criterion 14.3.

111111000212010000 Student 21 (least successful case)
111112212323132111 Student 65 (most successful case)

To perform a PCM analysis on the data file generated from this investigation, we need to indicate the following to the Rasch analysis software:

The number of "items" and their location in the data file. In this case there are 18 items in columns 1 to 18.
What the valid codes are in the file. Codes 0, 1, 2, 3 cover all the response possibilities here. We took the care always to use 0 as the code for the lowest possible observable response category for each item.

The estimation procedure should use the PCM. For some software, this is the default estimation procedure for polytomous data. For example, in QUEST, the PCM is used with polytomous data unless the qualifier "estimate rate" is used to constrain the threshold estimates to be the same for all items, as discussed in chapter 6.

PARTIAL CREDIT MODEL RESULTS

Figure 7.1 displays the item estimates and fit statistics from the partial credit analysis of the *méthode clinique* interview data from the pendulum problem, using the developmental pathway principles adopted earlier in this text. Figure 7.1 combines features of the displays from the dichotomous data analyses in chapters 4 and 5 and some features from the rating scale analysis of polytomous data in chapter 6.

First, the fit of items ($-2 <$ infit $t < +2$) is displayed using the parallel dotted lines. In this case, all the 18 items fit the Rasch model sufficiently according to this criterion. They are all located between those lines. For each of those items that were scored dichotomously (1, 2, 3, 4, 5, 16, 17, and 18), one item difficulty estimate per item is plotted, indicating the threshold at which the probability of scoring 0 or 1 is 50%. For those items that are scored polytomously (0, 1, 2 or 0, 1, 2, 3), either two or three difficulty thresholds are plotted. Three response categories (0, 1, 2 for item 6) are separated by two thresholds (e.g., estimate 6.1 separates the likelihood of scoring 0 on aspect 6 from the likelihood of scoring 1 on aspect 6; estimate 6.2 separates the most probable response zones for scores of 1 and 2 on aspect 6), whereas four response categories (0, 1, 2, 3) are separated by three threshold estimates (e.g., aspect 12: four response categories with three estimates).

Therefore, the item map in Fig. 7.1 will show a number of item estimate formats:

		Likely to score '3'
	Likely to score '2'	
		Threshold estimate 12.3
	Threshold estimate 6.2	
Likely to score '1'		Likely to score '2'
	Likely to score '1'	*Threshold estimate 12.2*
Estimate threshold for 1		Likely to score '1'
Likely to score '0'	*Threshold estimate 6.1*	*Threshold estimate 12.1*
	Likely to score '0'	Likely to score '0'
Item 1	**Item 6**	**Item 12**

The format shown depends on the number of threshold estimates needed to separate the response categories in Table 7.2. Both QUEST and WINSTEPS PCM procedures can handle up to 10 ordered response categories per item (0, 1, 2, 3, 4, 5, 6, 7, 8, 9), but whether any particular testing situation can make practical

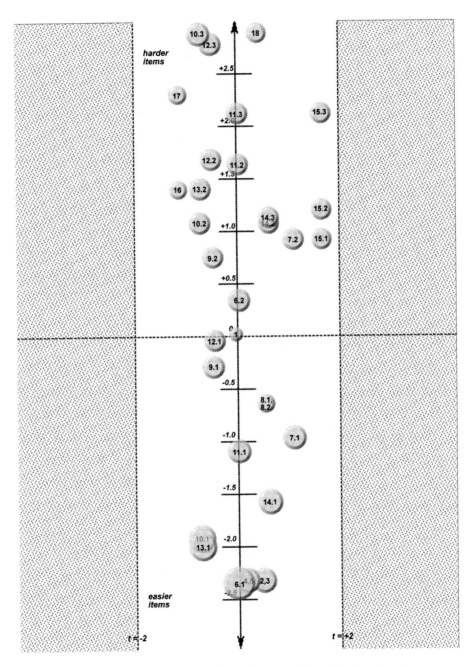

FIG. 7.1. Developmental pathway for Pendulum interview items.

and meaningful use of 10 response categories is an empirical question discussed in chapter 11.

As we would expect from a task designed to elicit partially correct responses from a broad band of respondents, say, 5- to 18-year-olds, the pendulum task items cover a span of nearly 6 logits from the least difficult (6.1 at -2.41 logits) to that with the criterion most difficult to satisfy (a score of 1 on item 18 at $+3.12$ logits). Given that this groundbreaking research was conducted by one undergraduate student in a very short time, and that each individual interview takes a considerable time to plan, implement, transcribe, and score, a rather small sample size of 58 students was used. As a result, the error estimates for the items and steps remain large, even unacceptably large in some instances. Three factors that were mentioned before have an influence on the size of error estimates. All other things being equal (and they never are), imprecision will increase when items are off target for the population, when the number of response categories per item increases, and when the sample is small. Take a moment to look at the error estimates in Table 7.3 and identify the more imprecise item difficulty locations (yes, they have the larger circles in Fig. 7.1). Then take a look at the complete item–person map in Fig. 7.2 to see which of the preceding influences have contributed to the large error estimates you have identified.

INTERPRETATION

What guidelines do these considerations provide for sample selection for further research using the pendulum task? First, we need to give the task to a larger sample, but what sort of larger sample? When we see that the items at the extremes of the difficulty range are dichotomous items, but that they have error estimates about the same size as those for the step estimates in the polytomous items 11, 12, and 13, we should conclude that the next sample should include both more able persons on the pendulum task to make estimates for 16, 17, and 18 more precise and less able persons to enhance the precision of items 1, 2, 3, 4, and 5.

This is in keeping with what we already know: Inhelder and Piaget (1958) designed this task for use with a broad age range (say, 5–18 years), whereas the breadth of the sample for this study was restricted deliberately to 12- to 15-year-olds, for two important reasons. First, it was the transition from concrete to formal thought that Bond and Bunting (1995) were investigating, not early concrete or mature formal thinking. Second, Bond and Bunting (1995) sought to avoid compounding the measurement of cognitive development with other age-related variables such as amount of education or exposure to formal science instruction. An increase in sample size would implicate both of these variables, as well as the possibility, indeed likelihood, that the team of interviewers/scorers necessary to administer the task to a larger sample would not do their work with the consistency that investigator aimed to achieve with the $n = 58$. The many-facets

TABLE 7.3
Item Estimates for Pendulum Interview Task

Item	Difficulty Estimate	Error Estimate	Infit t	Outfit t
1		Item has perfect score		
2	−2.36	0.73	+0.3	+0.5
3	−2.36	0.73	+0.3	+0.5
4	−2.36	0.73	+0.1	−0.4
5	−2.36	0.73	+0.1	−0.5
6.1	−2.41	1.25	0.0	−0.2
6.2	+0.36	0.63	0.0	−0.2
7.1	−0.97	0.72	+1.0	+0.6
7.2	+0.92	0.53	+1.0	+0.6
8.1	−0.65	0.30	+0.6	+2.3
8.2	−0.65	0.30	+0.6	+2.3
9.1	−0.28	0.59	−0.5	−0.3
9.2	+0.72	0.55	−0.5	−0.3
10.1	−2.03	0.94	−0.3	−0.2
10.2	−1.23	1.08	−0.3	−0.2
10.3	+3.10	0.66	−0.3	−0.2
11.1	−1.19	1.08	0.0	+0.3
11.2	+1.65	0.55	0.0	+0.3
11.3	+2.14	0.64	0.0	+0.3
12.1	−0.03	0.66	−0.7	−0.7
12.2	+1.73	0.52	−0.7	−0.7
12.3	+2.88	0.55	−0.7	−0.7
13.1	−2.06	0.53	−0.8	−0.9
13.2	+1.44	0.53	−0.8	−0.9
14.1	−1.56	0.64	+0.7	+0.5
14.2	+1.07	1.00	+0.7	+0.5
14.3	+1.13	0.55	+0.7	+0.5
15.1	+0.97	0.75	+2.0	+1.8
15.2	+1.27	0.49	+2.0	+1.8
15.3	+2.22	0.49	+2.0	+1.8
16	+1.41	0.47	−1.3	−1.0
17	+2.33	0.47	−1.4	−1.5
18	+3.02	0.51	−0.7	−1.1

Rasch model that we introduce in chapter 8 addresses the issues of rater behavior and has the promise of modeling the effects of such influences.

First, we must acknowledge that empirical results such as these, derived from small and restricted samples, can do hardly more than to point the way to the undoubted promise of larger scale investigations, although there are some hints in these results that show the possibility for theory–practice dialogue. In this case, the data from the pendulum task, at its first iteration, demonstrate sufficient adherence to the Rasch measurement specifications to be regarded as producing measures of cognitive development. These results are not bad for an explicitly

```
                        X    |
  4.0                        |
                             |
                        X    |  10.3                    18
  3.0                        |
                             |          12.3
                        X    |                    17
                       XXX   |  11.3     15.3
  2.0              XXXXXXX    |
                   XXXXXX     |  11.2 12.2
                    XXXX      |     13.2          16
                    XXXX      |                              15.2
  1.0                XX       |  10.2    14.2 14.3
                   XXXXXXX    |                   7.2 15.1
                    XXXX      |                         9.2
                   XXXXXX     |
                   XXXXXX     |                   6.2
   .0                        |     12.1
                       XXX   |
                        X    |                              9.1
                        X    |                      8.1 8.2
 -1.0                        |                         7.1
                        X    |  11.1
                             |
                             |     14.1
 -2.0                        |  10.1
                             |     13.1
                             |  2   3   4   5   6.1
```

FIG. 7.2. Item–person map for Pendulum interview.

qualitative approach that has faded from favor, in part, for not yielding suitably quantifiable results using traditional statistical approaches. Those who are interested can refer to the original research report (Bond & Bunting, 1995) to see the correspondences, and lack of them, between interpretations derived from Piaget's theory and the empirical results. If those results hold in further investigations, some fine-tuning of the underlying theory will be required. Although that report recommended that future replications of the task include the provision of a suitable timing device for accurately assessing the pendulum's swing, this conclusion was derived from the opportunity that interviewer had to pursue children's responses actively in the interview situation, not as a result of the

Rasch analysis. We are not suggesting that Rasch modeling is the universal panacea for measurement in the human sciences. Nothing replaces thoughtful theory-driven research.

The use of Rasch modeling in the Bond and Bunting (1995) research showed the value that the concept of order has within a framework of unidimensionality. Interpretations of item and item step order as well as person order are clearly central in developmental and educational research, with clear implications for measuring physical skill acquisition and medical rehabilitation as well. Hand in hand with a clear concept of the variable under examination is the Rasch concept of unidimensionality. Although this might seem a little esoteric to some, the point is an important one in the application to Rasch measurement, especially in novel settings.

In an address to the Rasch Special Interest Group (SIG) at the American Educational Research Association (AERA), Keeves (1997) reminded the audience of the primary role of unidimensionality in the longitudinal testing of educational achievement such as the international studies regularly being conducted by the International Association for the Evaluation of Educational Achievement (IEA). For the sort of scaling and equating required for these efforts, he indicated:

> Fulfillment of the requirement of unidimensionality is a matter of degree not just a matter of kind as Bejar (1983, p. 31) has pointed out:
>
>> Unidimensionality does not imply that performance on items is due to a single psychological process. In fact, a variety of psychological processes are involved in responding to a set of test items. However, as long as they function in unison—that is, performance on each item is affected by the same process and in the same form—unidimensionality will hold.
>
> Thus a science test can involve physics, chemistry, or biology content and test different skills, knowledge, understanding, application and analysis (to use the terms of the Bloom taxonomy, in the tradition of the University of Chicago) provided the processes involved operate in concord, the requirement for unidimensionality will be satisfied. This demands empirical testing as well as logical analysis. (Keeves, 1997, p. 4)

This provides an interesting context for the interpretation of Rasch modeling results in terms of the theory–practice dialogue. If our aim is to put into systematic practice a particular conception of one psychological or educational construct at a time, our success at that is represented empirically by the development of a unidimensional test. The unsuccessful aspects of that attempt, especially in terms of inadequate item fit, or item disorder, require us to revisit our theory-driven intentions or our effort to operationalize the theory into practice via a test, an observation schedule, or a marking scheme. Items should be included in tests because very good reasons exist for having them there. Test developers should be committed to the items they develop: Item misfit then signals to the investigator "Think again!" not the usual "Throw it out!"

When both our theoretical considerations and our empirical evidence suggest to us that our efforts to develop a test of some underlying latent trait have been successful, then evidence of misordered items or persons suggests that refinement of our ideas is necessary. As a principle that can be applied more generally in test development and use, however, we have indicators of both unidimensionality and order that beg for interpretation in the context of the theory that generated the test and the practical situation that produced the results.

Control file for QUEST:

```
Title PCM Analysis of Piagetian Interview data
Data chap7.dat
Format items 17-34
Codes 01234
Est
show item>>PCMitem.doc
show cases>>PCMcase.doc
Quit
```

Title line gives a title, "PCM Analysis of Piagetian Interview data," to each output file.

Data names the data file as "chap7.dat."

Format indicates the columns in the data file where the responses for the 18 interview codes are located.

Codes indicates which codes in the file are valid.

The "estimate" command performs partial credit analysis as the default for polytomous data.

Show commands direct the output to files that will open with a word processor.

Control lines for WINSTEPS:

```
&INST
TITLE="PCM Analysis of Piagetian Interview Data"
NI=18
ITEM1=17
CODES=01234
GROUPS=0
&END
Item1
Item2
. . .
End Names
```

The first line is required by WINSTEPS.
Title line gives a title to the output file.
NI is the number of items to be analyzed.
ITEM1 is the column number where the data begin.
Codes lists the possible codes for the responses.
Groups=0 specifies partial credit analysis.

8

Measuring Facets Beyond
Ability and Difficulty

Many of those who use other statistical methods for analysis in the social sciences tend to criticize the Rasch measurement approach for being simplistic. How could any human abilities be seriously regarded as unidimensional? Surely, even in the simplest forms of testing (e.g., flick and tick multiple-choice testing) shouldn't we make some allowance for guessing, lack of concentration, and the like?

The response is that the Rasch approach is simple, not simplistic: The aim is to develop fundamental measures that can be used across similar appropriate measurement situations, not merely to describe the data produced by administering test a to sample b on day c. Rasch modeling addresses itself to estimating properties of persons and tests that go beyond the particular observations made during any testing situation. Wright (1998b) summarized it succinctly: "I don't want to know which questions you answered. I want to know how much . . . you know. I need to leap from what I know and don't want to what I want but can't know. That's called inference."

So far, we have focused on just two aspects of the measurement situation, on just two facets of the single underlying dimension being measured: One facet is the level of ability or attitude expressed by the person, whereas the second facet is the level of difficulty or endorsability of the item, stem, or prompt. The testing situation, therefore, can be viewed as an opportunity to collect data, some observable evidence of the interaction between the person and the test that provides empirical evidence about the existence of a latent trait revealed in the test items and person's performance on them.

Of course, it does simplify matters quite remarkably to regard the person simply in terms of which items were "bubbled" on a computer scan sheet, and to regard the discipline of, say, mathematics in terms of 150 multiple-choice stems with four response options each. Surely, reading ability plays a part, along with the person's motivation, propensity to guess, and the like. Surely, some items are more clearly written; some have better diagrams; some are based on everyday experiences, whereas some are a little esoteric. This undoubtedly is the case, but Rasch modeling works from the principle that the key predominant underlying attribute of the measurement situation is the latent trait expressed in the items, elicited from the candidates, and recorded in the performances when each test candidate and each test item interact. To the extent that the test performances are driven primarily by the person's ability and the item's difficulty, the Rasch model principles hold. Any aberrant performance, either by items or persons, would be flagged by the fit statistics for closer monitoring.

However, we can easily imagine measurement situations in which other aspects of the testing situation routinely interpose themselves between the ability of the candidates and the difficulty of the test (e.g., when judges are used to evaluate test performances in terms of performance criteria). The most notorious of these usually occurs at Olympic Games time, say, in the platform diving or gymnastics sections of the summer games, or the figure skating competition of the winter games. Even the least-informed of us sit stunned in front of our television screens at what appears to be, shall we say, inconsistent behavior among and between judges. The TV score cards usually show the country of origin for each judge, and many of us shake our heads in disbelief at what appear to be obvious, and repeated, discrepancies between judges' score cards. Two general properties of judges' behavior seem worthy of note. The first is that some judges seem to be more lenient or more severe than other judges, right across the board. The second, the one that gets us the most riled, is what we would call bias, judgment that seems to be more lenient or more severe depending on the competitor, the competitor's country, that country's political alliances, and so on.

Why then, in important evaluation situations, do we continue to act as though the judge, rater, or examiner has merely a benign role? On a personal level, we might try to avoid the tough marker, complain that some judges are biased against us, or avoid the examiner's specialist topic, but we might as well face it, in high-stakes testing, we often have the suspicion that the marker, not the candidate or the test, might mean the difference between pass and fail, that the scorer rather than the performance determines silver, not gold.

Does this then not show the inadequacy of the fundamental Rasch principle of unidimensional measurement? Do we not need to consider more than just the test and the candidate? Well, no and yes, in that order! Clearly, we have suggested here that rater severity, at least, needs to be taken into the equation. This chapter argues that many other facets of the testing situation can profitably be considered as key aspects of the measurement process. Moreover, we show how the many-facets Rasch model, developed in the work of Mike Linacre of Chicago, successfully models these more complex situations, and does that successfully, all within the requirement of measurement along one dimension at a time.

A BASIC INTRODUCTION TO THE
MANY-FACETS RASCH MODEL

Let us reconsider our earlier proposition that person ability and item difficulty are the key contributors to the performances that we wish to measure. If we had a little logit scale of item difficulty, it might look like this:

```
........1........2........3........4........5........6......
easier                                                   harder
```

so that a person who is successful on harder and harder items has ability located further towards the "harder" end of the scale.

```
.......1.......2.......3...B......4....W....5.......6......
easier                                                   harder
```

where Bill has 1 logit less ability than Wendy. Now consider that their performances, say short written answers to questions, are rated by two different judges, one who generally is tough, and another who generally is more lenient:

```
.......1.......2.......3.......BW.......5.......6......
easier                                               harder
```

Now the ability estimates for Bill and Wendy are so close that they cannot be meaningfully separated by this testing situation. We can guess that Bill got the easy judge, whereas Wendy got the tough one. If the situation were reversed, we could have expected a result such as the following:

```
........1........2.....B..3........4........5 W........6......
easier                                                   harder
```

It seems reasonable to presume that the examiners are not behaving in a random or precipitous way. They do know their area of expertise; they can discriminate better from lesser displays of ability; they both understand and use the marking guide sensitively and diligently; and both would be able to argue the "correctness" of the scores they give. As examiners, one is routinely tougher, and one is routinely easier.

Let us imagine giving the same small set of short-answer examination papers to examiner Tough and then to examiner Easy for rating. Look at the outcome:

```
Judge Easy:
......1......2....C....3..J.....B.......5 W....H...6......
less ability                                    more ability
```

Judge Tough:

. . . . . . 1 . . . C . . . 2 . . J . . . . . B 3 . . . . 4 W . . . . H . . 5 . . . . 6 . . . . .

less ability   more ability

We will put the pass mark at 3 on this scale. Greater than 3 is a passing grade. Judge T will fail both Bill and Jenny, but Judge E will give them a passing grade. Sure, you might be happy if Judge T (rather than Judge E) were accrediting your future brain surgeon, but what if the testing result was that your kid just missed the entrance cutoff for college? Either way, if we were serious about measurement of ability in a judged situation, we would want to be sure that passing or failing depended more on ability than on luck of the draw with examiners. We could fire one of the examiners, but which one? We could give one or both of them some retraining in use of the marking guide. Better still, we could model the difference in the severity of the judges, check the probability that the differences are systematically applied by each, and use all the available information we have to decide the cutoff point for the test.

WHY NOT USE INTERRATER RELIABILITY?

We can imagine that the interrater correlation shown in the preceding example will be just about perfect (i.e., +1), although the effects on passing or failing at the level of 3 would be quite different depending on which judge the candidate got. Try it. Use your spreadsheet or calculator to work out the correlation between the following sets of scores:

Candidate	Judge Easy	Judge Tough
a	7	6
b	6	5
c	5.5	4.5
d	5	4
e	4.5	3.5
f	4	3
g	3.5	2.5
h	3	2
i	2	1

The correlation is +1.0 (perfect), but Judge T fails *f*, *g*, *h*, and *i*, whereas Judge E fails only *h* and *i*.

A candidate in any of the preceding situations has to be considerably more able to get the same rating from the severe judge than a less able candidate would receive from the lenient judge. Because we have a complete set of data for raters, we can conclude that Judge T is just one 1 logit harder on candidates than Judge E: Adjusting Judge E's ratings by one logit to the left or Judge T's ratings by one logit to the right reveals the general consistency in the judging behavior. Therefore, the problem with intercorrelations between judge ratings is that they can demonstrate only consistency among the rank orders of candidates. They do not tell us anything about the severity or leniency differences between judges (i.e., judge discrepancies in difficulty levels).

When we understand that raters involved in the evaluation process might influence the location of person ability estimates, we can imagine how various other facets of human performance measurement might intervene in that process in a lawful (i.e., measurable, and therefore accountable) way. We might want to determine whether the short form and the standard form of a test treated candidates equally, and, if not, how much they differed. While we are looking at the test facet, we could consider whether parallel tests actually produced equivalent measures of candidates. If we routinely change our accreditation or entrance tests to keep them secure, we would want to monitor whether we could rely equally on all forms of such tests. Likewise, if we reasonably harbor a suspicion that some attributes of the candidates are consistently important aspects of their performances, we could examine one or more facets related to candidates, such as gender, first language, cultural grouping, and the like.

RELATIONS AMONG RASCH FAMILY OF MODELS

We can now enlarge our understanding of Rasch's original (i.e., two-facets) model that the probability of any correct response is a function of the ability of the person and the difficulty of the item (i.e., probability = function of (ability–difficulty)), to include other additional facets of the examination process. The probability of any correct response is a function of the ability of the person and the difficulty of the item, with allowance made for the severity of the rater, and for which particular form of the test was taken (i.e., probability = function of (ability–difficulty–rater–test)).

Linacre's (1989) conception of the many-facets Rasch model shares an interesting property with the rating scale and partial credit models: When the extra facets (e.g., rater, test, or candidate) are not required to model the added complexities of the measurement situation, then the equation conflates to the basic two-facets Rasch model: probability = function of (ability–difficulty).

DATA SPECIFICATIONS
OF THE MANY-FACETS RASCH MODEL

Interestingly, evaluations and examinations that do not adopt the many-facets Rasch model to deal with the "rater severity" problem, deal with the role of the examiner in two remarkably contrasting manners. The first, of course, is just to ignore the problem: All grades or scores are taken at face value, and no attempt is made even to check whether the scores assigned by raters differ at all. The second approach goes to the other extreme: It requires that all examiners grade the same set of papers in an attempt to ensure that all raters assign the same grade to any one paper. Of course, as we have seen, correlation indices are not indicators of this exact agreement intention, and interrater agreements of 90% mean little if agreement, say within one grade level, is counted as perfect. Although it might not be necessary for all examiners to score all tests, the subset of double-, triple-, or quintuple-marked papers must be large and be graded by all examiners. Any paper not marked by all examiners cannot be used to check rater behavior.

Now, with the Rasch model, we can take advantage of a property of the model that we have come across before. The Rasch model is quite robust in the face of missing data: It does not require a perfectly complete matrix of values as the starting point for calculations. True score-based statistics require a complete data set, so perfectly good data often are discarded because the set is incomplete, or some inauthentic datum (e.g., an average or typical score) is interpolated into the gap. On the other hand, the Rasch model requires only sufficient density of data to permit the calculations. Where the data matrix is empty, no information is interpolated. Therefore, a data set to detect rater severity effects does not require the very costly procedure of having all five judges rate all 500 papers. Provided the examiners' rotation roster is carefully thought out to provide sufficient links through the data set, it should not be necessary for any paper to be assessed by more than two examiners. The many-facets Rasch model's approach to monitoring the rater severity effect provides for the most parsimonious allocation of double-marking that is consonant with the calculation of rater effect estimations. Linacre provides quite detailed requirements for minimal marking schedules in a number of places (Linacre, 1997; Lunz & Linacre, 1998).

Of course, given what we already know about the density of the data submitted for Rasch analysis, that more targeted data will produce more precise estimates than less data, we can be sure that the scoring roster requiring all raters to grade all questions for all candidates will produce the most precise estimates of ability, difficulty, and rater severity. The point is that a complete scoring roster can be too demanding, too expensive, or too time-consuming, or it often can be just plain impractical in a practical examination situation. The robust nature of the Rasch model in the face of missing data means that sufficiently accurate estimates of these three facets can be calculated with much less demanding (i.e., substantially incomplete) marking rosters.

Linacre (1997) displayed three judging rosters for ratings from the Advanced Placement Program of the College Board. The complete judging plan of 1,152 ratings illustrates the ideal plan for both conventional and Rasch analysis. This complete judging plan meets the connection requirement between all facets because every element (essays, examinees, and judges) can be compared directly and unambiguously with every other element.

A much less judge-intensive plan of only 180 ratings also is displayed, in which less precise Rasch estimates can be obtained because the facet-linking overlap is maintained. The Rasch measures would be less precise than with complete data because 83% fewer observations are made.

Linacre's final table reveals the minimal judging plan, in which each of the 32 examinees' three essays is rated by only one judge. Each of the 12 judges rates eight essays, including two or three of each essay type, so that the examinee–judge–essay overlap of these 96 ratings still enables all parameters to be estimated unambiguously in one frame of reference. Of course, the saving in judges' costs needs to be balanced against the cost of low measurement precision, but this plan requires only 96 ratings, 8% of the observations required for the complete judging plan. Lunz et al. (1998) reported the successful implemention of such a minimal judging plan (Linacre, 1997).

MANY-FACETS ANALYSIS OF EIGHTH-GRADE WRITING

The many-facets Rasch model exemplar included here is taken from the work of Engelhard (1992, 1994), in which he examined rater severity and other aspects of the writing ability assessment in the high-stakes Eighth Grade Writing Test administered annually to all eighth-grade students in the state of Georgia. Each student was asked to write an essay of no more than two pages on a writing task randomly assigned from a set of eight topics (labeled a–h). The 1,000 marked scripts were selected randomly from the spring 1990 cohort of examinees, with 82 raters (or essay markers) having graded the essays. The essays were graded "by two raters, on each of the following five domains: content/organization, style, sentence formation, usage and mechanics," using "a four-category rating scale (ranging from *inadequate* [1] to *minimal* [2] to *good* [3] to *very good* [4]) . . . The final rating pattern used to estimate student writing ability consists of 10 ratings (2 raters × 5 domains = 10 domains)" (Engelhard, 1992, p. 177).

Of course, reliance on rater allocation of grades on five criteria across assigned topics in a high-stakes statewide educational assessment requires that the raters grade with the same severity, that the essay topics be equally demanding, and that the grades across domains reflect similar ability. Indeed, raters for the Georgia writing tests must meet rigid training and testing requirements. The estimated interrater reliability for this set was .82, which is comparable with the usual requirements of state education authorities. The essay topics were constructed with the explicit intention of producing tasks of equal difficulty.

Engelhard's (1992) many-facets Rasch analysis of the writing assessments used the following facets: essay writing ability (B), the difficulty of the assigned writing task (T), the severity of the rater (R), the difficulty of the writing domain (D), and the difficulty of the rating scale step (F). Engelhard's conception of his measurement problem would take the following form: probability = function of $(B - D - T - R - F)$.

As expected, the writing ability estimates of the 1,000 students varied considerably: Raw scores from 10/40 to 39/40 yielded estimates that varied from a low of −6.84 logits to a high of +7.07 logits. Figure 8.1 (Engelhard, 1992, p. 179) reports the estimates for raters (R), tasks (T), and domains (D).

The map of the task difficulty (T) facet shows that the examiners' intention to produce eight essay writing prompts of equal difficulty has almost been realized: The most difficult writing task (c, "all-expense-paid trip"; estimate = +0.12; error = 0.06) is measurably more difficult than the easiest task (b, "experience that turned out better"; estimate = −0.16; error = 0.06). Therefore, although these writing prompts/tasks show small, statistically significant differences in difficulty, for all practical purposes, the prompt writers have succeeded in producing essay-writing topics of approximately equal difficulty. In the absence of evidence showing such empirical equivalence of task difficulty, students' final grades would be fairer if their scores were adjusted to account for the differential difficulty of writing tasks.

The calibrations for writing domains (D) show greater variation in difficulty. Whereas the domains of content/organization, usage and mechanics, style, and sentence formation could be regarded as equally difficult, allowing for the error of the estimates, the style domain was the most difficult at +0.50 logits (error = 0.05). Sentence formation, with a difficulty estimate of −0.28 (error = 0.05), was significantly easier to score well on.

The plots of rater severity in Fig. 8.1 tell a much more varied tale, however. A group of approximately 20 raters (located around the 0 origin of the scale) could be regarded has having graded the essays with the same middling severity (allowing for measurement error). However, the remaining 60 raters are spread across more than a 3.5-logit severity range, with the most severe rater (11) estimated at +1.78 logits (error = 0.66) and the most lenient rater (19) estimated at −1.74 logits (error = 0.48).

Engelhard (1992, p. 177) pointed out that these raters were highly trained. They had to undergo rigorous training and then qualify by achieving at least 62% perfect agreement and 38% adjacent category agreements to become operational raters. During the actual essay grading period, unidentifiable "validity" papers were included in each packet of 24 essays for grading so that rater agreement was continuously monitored. Every essay was graded by two raters, with

	Raters	Writing Tasks	Domains
	Severe	*Hard*	*Hard*
+2.0			
.	11		
.			
+1.5			
.	101 82		
.	106 77 66		
+1.0			
.	35 18		
.	110 3 61 96 60 63		
.	31 65 79		
.	120		
+0.5	41 23 48 53		S
.	32 20 72 100		
.	103 14		
.	80 105 69 45 74 16		
.	7 75 52 70 40 34	d c	
0.0	85 102 93 71 58	g h f a e	M
.	114 113 21		C/O U
.	94 64	b	
.	12 119 73 118 37		SF
.	4 95 112 90 104 49		
-0.5	116 51 57 97		
.	24 76 111 86 26		
.	59		
.	27 44 115 55		
-1.0	109 117		
.	6		
.	89 87		
-1.5			
.	25		
.	19		
-2.0			
	Lenient	*Easy*	*Easy*

FIG. 8.1. Calibrations of rater severity, writing task and writing domain difficulties (Engelhard [1992]. The measurement of writing ability with a many-faceted Rasch model. *Applied Measurement in Education, 5*(3), 171–191.)

papers showing large between-rater discrepancies being rescored by a third rater. The high interrater reliability mentioned earlier (.82) reveals how successful rater training and monitoring was when monitored through the eyes of conventional statistics.

Despite these remarkable efforts, the measurement of rater severity, using the many-facets Rasch model, reveals that variation in rater severity could have a remarkable effect on student writing assessment scores. Table 8.1 has been derived from Engelhard's (1992) Table 5 (pp. 185–186) to show the impact of the variations in rater severity on the observed and expected ratings of essay writing for four selected students.

Students 43 and 522 from this sample received identical total raw scores of 27/40 when their identical ratings across five writing domains by two raters were added together. They even shared a common rater (106), who is shown in Fig. 8.1 as a moderately severe rater (estimate = +1.13), well above the mean. However, the essay of student 43 received its other ratings from a lenient rater (26, estimate = −0.65 on Fig. 8.1), whereas the second rater for student 522 was another severe rater (82, estimate = +1.29). The Rasch ability estimates of writing ability in the right column are based directly on the identical raw scores (27/40 for students 43 and 522), but incorporate allowances for the unequal severity of the rater pairs derived from the modeled estimates of rater severity plotted in Fig. 8.1. Relying on raw scores alone would cause the analyst to underestimate the writing ability of student 522 by a considerable amount (1.99 − 1.16 = 0.83 logits).

Similarly, students 621 and 305 received identical ratings yielding equal raw score totals of 22/40 each. The essay of student 621 was graded by two severe raters (82, estimate = +1.29; and 66, estimate = +1.06), whereas the 22/40 of student 305 came from a severe rater (61, estimate = +0.81) and a lenient rater (55, estimate = −0.85). This was a tough break for student 621 because relying on raw scores alone and ignoring rater severity would have underestimated that student's writing ability by more than 1 logit this time (0.08 − [−1.18] = 1.26 logits).

It should be kept in mind that the pairs of raters for each preceding essay were in perfect accord with their allocation of grades for each essay (i.e., interrater reliability would be high for these essays). They met or exceeded the stringent agreement demands of the assessment system. However, the many-facets Rasch modeling of the essay-grading data, made possible because raters could be linked together across common essays, showed very considerable differences in rater severity. The range of rater severity in this tightly monitored grading system (more than 3.5 logits) clearly overwhelms the difficulty differences in the allocated writing topics, and more importantly, has the potential to confound severely the essay-writing ability estimates of these eighth-grade students. The fit statistics of these raters and ability estimates suggest that these effects are not the result of erratic judge behavior. The judges performed very con-

TABLE 8.1

Observed and Expected Ratings for Selected Students

Student	Domain					Domain					Raw Score	Infit Mean Square	Outfit Mean Square	Rasch Ability
	C/O	S	SF	U	M	C/O	S	SF	U	M				
43	2	3	3	3	3	3	3	3	2	2	27	0.9	0.9	+1.16
			Rater 26					Rater 106						
522	2	3	3	3	3	3	3	3	2	2	27	0.9	0.9	+1.99
			Rater 82					Rater 106						
621	2	2	3	2	3	2	2	2	2	2	22	0.6	0.6	+0.08
			Rater 66					Rater 82						
305	2	2	3	2	3	2	2	2	2	2	22	0.5	0.4	-1.18
			Rater 55					Rater 61						

Note. C/O = Content Organization; S = Style; SF = Sentence Formation; U = Usage; M = Mechanics.

sistently, well within the Rasch model's stringent expectations. However, the judges are consistently more or less lenient than each other, so much so that it would be unfair not to adjust students' final grades according to the allocation of examiner pairs.

Engelhard (1992) further pointed out that misfitting raters could be identified. Their apparently erratic grade allocations could be identified by student essay number. Therefore, the essay could be reexamined, and the occasional inconsistencies of these examiners could be monitored more effectively. When the grade allocations of overfitting raters were examined, they typically showed little variation of grade allocation within essays (e.g., giving 444444, 33333, or 22222 across the five writing domains), indicating a holistic rather than an analytic approach to essay evaluation. In a later paper based on a section of similar eighth-grade essay-grading data (15 raters across 264 compositions), Engelhard (1994) showed how the many-facets Rasch model could be used to reveal typical rater errors other than severity, such as halo effect, central tendency, and restriction of score range.

RASCH MEASUREMENT OF FACETS
BEYOND RATER EFFECTS

We could go a little further with this many-facets Rasch model study to investigate whether some other facets of essay writing assessment could be profitably modeled.

The many-facets model allows all the relevant facets of a measurement situation to be modeled concurrently but examined independently. What is termed "differential item functioning" (DIF) in the less complex models of the Rasch family can be generalized to the concept of "differential facet functioning" (DFF) in this model to detect whether the invariance expected under the model's requirements actually are instantiated empirically or whether some sort of bias exists.

The basic Rasch measurement model is both strict and simple. It prescribes two attributes that matter when the interaction between a person and an item is modeled: the ability (agreeability) of the person and the difficulty (endorsability) of the item. We have illustrated, however, several instances in which it might be more reasonable to determine whether test responses are affected by other sources of systematic variance in the data collection situation such as the time of the test, the particular task, or the severity of the judge. We could regard these additional facets as decompositions of the original single Rasch difficulty facet, for example, in which a number of aspects of the examination process contribute to the difficulty that the candidates face in revealing their abilities. In these demonstrably more complex circumstances, we then can estimate the extent of those influences on the quality of our measures. The values for these separate facets, created on the same logit scale as person ability and item difficulty (i.e., in the same manner as thresholds are represented), are estimated while the parameter separation so fundamental to the construction of sound and reproducible measures is maintained. The many-facets Rasch model provides for the simultaneous estimation of facet parameters so that they may be examined separately.

In the face of these developments, further reliance on interitem correlations between judges as the criterion for high-quality ratings is, at best, ill informed. Interjudge correlations tell us only about the consistency between judges in their rank ordering of candidates, and consistency is a necessary but not sufficient condition for producing valid ratings. We need to know whether the judges' ratings (or different tasks or examination timings, for example) result in the same decisions for candidates of the same ability. But how can we know this without estimating the relative severity of the different judges? We cannot, yet we need exactly this type of information to make valid, equitable comparisons among respondents. Without separately estimating such relevant individual facets, these sources of systematic variance go unmonitored, confounding our efforts to construct useful measures, and hence biasing important decisions.

9

Revealing Stage-Based Development

One fundamental benefit from constructing measures of psychological and other human science variables is the consequence that the estimates derived from Rasch procedures are located on an interval scale where the unit value of the scale is maintained at all points along the scale. Then displays such as Rasch item–person maps convey, in more complete ways, the nature of the relations between the difficulties of the items that form the test and the abilities of the persons who took the test. Consequently, the construction of mathematically meaningful measurement intervals into what is otherwise merely ordinal data paves the way for closer meaningful inspection and statistical analyses of investigation results. Following the example of the physical sciences, we claim that statistical analyses will be effective only if fundamental measures have been constructed in the first place.

Stagelike development has been one of the major themes in developmental psychology, especially in the field of cognitive development. The stage notion in cognitive development is associated mainly with the work of Piaget and his co-workers, but the concept exists as well in the classic work of Sigmund Freud, Kohlberg's stages of moral development, and Maslow's hierarchy of needs. In general, changes occurring during development result in the construction of each new stage, which integrates the preceding stage while being qualitatively more sophisticated.

This raises the notion of discontinuity in stagelike development and, more particularly, given the apparently continuous and gradual nature of human development, suggests how empirical evidence for stages might be collected and measured. In order to illustrate how Rasch item measures might be analyzed statistically to detect stagelike qualities of development, we have selected an example based on cognitive tasks developed by Noelting and his collaborators. Noelting's study was inspired by Piaget's qualitative framework research, but each task involved a collection of individual items with various degrees of complexity (Noelting & Rousseau, in press). The structure of each item corresponded to a form of thinking characterizing a stage of cognitive development.

SHOWING DEVELOPMENTAL STAGES CROSS-SECTIONALLY

An example of the items comprising the three tasks is shown in Fig. 9.1. The mixing juices (MJ) task (Noelting, 1980a, 1980b) consists in assessing which set of glasses will have a stronger concentration of juice after the liquids are mixed in a beaker. The caskets task (CT) derives from a logical puzzle by Smullyan (1978) and involves propositional logic. It consists of statements about the presence or the absence of an object in the caskets. Only one object exists, and it must be in one casket. The aim is to discover the casket in which the object is hidden. Finally, the coded orthogonal views (COV; Gaulin, Noelting, & Puchalska, 1984; Noelting, Gaulin, & Puchalska, 1985) involves the drawing and coding of a three-dimensional object composed of cubes. The task concerns the reproduction of three-dimensional objects on a paper using coded drawing. Subjects are asked to draw an outline of the object from a frontal point of view, using signs in appropriate locations to account for the third dimension. An item is mastered if it is possible to reconstruct the object from the subject's drawing, which includes a coding system and a legend.

Criteria for cognitive developmental stages were established in Noelting's (1982) previous work from an analysis of children's behavior on each task. The criteria were then used to examine the correspondence between qualitative and quantitative stage characteristics. The cognitive developmental range covered by the tasks included the intuitive, the concrete, and the formal operational stages. Because the sample reported here consists of late adolescents and adults, data concerning the concrete operational and formal operational stages only are analyzed here.

Previous Rasch analyses of data collected with the three tasks have shown a good intratask fit of items to the model's requirements. The data reported here come from an experiment conducted by Brunel, Noelting, Chagnon, Goyer, and Simard (1993), using versions of MJ, CT, and COV comprising 18, 16, and 7 items, respectively. The tasks were submitted to a sample of 350 subjects ranging in age from 16 years to adulthood. The written answers collected during group administration of the tasks were dichotomously scored according to stage criteria for each task.

The Rasch analysis of the data from the three tasks together are shown in Table 9.1. Items range on the difficulty scale from −5.97 logits for the easiest item

a) Mixing Juices (MJ)

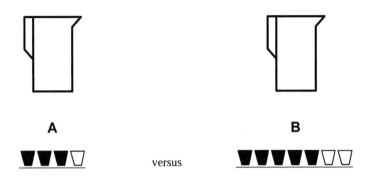

A   B

▼▼▼▽   versus   ▼▼▼▼▼▽▽

b) Caskets Task (CT)

Of these three inscriptions, two are FALSE, one is TRUE

c) Coded Orthogonal Views (COV)

Item   **Coded drawing**   **Legend**

3		1,2
3		2
3	3	2,3

1 = cube on 1st layer
2 = cube on 2nd layer
3 = cube on 3rd layer

FIG. 9.1. The three Noelting tasks.

TABLE 9.1
Rasch Analysis of the Three Tasks: Item Statistics

Item		Logit Measures		Fit Statistics		Item		Logit Measures		Fit Statistics	
Name	Stage	Difficulty	Error	Infit t	Outfit t	Name	Stage	Difficulty	Error	Infit t	Outfit t
COV7	3C	4.61	0.20	0.0	-0.2	CT9	2C	-0.78	0.18	-0.7	-0.5
MJ19	3C	4.13	0.17	-1.4	-1.6	MJ9	2B	-0.85	0.19	0.8	-0.5
MJ18	3C	4.01	0.17	-1.0	-1.6	MJ10	2A	-1.15	0.20	0.0	-0.9
CT18	3B	3.55	0.15	0.3	0.6	CT8	2B	-1.23	0.20	-0.1	-0.1
CT16	3B	3.41	0.15	2.0	1.0	CT7	2A	-1.27	0.21	-0.1	0.4
MJ16	3B	3.30	0.15	-2.8	-2.3	CT4	2A	-1.45	0.22	-0.8	0.2
COV6	3B	3.26	0.15	-0.3	0.4	CT6	2A	-1.71	0.23	-1.7	-1.5
MJ15	3B	3.16	0.14	-3.5	-2.7	CT3	1B	-2.08	0.26	-0.3	0.4
CT17	3B	3.12	0.14	1.7	0.1	CT2	1B	-2.15	0.27	0.4	1.8
CT15	3B	3.10	0.14	-0.1	-0.4	CT5	1B	-2.15	0.27	-0.4	0.9
MJ13	3A	2.48	0.13	-1.5	0.1	MJ8	1C	-2.23	0.28	-0.3	-1.3
MJ14	3A	2.48	0.13	-1.1	0.3	MJ5	1B	-2.31	0.29	0.0	1.2
COV5*	3A	2.41	0.13	4.0	3.3	COV1	2B	-2.31	0.29	-0.1	0.7
COV4*	3A	1.95	0.13	3.9	2.9	MJ6	1C	-2.58	0.31	0.0	-0.8
COV3*	2C	0.51	0.14	3.1	1.7	MJ7	1B	-2.58	0.31	0.1	0.8
MJ12	2B	0.30	0.15	-1.3	-1.7	MJ4	1C	-3.37	0.43	0.0	0.9
CT12	3A	0.22	0.15	-1.7	-1.4	CT1	1A	-4.12	0.59	0.2	1.9
COV2*	2C	-0.02	0.16	2.6	2.4	MJ2	1A	-5.26	1.01	0.0	-0.2
MJ11	2B	-0.10	0.16	-1.2	-1.4	MJ3	1A	-5.26	1.01	-0.1	-0.6
CT10	2C	-0.44	0.17	-2.4	-0.9	MJ1	0	-5.97	1.42	—	—
CT11	3A	-0.59	0.17	1.3	0.6						

*Does not fit the Rasch model ($t > 2.0$).

to +4.61 logits for the most difficult item (a late formal item of COV). The spread of subjects on the same scale goes from −2.79 logits to +6.76 logits, with a person ability estimate mean +1.74 logits higher than the mean item difficulty estimate, which is centered routinely on 0 logits. Four items (COV2, COV3, COV4, and COV5) present infit and outfit values beyond the conventionally acceptable range for a t distribution (between −2.00 and +2.00), whereas negative fit values for items MJ15, MJ16, and CT10 indicate less variation in performance than expected.

EVIDENCE OF DISCONTINUITY

The item–person map of the cognitive development trait shows gaps between item difficulty allocations on the logit scale. One way to assess the significance of the empirical gaps could be to perform t tests between successive pairs of items along the logit scale (Fig. 9.2). The items are labeled by stage and located by task in different columns. The item hierarchy of difficulty presents some gaps. The results show seven statistically significant gaps in the scale, with the widest gap ($t = 10.67$) separating the concrete and the formal operational stages (stages 2 and 3 in Fig. 9.2). These results provide a quantitative empirical demonstration of the qualitative changes that occur in thought processes during development, with the crucial passage from the concrete stage to the formal operational stage showing as the largest gap.

Smaller, but still significant, gaps in item difficulties show the locations of less comprehensive intrastage developmental changes in thinking. Therefore, the qualitative discontinuity postulated between concrete and formal stages is supported quantitatively. The major gap obtained between 14 concrete level items and 14 formal level items indicates that the addition of a new component is not mastered gradually, but takes the form of a new organization. The size of this gap between stages demonstrates the important cognitive change associated with the passage from one stage to the next as compared with the within-stage transitions. The application of Rasch modeling to these data has opened a whole new world of analysis to Noelting and his colleagues, resulting in a complete new book (Noelting & Rousseau, in press) based on the interpretation and retheorizing of his work, which has its basis in Rasch modeling of data from a lifetime of such testing.

MODELING AND MEASURING DEVELOPMENTAL DISCONTINUITY

Indeed, the measurement of stage-governed development is of such importance that it has been the focus of Mark Wilson (University of California, Berkeley), who has developed the Saltus model (a latent group model) from the basic

Logit Scale	Subjects	Items		
		By Task	**By Stage**	**Significant Gap**
7.0	.#			
6.0	.			
	### Q			
5.0	.##	COV	3C	t = 2.59
	##			
4.0	.####	MJ MJ	3C 3C	t = 2.88
	.#####	CT	3B	
	.#####	MJ CT COV	3B 3B 3B	
3.0	#############	MJ CT CT	3B 3B 3B	t = 4.59
	########## S			
	########################	MJ MJ COV*	3A 3A 3A	t = 3.54
2.0	.#############	COV*	3A	
	#############			
	.##########			t = 10.67
1.0	##########			
	.###############	COV*	2C	
	.####	MJ **CT**	2B **3A**	
.0	.##### M	MJ COV*	2B 2C	t = 2.06
	#####	CT	2C	
	.######	**CT** CT	**3A** 2C	
1.0	.##	MJ MJ	2A 2B	
	.####	CT CT CT	2A 2A 2B	
		CT	2A	
2.0	.	CT CT CT	1B 1B 1B	
	#	MJ MJ COV	1B 1C 2B	
	. S	MJ MJ	1C 1B	t = 2.13
3.0		MJ	1C	
4.0		CT	1A	
5.0				
	Q	MJ MJ	1A 1A	
6.0		MJ	0	

FIG. 9.2.   Map of subjects and items on the logit scale for the three Noelting tasks. The 3A items of caskets task with a concrete operational difficulty level are in bold. Items marked by * do not fit (t > 2.0).

Rasch model to detect discontinuity in development (Wilson, 1985). Two key papers by Wilson (1989) and Mislevy and Wilson (1996) cover the key theoretical and technical issues in the application of the Saltus model. The term "Saltus," from the Latin meaning "leap," is designed to represent Wilson's conception of the relatively abrupt changes in the relative difficulty of items for a person who moves from one stage to the next. Although the tradition in developmental and other research had been to use Guttman scalogram analyses, Wilson (1989) summarized:

> This technique, derived from attitude questionnaires, assumes that there is just one item per level and assigns subjects to levels according to the following crite-

ria. (a) A subject is in level n if he or she has responded correctly up to and including the item representing level n and has failed the remainder of the items: Such a response is said to be *scalable*. (b) A subject with any other response is of a *nonscale* type. (p. 277)

A far more realistic method would involve the development of a testing situation having many items or tasks at each of the developmental levels or stages, with the expectation that as a person moves into a new stage, discontinuity in development would be marked by a rather rapid transition from passing no, or few, tasks to passing many or most tasks indicative of the new level. Indeed, the Guttman requirements for ordinal scaling are rarely met even with continual refinement of testing procedures. There will always be some error in our recorded observations of human behavior. Some errors will be the result of deficiencies in our observation methods, whereas others will result from the nature of human behavior itself: the role of individual differences and the sheer unpredictability of humans. Under these pervasive conditions, Guttman scaling, while fundamentally correct on the crucial issue of order but ignoring the equally important aspect of stochasticity, has much more stringent requirements about human performance than the developmental theories it is being used to assess (Kofsky, 1966; Wilson, 1989).

The results from Noelting and Rousseau (in press) reported earlier in this chapter reveal what Wilson terms *segmentation*, prima facie evidence for first-order developmental discontinuity: When tests with many items at each level are submitted to Rasch analysis, items representing different stages should be contained in different segments of the scale (Fig. 9.2), with a nonzero distance between segments, and, of course, the items should be mapped in the order predicted by the theory. When item estimates are being tested for segmentation, the idea of a segmentation index must reflect the distance between the levels in terms of the errors of measurement of the item difficulty estimates. Given that the t test used to calculate the between-stages differences in the Significant Gap column in Fig. 9.2 is the ratio of the "difference between adjacent item estimates" and the "sum of the measurement errors for those two items," then Noelting's results provide evidence of stagelike developmental discontinuity (Noelting, Coudé, Rousseau, & Bond, 2000; Wilson, 1989).

The more subtle type of leap that the Saltus model is uniquely designed to detect and model (i.e., second-order developmental discontinuity) can be appreciated readily from consideration of the following Saltus principles. Although the Saltus method can be applied to a number of hierarchical developmental levels in one analysis, the key points are encapsulated more easily in a situation of less complexity: one in which person abilities and item difficulties can be seen as representing either of two developmental levels, as shown in Table 9.2.

For each group of subjects in turn, we shall presume to view the two types of items from their perspectives. In each situation, we summarize the ability levels of the persons at a certain level by the mean of the ability estimates and summa-

TABLE 9.2

Subjects and Items Grouped for Saltus Example

Stage	Subject Groups	Item Types
Higher level	Higher level subjects II	Higher level items B
Lower level	Lower level subjects I	Lower level items A

rize the difficulty levels of the items at a certain level by the mean of the difficulty estimates. The vertical arrow indicates increasing person ability or item difficulty (see Fig. 9.3).

First, we present the perspective of the lower level group:

The reasoning is that from the perspective of the mean ability of the lower level subjects (β Group I), the mean difficulty of the lower level items (θ_A) appears to be relatively easy, whereas from that same perspective (β_I), the mean difficulty of the higher level items (θ_B) appears to be hard (i.e., $[\theta_B] - [\beta_I] >> [\theta_A] - [\beta_I]$). Wilson referred to the difference between these two values as D_I (the group I gap): $D_I = ([\theta_B] - [\beta_I]) - ([\theta_A] - [\beta_I])$. This represents the relative difference in difficulty between higher (θ_B) and lower (θ_A) items for the lower level group of persons (β_I).

Now, we present the perspective of the higher level group (see Fig. 9.4). From the perspective of the mean ability of the higher level subjects (β_{II}) the mean difficulty of the lower level items (θ_A) appears to be relatively easy, and

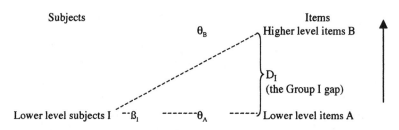

FIG. 9.3.   Group I subjects regard items grouped for Saltus example.

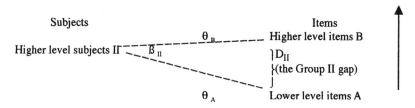

FIG. 9.4.   Group II subjects regard items grouped for Saltus example.

the mean difficulty of the higher level items (θ_B) appears to be relatively easy as well (i.e., $[\theta_B] - [\beta_{II}] > [\theta_A] - [\beta_{II}]$). Wilson referred to the difference between these two values as D_{II} (the group II gap): $D_{II} = ([\theta_B] - [\beta_{II}]) - ([\theta_A] - [\beta_{II}])$. This represents the relative difference in difficulty between higher (θ_B) and lower (θ_A) items for the higher level group of persons (β_{II}). The asymmetry index, $D = D_I - D_{II}$, is used then in the Saltus model to detect a less immediately obvious form of developmental discontinuity.

Therefore, a positive asymmetry index (i.e., $D_I > D_{II}$) indicates that the item types are closer together in item difficulty terms for group II than for group I, and a large $D_I - D_{II}$ difference is the indicator of second-order developmental discontinuity: Type B items are much harder than type A items for subjects in group I (i.e., their probability of success on type B items is low). Once the leap is made across the developmental levels (i.e., for subjects in group II), the difference between the two item types becomes much less.

When the asymmetry index is 0, second-order developmental discontinuity has not been detected, and the principles of the basic Rasch model can be applied to the detection of first-order developmental discontinuity (as in the Noelting example). Wilson (1989) claimed that the further the asymmetry index is from 0, the greater the need for the Saltus model to interpret what the Rasch model could detect only as misfit. Importantly, Saltus results include both a probability of a person being in each stage and a location in each.

A SALTUS EXAMPLE

The data for the example given here from the work of Draney (1996) are also from a set of responses to Noelting's (1980a, 1980b) MJ task for assessing proportional reasoning, which were administered to a group of 460 subjects ranging in age from 5 to 17 years. Although the Noelting MJ task contains 20 items that are scored dichotomously, Draney raised an important issue regarding the Rasch modeling of such items. When subsets of dichotomous items are essentially replications of one another, there sometimes is the concern that the requirement of local independence of items, necessary for Rasch models, will be violated. Local independence requires that the success or failure on any item should not depend on the success or failure on any other item. This might not be the case when several questions relate to the same test premise. One method used to deal with this possibility is to group such related dichotomous items together into what could be called "superitems" (Wilson, 1989; Wilson & Iventosch, 1988). The person's score on any superitem is the summed scores of its individual subitems. Thus, a superitem is polytomous (i.e., if there are three items in a superitem, the subject might get 0, 1, 2, or 3 of them correct). This was the approach used in the Saltus modeling of the MJ data reported here (Draney, 1996).

Although the MJ task comprises three hierarchical groups of items (intuitive, concrete operational, and formal operational items), which in the analysis reported at the start of this chapter yielded information about three hierarchical groups of children (intuitive, concrete operational, and formal operational thinkers), the Saltus analysis reported here compares the set of intuitive superitems to the set of concrete operational superitems. Although the analysis uses only those six items (three for intuitive and three for concrete), all 460 members of the sample were included. In this case, the Saltus-based hypothesis is that the difference in difficulty between the intuitive and concrete items should be much greater for children in the intuitive stage than for those in the higher (concrete or formal operational) stages. To model this expectation, the youngest children were classified into the lower Saltus group (group I) and all of the older children into the upper Saltus group (group II). The Saltus parameter, or asymmetry index, $D = D_I - D_{II}$, describing the difference in difficulty between group I and group II, is predicted to be positive, indicating a developmental discontinuity between the intuitive and the operational stages of cognitive development (Draney, 1996).

Table 9.3 reports the average item difficulty estimates for each of the intuitive (1a, 1b, 1c) and concrete (2a, 2b, 2c) substages described by Noelting. Difficulties are ordered hierarchically across the greater than seven logit range.

The interpretation of item difficulties and mean abilities for Saltus groups is easier when these locations are displayed in the form of the item–person map that we have used in earlier chapters. Figure 9.5 provides the item–group map of the MJ intuitive versus concrete Saltus analysis. The logit scale is shown on the left side of the figure. The column to the right of this contains the mean abilities of the two person groups, with a range of one standard deviation on either side of each group mean. The mean ability estimate for the intuitive group (M1) is located between the upper and lower limits of the +1 standard deviation range (S1), as it also is for the operational group (M2 and S2). Following the display principles in Figs. 9.3 and 9.4, the difficulty levels for the items as seen by

TABLE 9.3
Average Mixing Juices Subitem Difficulties for the Intuitive
Versus Concrete Operational Saltus Comparison

	Developmental Substage	Average Difficulty
	Concrete 2c	+3.50
	Concrete 2b	+3.12
	Concrete 2a	+0.53
	Intuitive 1c	−1.22
	Intuitive 1b	−2.33
	Intuitive 1a	−3.79

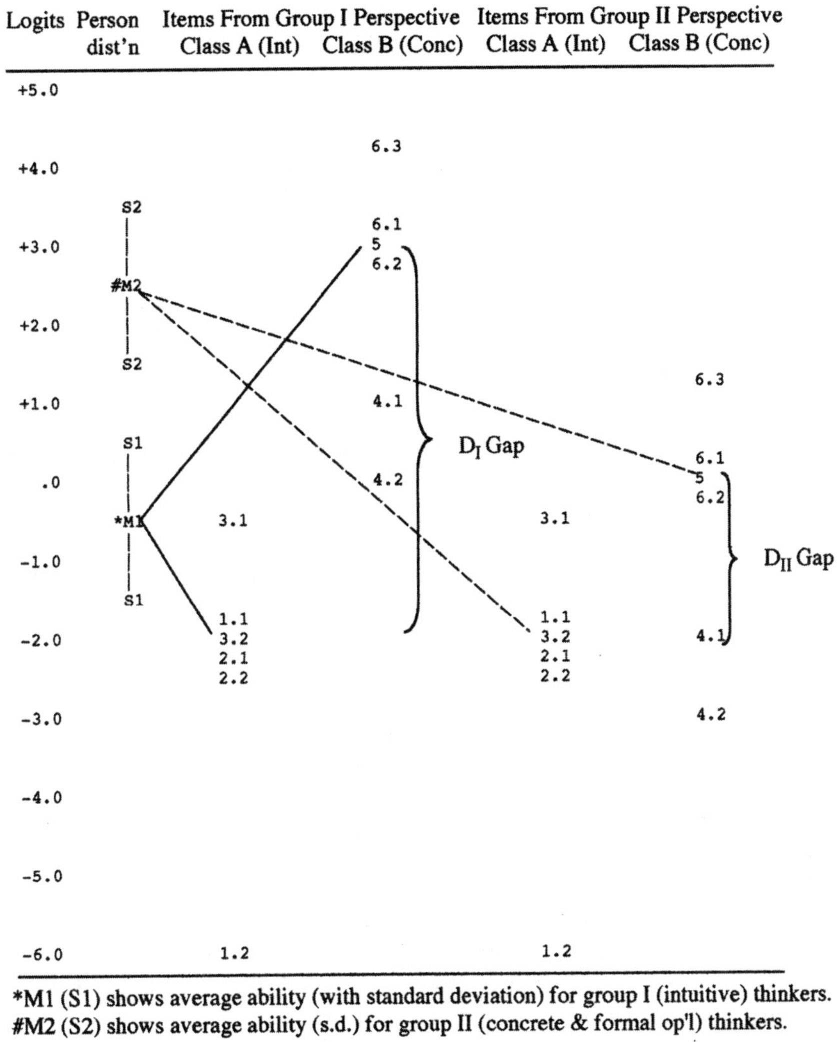
Logits
Person dist'n
Items From Group I Perspective
Class A (Int)
Class B (Conc)
Items From Group II Perspective
Class A (Int)
Class B (Conc)
+5.0
+4.0
+3.0
+2.0
+1.0
.0
-1.0
-2.0
-3.0
-4.0
-5.0
-6.0
S2
#M2
S2
S1
*M1
S1
6.3
6.1
5
6.2
4.1
4.2
3.1
1.1
3.2
2.1
2.2
1.2
D_I Gap
3.1
1.1
3.2
2.1
2.2
1.2
6.3
6.1
5
6.2
D_{II} Gap
4.1
4.2
*M1 (S1) shows average ability (with standard deviation) for group I (intuitive) thinkers.
#M2 (S2) shows average ability (s.d.) for group II (concrete & formal op'l) thinkers.

FIG. 9.5. Item–group map of intuitive versus concrete Saltus analysis of mixing juices.

group I are shown in the section labeled Items From Group I Perspective, as they also are for items as seen by group II. More difficult item steps and more able persons are toward the top of the logit scale, and less difficult item steps and less able persons are toward the bottom of the scale.

In this figure, the effect of the Saltus parameter is clear. The intuitive item difficulties are held fixed for both groups, but from the perspective of the intu-

TABLE 9.4
Exemplar Persons for the Mixed Juices Intuitive
Versus Concrete Saltus Comparison

Person	Response String	Probability of Belonging to Group I	Ability I	Standard Error I	Ability II	Standard Error II
A	000000	1.00	−3.02	0.68	−2.30	0.57
B	222000	1.00	−0.30	0.69	−0.28	0.61
C	222100	1.00	0.19	0.70	0.10	0.63
D	212200	0.97	0.19	0.70	0.10	0.63
E	222001	1.00	0.19	0.70	0.10	0.63
F	222213	0.00	2.79	0.71	2.85	0.89
G	222212	0.01	2.28	0.72	2.11	0.82
H	222102	0.68	1.22	0.73	0.97	0.70
I	222210	0.68	1.22	0.73	0.97	0.70

itive group subjects, the concrete items seem to be much more difficult indeed (large D_I gap). The higher ability of the operational group II means that this group does considerably better on the intuitive items than does group I, but from the perspective of the operational group subjects, the concrete items seem to be not difficult at all (small D_{II} gap). The Saltus parameter (or asymmetry index, $D = D_I - D_{II}$) describing the relative difference in difficulty between group A and group B items is estimated at +2.99 logits (error = 0.003), both large and positive as predicted by the preceding account based on Draney (1996).

Table 9.4 provides the observed response strings, the probabilities of intuitive group membership, and the estimated abilities with standard errors for a subset of the sample chosen to be representative of typical persons. Persons who tend to score 0 on all of the concrete items, such as persons A and B, are given a greater than 0.99 probability of being in the intuitive group (I), regardless of scores on the intuitive items. Even persons such as C or D, who score either one or two on the easiest of the concrete items (superitem 3), also are placed into the intuitive group, with a probability between 0.97 and 0.99. Even person E, someone who answers one of the subitems of concrete superitem 6 correctly while missing all of the other concrete items, is classified in group I ($p = 1$). Persons who tend to answer most, or all, of the concrete items correctly are placed into the operational group (II). Students such as person F, whose score on all six items is perfect, has a higher probability (> 0.99) of being in the higher group (group II) than person G, who misses only one possible point on the concrete items.

Although the classification of person H, who scores two out of three on the last concrete item, misses item 5, and scores one out of two on (concrete) item 4, is more equivocal (group I classification has 0.68 probability), in the sample of 460 persons there are only 17 such persons, or less than 5%. Response strings like that of person I (scores 0 on concrete superitem 6, but does well on all the other items) all have group II membership probabilities of 0.68.

LONGITUDINAL ANALYSES

It is unfortunately true that whereas development routinely encompasses at least the idea of change over time (part of the life span), genuine longitudinal research design is the exception rather than the rule. Cross-sectional studies, in which subjects across an age range are tested simultaneously, comprise the vast majority, whereas longitudinal studies, in which a cohort of subjects is tested repeatedly as the subjects age, remain in the minority. Longitudinal studies are more expensive. Repeated studies risk challenges to validity such as mortality, whereas the publish-or-perish prerogative pushes for short-term rather than long-term research commitment. Of course, longitudinal studies, which involve fundamental measures of developmental or other attributes, are even scarcer on the ground. Although statistical analyses will never be replaced by the development of measures, statistical analyses based on measures have the potential to answer these questions more meaningfully than before.

LONGITUDINAL DATA: THE SHORT HAUL

Data for a study by Endler (1998) were collected over a 5-year period to investigate the progressive changes in the Piagetian level of cognitive development in a cohort of students during the course of their secondary education. Estimates of cognitive development were based on responses to Bond's Logical Operations Test (BLOT; Bond, 1976/1995; see also chapters 4 and 5). All data collected from the years 8, 10, and 12 cohorts were used to provide three separate empirical developmental accounts of the students in the year groups of 1993, 1995, and 1997. Figure 9.6 plots the track of the mean ability estimate for the cohort over the 5-year span. The graph depicts results that support the commonly understood progress of cognitive development across the adolescent years. Moreover, the use of the Rasch logit as the measurement unit allows us to make direct visual comparisons about the relative size of the developmental changes. By and large, early adolescents (as 13-year-olds in eighth grade) are, on the average, at the stage of mature concrete operational thought (stage IIB). By the time their 15th birthdays have rolled around, as 10th graders, they show early formal operational thought (stage IIIA), and by the time they are ready to graduate from high school (as 17-year-olds in the final year 12), mature formal thought (stage IIIB) is in evidence. The addition of measurement error bars (in logits) for each of the mean ability estimates makes the significance of the size of change (compared with size of error) directly appreciable. The graph of these summary data portrays continued but modest change over the 5-year period as the developmental rule.

More importantly, however, the individual developmental profiles of particular students tested on more than one occasion over the 5-year period were

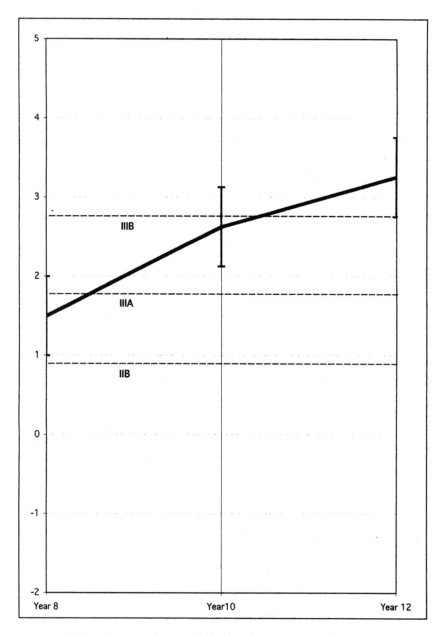

FIG. 9.6.   Average cognitive development over five years.

tracked individually to trace each child's intellectual growth over time. These longitudinal results, shown in Fig. 9.7, clearly show periods of rapidly developing formal operational thought along with periods of relatively little change. Given that this plotting of cognitive ability measures shows how developmental spurts occur at different periods, the longitudinal/cross-sectional contrast reveals the inadequacies of empirical accounts of cognitive development that rely on cross-sectional summaries alone. Individual growth summaries based on the use of interval measures show that the matching of educational strategy to intellectual abilities is a much more complicated task than cross-sectional data or group longitudinal trends could possibly reveal.

ESTIMATES FOR PERFECT SCORES

Technically speaking, Rasch modeling cannot provide estimates for perfectly good (all ✔s) or completely failing (all ✘s) scores. As detailed in chapter 3, Rasch estimates are based on probability of success to probability of failure ratios. Whereas 80% success has 20% failure from which to construct a ratio, 100% success has 0% failure, and 0% success has 100% failure. Then, the 100/0 fraction produces an infinitely large estimate, and conversely, 0/100 yields an infinitely small result.

In keeping with that requirement, the QUEST software used in the Endler (1998) study does not provide Rasch ability estimates for perfect scores (all 1's, or all 0's). However, users of the BLOT would expect that the performances of many students would show ceiling effects during adolescence. Many students "top out" on the test with a perfect score of 35/35. Whereas the ceiling effect itself can result in underestimation of ability and growth, removing all 35/35 perfect scores from the data sets for Figs. 9.6 and 9.7 would be even more misleading. Wright (1998) provided guidelines for the extrapolation of approximate measures for perfect scores. Endler (1998) chose to adopt the conservative approach that "(n)o extreme score extrapolation can be less than one logit" (Wright, 1998a), adding 1 logit to the +3.99 logits (for 34/35) to give the +4.99 logits estimate for 35/35 on the BLOT used to construct the preceding figures.

On the other hand, WINSTEPS Rasch software routinely provides an approximate estimate for perfect scores using an almost-perfect score as the basis for its estimation. That procedure yields an estimate of +5.16 logits for a perfect BLOT score in place of the +4.99 used by Endler (1998). Linacre (1999b) advised: "The measure for an extreme score is estimated as the measure for (maximum score − x) or (minimum score + x) in which $0.5 \geq x > 0$. The default for WINSTEPS is 0.3. This takes the position that the extreme score is only barely extreme." The estimate from WINSTEPS of +5.16 logits is based on the fraction 34.7/0.03 (i.e., on a BLOT score of 34.7 out of a possible 35).

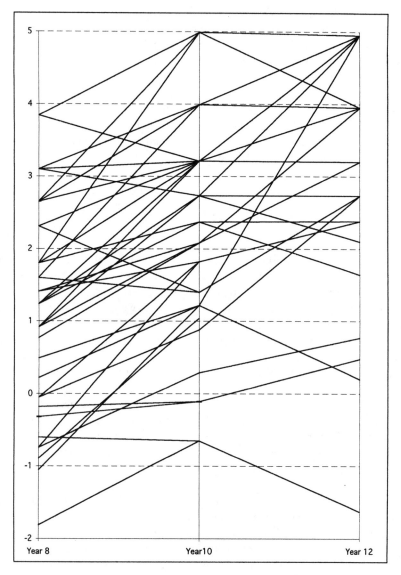

FIG. 9.7.   Individual changes in cognitive development over five years.

LONGITUDINAL DATA: THE LONG HAUL

Dawson's (2000) Rasch modeling of data collected by Armon (1984) to investigate the longitudinal development of moral judgment and ideas of the good provides an excellent exemplar of Rasch measures used to address the existence and nature of stagelike change in persons over time. Dawson argued that Rasch measurement, using the partial credit model, was well suited to answer questions about whether development is steplike or gradual, about the relation between development in different domains, and about the relations between stages assessed with different data collection instruments, all of which are seen as difficult for traditional quantitative methods even to address.

In her longitudinal study of moral reasoning and evaluative reasoning about the good, Armon interviewed a total of 42 individuals (19 males and 23 females) on four separate occasions: 1977, 1981, 1985, and 1989. The youngest commencing subject was 5 years of age, whereas the oldest was age 86 years on the final interview occasion. At each occasion, three dilemmas from the Moral Judgment Interview (MJI; Colby & Kohlberg, 1987) were used to assess moral reasoning along with Armon's (1984) Good Life interview which includes questions about the good life, good work, good friendship, and good person. The interviews were open ended. They were administered individually to each participant, tape-recorded, and transcribed, with seven participants missing two out of four interviews. Both the Colby and Kohlberg and the Armon scoring systems produce scores that can be reported as global stage scores (GSS) ranging from 1 to 5 in increments of one half stage (Armon, 1984; Colby & Kohlberg, 1987). All the interview examples in each of the five domains for each participant were scored individually and averaged, using a standard weighting system (Armon, 1984). This resulted in a single score for each participant in each domain (i.e., five scores per person per test time).

The Rasch analyses reported in Fig. 9.8 were conducted on the pooled longitudinal and cross-sectional data. All observations were treated as independent, giving an n of 147 separate observations from the total number of 42 participants. This effectively increased the analytical power. This is a useful and permissible strategy when a study design involves more than two test times separated by relatively long intervals (Rogosa & Willett, 1985; Willett, 1989). More importantly for this exemplar, the longitudinal information incorporated into the Rasch estimation analysis in this way shows that any age differences reflect actual individual trends rather than mere statistical artifacts.

The item–person map in Fig. 9.8 presents a thorough and comprehensive display of the results from the analysis, with the logit scale represented as a long vertical gray band toward the right of the figure. Estimates for individuals (represented by case numbers) at each of the four times of testing are in separate columns to the left of this band, arranged in ascending order from left to right. Tracing the developmental trajectory of the developmental trajectory for each individual then is simply a matter of joining the appropriate identification numbers.

Conservative, qualitatively judged locations for individuals with 0 scores (all items scored stage 1) have been added to the bottom of the logit scale, whereas locations for individuals with perfect scores (all items scored stage 5) have been added to the top of the logit scale. The few case numbers shown in bold indicate

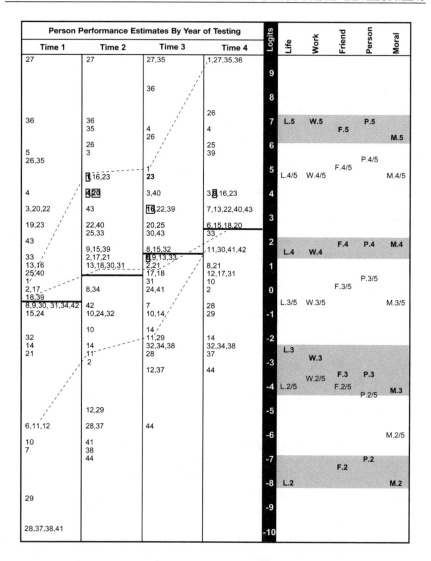

FIG. 9.8.   Moral and evaluative reasoning: item and person performance estimates with means.

that their performance patterns did not fit the model. Table 9.5 shows the actual scores, infit mean squares, and standardized t infit values for those individuals. Dawson (2000) argued that although cases 35 and 26 (twice) had scores across items that were very similar, too similar to fit the Rasch model, these cases were not problematic from her theoretical perspective because the similarity of their

TABLE 9.5

Moral and Evaluative Reasoning:
Person Performances That Do Not Fit the Model

ID No.	Year	Actual Scores					Infit Mean Square	Infit t
		Good Life	Good Work	Good Friendship	Good Person	Moral Judgment		
26	1977	4.5	4.5	4.5	4.0	4.5	0.18	−2.18
35	1977	4.5	4.5	4.5	4.0	5.0	0.18	−2.18
26	1989	4.5	4.5	4.5	4.5	4.5	0.90	−2.91
1	1989	4.0	4.0	3.5	5.0	3.5	3.97	+2.58

scores is consistent with the hypothesis that individuals tend to think in structurally similar ways across these different contexts.

To the right of the logit scale are the item estimates for the good life, good work, good friendship, good person, and moral judgment, respectively. Dawson (2000) has helpfully added large horizontal gray bands to indicate the approximate range for each level of reasoning from stage 2 to stage 5 across the five items. With the exception of moral judgment at stage 2.5, stage scores across items cluster within relatively narrow bands of the logit scale, indicating that individual stage scores across all five items appear to measure the same level of reasoning. Not only does this provide evidence for structural coherence across test contents, it also allows interpolation of stage boundaries and stagewise progress onto the interval logit scale. The stage 2.5 exception seems to be a consequence of the greater immediate relevance of a concrete moral dilemma, as opposed to the abstract concept of "good," for young children. There is an absence of any result in the distribution of the stages that would suggest that developmental level in any one testing context item progresses more rapidly.

Finally, four narrow horizontal gray bands show the means of the person performance estimates at each of the test times. Mean development in this group over the course of the study spanned 4 logits, or approximately one full stage. An analysis of variance (ANOVA) comparing means at the four test times indicates that mean stage advance is significant: $F(3, 144) = 7.29$, $p < .001$.

In Fig. 9.8, the developmental trajectories of three of the subjects have been made more obvious by the simple technique of joining the person estimates across the four data-collection occasions for subjects 1, 11, and 18. In spite of the large differences in starting and end locations for persons 1 and 11, their developmental profiles show remarkable similarities in pattern/slope. While persons 1 and 18 start at similar locations, their endpoints are quite different. However, persons 11 and 18, who end up at about the same developmental point, have dramatically different starting points 12 years earlier. Nevertheless, for all three cases, the profiles are quite comparable: growth in period one, consolidation in period two, followed by more growth in period three.

Variations on the item–person map principle of representing the variable of interest have particular applications in the investigation of stagelike development of human abilities and attributes. The use of a genuine interval scale with such data allows for more informative results from these analyses. In the studies described in this chapter, the logit-scale person measures then were used as the input into a variety of statistical analyses for examining developmental trends.

10

The Rasch Model Applied
Across the Human Sciences

DICHOTOMOUS ANALYSIS
OF CHECKLISTS

We have already lamented that the large majority of empirical studies do not include the deliberate construction of a variable before performing the statistical analysis. Raw scores, or counts, are treated as measures, and analyses often are conducted at the item level rather than the variable level. For example, the ubiquitous checklist is an item format commonly used in surveys, particularly in the discipline of health education. A researcher who wished to know respondents' perceived barriers to getting involved in determining public health policy might ask them to check all statements that apply to them. Some of the options offered to the respondent might include the following: lack of time, lack of money, involvement not personally gratifying, and so on (Boardley, Fox, & Robinson, 1999).

The usual way to analyze data such as these is at the item level: Whether the respondent checked the item (a dichotomous answer) is investigated with regard to respondent characteristics such as sex, ethnicity, or level of education, usually with a chi-square analysis. Another common technique is to treat the items as a pseudoscale (i.e., by summing the total number of items checked by each respondent). In this example, scores could range from 0 to 8. Thus, subjects with higher counts are treated as having "more perceived barriers" to involvement than those with lower counts. As probably can be ascertained by now, these types of data analyses do not consider the pattern of responses, nor do they provide any understanding of the data at the level of the policy involvement variable. How then can Rasch analysis of checklist data provide a better alternative to these two options?

Boardley, Fox, and Robinson (1999) were interested in understanding what personal characteristics were related to the public policy involvement of nutritional professionals. Using the dichotomous Rasch model, the investigators constructed an involvement variable from a checklist of activities to create an interval-level measure in which higher estimates meant more involvement and lower estimates meant less involvement. These measures (the Rasch logit estimates) then were used in subsequent statistical analyses to determine whether certain groupings of persons differed significantly on involvement.

Figure 10.1 shows a WINSTEPS (Linacre & Wright, 2000) person–item map for the public policy involvement variable. As expected, the items with fewer checks indicate higher involvement items, such as volunteering as an elected official or serving as a public official, whereas the items with more checks indicate lower levels of involvement, such as voting. Both the items and the persons span a large logit range (approximately 7 logits), indicating that a variable from more to less involvement was clearly defined. When the distributions of the sample are compared with the distribution of items, it is clear that this sample is less involved than the mean involvement level defined by the items in the checklist.

A noticeable gap in the variable definition appears between "voted for a candidate or proposal" and "gave money to a campaign or official." This gap in the variable occurs just where many of the respondents are located. Thus differentiation in public policy involvement is inadequate at this lower level of involvement. This is further reflected in the person separation statistics (a rather low 1.34).

This variable construction provided a better understanding of the analysis in several ways. First, the variable of public policy involvement was constructed, allowing for inferences to be made at the variable, not the item, level. Second, the investigators not only could visualize a continuum of involvement, but they also could measure individuals along that continuum. Third, suggestions for scale improvement were highlighted by the analysis. For example, the gap in the variable along the low involvement levels suggested the addition of activities requiring more involvement than voting, but less involvement than giving money. Inclusion of such items (e.g., reading relevant newspaper articles, discussing policy issues with colleagues, reading political brochures, or attending public hearings) might help differentiate those people at the bottom of the scale.

Although a post hoc Rasch analysis might not always be fruitful, this analysis was a considerable step forward for researchers in this field of health education, a step toward conducting analyses at the variable level rather than the item level. It also shows the flexibility of the dichotomous Rasch model in its application to checklist analysis, in addition to its usual use with the multiple-choice format.

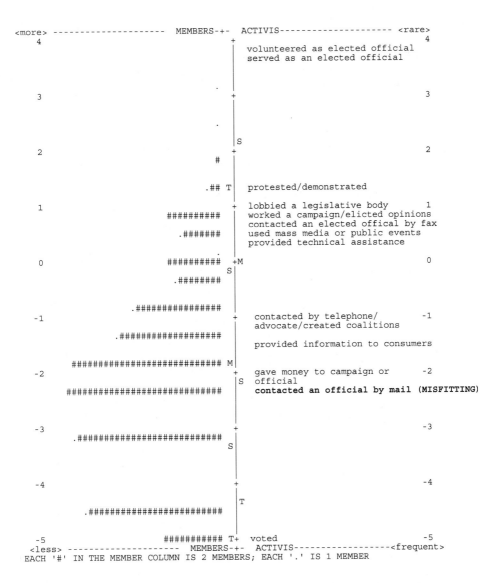

```
<more> -------------------- MEMBERS-+- ACTIVIS-------------------- <rare>
   4                                    +                               4
                                        |  volunteered as elected official
                                        |  served as an elected official

                                   .    |
   3                                    +                               3
                                        |
                                   .    |
                                        |S
   2                                    +                               2
                                   #    |
                                        |
                              .## T|  protested/demonstrated
   1                                    +  lobbied a legislative body    1
                      #########            worked a campaign/elicted opinions
                       .#######            contacted an elected offical by fax
                              .            used mass media or public events
                                           provided technical assistance
   0                  #########  +M                                     0
                       .#######  S|
                                        |
                  .###############       |
  -1                                    +  contacted by telephone/       -1
                                           advocate/created coalitions
             .#################           provided information to consumers

       ######################### M|
  -2                                    +  gave money to campaign or      -2
                                        |S official
       #########################           contacted an official by mail (MISFITTING)


  -3          .#########################  +                               -3
                                        |S

  -4                                    +                               -4
                                        |T
           .#######################
                                        |
  -5                  ########## T+  voted                               -5
<less> -------------------- MEMBERS-+- ACTIVIS-----------------<frequent>
EACH '#' IN THE MEMBER COLUMN IS 2 MEMBERS; EACH '.' IS 1 MEMBER
```

FIG. 10.1. Public policy involvement map for nutrition professionals.

141

CLIENT SATISFACTION ANALYSIS[1]

Rasch modeling of Likert scale data has paved the way for more sensitive, powerful, and meaningful analysis of customer satisfaction data. Bond and King (1998, 2000) reported on the competing demands of a School Opinion Survey of client satisfaction involving approximately 36,000 parents and 45,000 students and carried out over 1,200 government schools in one state in Australia. The framework used to guide questionnaire construction was Moos's (1979) scheme for classifying human environments. The final 20-item School Opinion Survey parent and student forms (Bond, King, & Rigano, 1997) were designed after feedback from the administration of trial forms. Recommendations to the group representing state peak educational bodies that oversaw instrument development were supported by the results of Rasch modeling. This analysis showed that the 20 items with the best Rasch psychometric indices were also the 20 items rated most important by the trial samples.

One of the specified outcomes of the School Opinion Survey contracted research project was the establishment of state parent and student satisfaction benchmarks. In a very large state education system, in which accountability of both the system as a whole and of individual school sites was to be undertaken in terms of quantitative outcomes, the benchmarks provided two complementary functions. The first function focused on the accountability of the individual education unit in which the role of the client satisfaction benchmarks would act as the standard against which satisfaction at any single school site could be compared. The second function focused on the education system as a whole, in which the benchmarks were to facilitate the tracking of changes in client satisfaction with public education over time. The contracted requirement that all state schools (more than 1,200 of them) were to be involved in the sample and would receive individual reports precluded the use of population proportional sampling.

To develop the satisfaction benchmarks for the School Opinion Survey project, Rasch analyses were performed by setting the mean of the persons, rather than the mean of the items, as the starting point (0 logits) for the estimation procedures. The item difficulties, or endorsability, then were plotted in relation to the mean satisfaction level (0 logits) for the benchmark group (i.e., how easy it was, on the average, for the members of the benchmark group, parents or students, to endorse each of the 20 School Opinion Survey items). For example, if, from the standpoint of the group average, an item was plotted as "more difficult to endorse" than another, then that group was judged to be less satisfied on that item. Each statewide satisfaction benchmark, then, consisted of 20 item difficulty estimates, one for each School Opinion Survey item, and an accompanying error value for that estimate.

---

[1]Disclaimer: Reproduced with the permission of the Queensland Department of Education. All inquiries concerning the original material should be addressed to the Copyright Officer, PO Box 33, Albert Street, Brisbane, Q 4002, Australia.

TABLE 10.1
Item Estimates for All Parents ($n = 35{,}928$)

Item No.	Estimate Logits	Error	Infit Mean Square	Outfit Mean Square
1	−1.637	0.008	0.95	0.97
2	−1.472	0.009	1.09	1.09
3	−1.273	0.007	0.88	0.89
4	−1.474	0.007	0.85	0.89
5	−1.411	0.007	0.73	0.76
6	−1.450	0.007	0.98	1.00
7	−1.352	0.007	1.02	1.04
8	−1.544	0.008	0.85	0.88
9	−1.587	0.008	0.92	0.94
10	−1.351	0.007	0.87	0.88
11	−1.280	0.008	0.82	0.84
12	−1.319	0.007	0.65	0.68
13	−1.334	0.008	0.81	0.83
14	−1.445	0.008	0.93	0.94
15	−1.747	0.008	0.71	0.77
16	−0.804	0.007	1.48	1.43
17	−0.615	0.007	1.62	1.53
18	−0.642	0.007	1.32	1.28
19	−1.560	0.008	1.16	1.18
20	−1.543	0.008	1.72	1.53

Table 10.1 shows the state benchmark item difficulty estimates when the mean satisfaction level of all responding parents (approximately 36,000) was set as the starting point (0) of the Rasch analysis estimation procedure: The higher the item estimate, the more difficult that item was for the group to endorse and the less satisfied the group was on that item. By way of an interpretative note, all of the item estimates are negative (below 0 logits), so the sample of parents found it relatively easy to agree with the 20 School Opinion Survey items.

Table 10.2 shows the corresponding state benchmark item difficulty estimates when the mean satisfaction level of all responding students (> 40,000) was set as the starting point (0) of the Rasch analysis estimation procedure: Again, the higher the item estimate, the more difficult that item was for the group of all students to endorse and the less satisfied the group was on that item. For example, the single positive value in the estimates column for item 18 means that the student sample had the most difficulty endorsing that item on the School Opinion Survey student form.

In Fig. 10.2, the benchmark estimate for the parents as a whole (from Table 10.1) is plotted along the heaviest line, representing the item difficulty estimates in graphic form. Furthermore, the statewide samples of parents and students were divided to produce 12 data sets, six each for parents and students. This was

TABLE 10.2
Item Estimates for All Students ($n = 40,371$)

Item No.	Estimate	Error	Infit Mean Square	Outfit Mean Square
1	−0.736	0.007	0.91	0.91
2	−0.487	0.006	1.01	1.01
3	−0.635	0.006	0.93	0.93
4	−0.448	0.006	0.95	0.96
5	−0.731	0.006	0.86	0.87
6	−0.656	0.006	0.98	0.99
7	−1.023	0.006	0.98	1.00
8	−0.457	0.006	0.98	0.99
9	−0.790	0.006	0.98	1.00
10	−0.631	0.006	0.92	0.93
11	−0.850	0.006	0.76	0.78
12	−0.033	0.006	0.96	0.96
13	−0.558	0.006	0.87	0.88
14	−0.730	0.006	0.84	0.87
15	−0.250	0.005	1.22	1.19
16	−0.110	0.005	1.18	1.16
17	−0.111	0.005	1.19	1.17
18	0.137	0.006	1.40	1.36
19	−0.706	0.006	1.08	1.09
20	−0.424	0.005	1.11	1.10

carried out according to the agreed-on notion of establishing benchmarks in which generally comparable schools would be grouped to allow fairer and more meaningful school-versus-benchmark comparisons to be undertaken and reported. Benchmarks were estimated and constructed separately for six groups of comparable schools. Figure 10.2 also shows the relative benchmark item satisfaction estimates for the parents for each of the six groups of comparable schools.

Rasch measurement showed that satisfaction with public education varied meaningfully across different types and sizes of schools. Consequently, school-versus-state benchmark comparisons that did not account for the wide variations in satisfaction level by school type would systematically give an advantage to some groups of schools over others.

PERSON-FREE ITEM ESTIMATES

The requirement that all state schools were to be involved in the sample precluded the use of population proportional sampling. In the smallest schools, the whole target population (parents and year 7 students) of each school was surveyed. At larger education sites, samples were selected using alphabetical

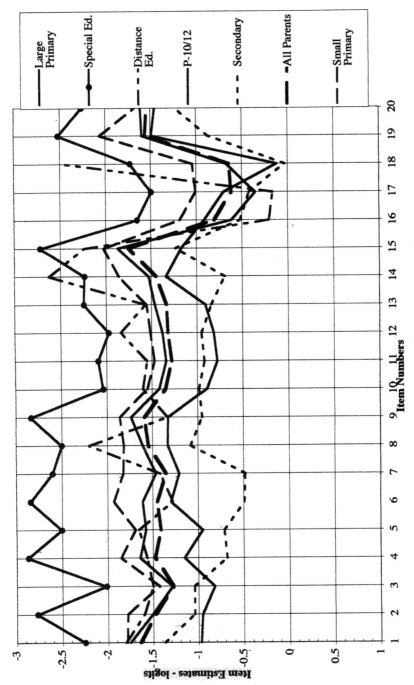

FIG. 10.2. Benchmark satisfaction estimates for parents.

145

groupings by family name, with fewer groupings being required for larger schools.

The Rasch modeling property of specific objectivity was verified empirically when calculation of identical benchmark estimates resulted from the construction of simulated population proportional samples using sample-to-population ratio weightings. Given that educational assessment and evaluation has been informed by true-score statistical presumptions since its inception, it should be expected that those enamored with traditional principles might be more than a little skeptical of some claims made for the Rasch family of measurement models. Often, the most difficulty is expressed concerning the assertion that the Rasch family of models exhibits the property of specific objectivity. *Specific objectivity* is the development of fundamental measures: person-free estimates of item difficulties (i.e., difficulty estimates independent of the distribution of abilities in the particular group of persons for whom the items are appropriate). To confirm that the properties of the Rasch model (sample-free measures of item difficulty) were maintained with these data sets, a probability proportional to size sample was constructed for each parent and student benchmark by weighting every person's responses according to the size of the school target population and the number of responses from that school.

Weighted versus unweighted benchmark comparisons were reported for all 12 groups of clients. Except for two cases, in which the weightings for parents from larger schools depressed the satisfaction levels previously calculated, the benchmark comparisons provided empirical confirmation for the Rasch specific objectivity claim. Given that the two exceptions did not meet the model's requirements, the lower benchmarks were used for 1997 comparisons, and a recommendation was made for the modification of comparable school groups in subsequent surveys. Examples of weighted versus unweighted benchmark comparisons are shown in Figs. 10.3 (no difference) and 10.4. Parents in larger school settings were less satisfied.

COMPUTERIZED ADAPTIVE TESTING (CAT)

The Rasch model has been indispensably useful in situations using computerized adaptive testing (CAT). CAT involves a special sort of computer-based test in which the difficulty of test items administered is specifically tailored to the ability level of the current test taker—thereby providing an individualized examination for each person. CAT operates on the principle that items that are too easy or too difficult for the candidate contribute little information about the test taker's ability.

There are two key elements at the heart of a well-developed CAT system. The first is a large bank of accurately calibrated items that cover a wide range of

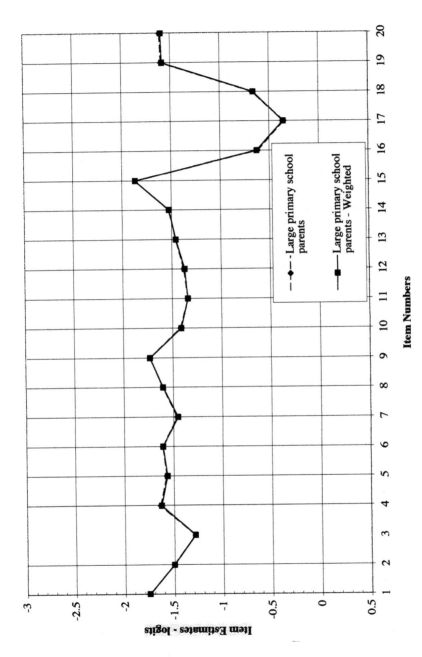

FIG. 10.3. Weighted versus unweighted benchmark estimates for large primary parents.

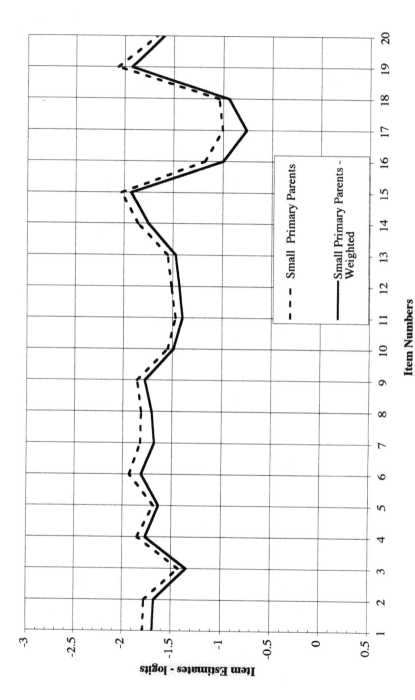

FIG. 10.4. Weighted versus unweighted benchmark estimates for small primary parents.

148

difficulties. The second is a test item presentation algorithm that determines the next item to be presented on the computer screen to the current test taker. Both of these elements derive considerable benefits from the application of Rasch measurement. The construction of calibrated item banks that provide for the presentation of almost unlimited versions of person-specific tests is a consequence unique to Rasch measured CATs. Moreover, when the intent is to operationalize another benefit of Rasch measurement, the item-selection algorithm is constrained to present items at the 50% probability of success for the current test taker, based on the success or failure on the current item. The presentations might follow, say, a 0.2 logit increase in difficulty with a successful response or a similar decrease in difficulty following an incorrect response to keep the future items well targeted for the respondent.

This type of flexible testing situation, then, quickly hones in on the test taker's demonstrated ability level with fewer questions, hence maximizing information and limiting both the amount of testing time and the number of test items exposed to any one examinee. When on-target information is maximized in this manner, the standard error measure is minimized and the test can be much shorter without sacrificing reliability. Furthermore, tests are more secure because two different students might take two entirely different tests when the test items have been previously equated. When an adaptive test is delivered from a Rasch-calibrated item bank, the estimates of test-taker ability are statistically equivalent across all exams whether the test taker has been administered easy or hard items. This level of generality is essential for a CAT.

CATs are currently used for human resources selection examinations, high-stakes certification and licensure examinations, large-scale admissions testing, diagnostic testing, aptitude tests, and achievement tests. Adaptive testing is particularly appropriate for heterogeneous populations and/or testing scenarios that cover a wide range of ability.

There are a number of topics related to CAT that are often canvassed in the literature. They include the level of confidence in the pass/fail decisions made from CATs, the equivalence of test items, and targeted tests, as well as the role of CAT in certification and licensure. Researchers have addressed whether examinees should be retested on items exposed to them in previous test administrations. Bergstrom and Lunz (1992) demonstrated that only half as many test items were needed to achieve the same level of pass/fail decision confidence with a CAT as with a paper-and-pencil test and that ability estimates were not affected when the targeted difficulty of a test was altered (Bergstrom, Lunz, & Gershon, 1992).

Although the traditional threats to test security, such as cheating on test items or even stealing parts or all of a test, draw interest from CAT administrators and researchers, Rasch-modeled CAT research provides particular insights into testing problems posed by guessing and student misrepresentation of ability. In the context of the development of a sound-file-enhanced CAT to measure second language ability, Stahl, Bergstrom, and Gershon (2000) suggested that incorrect responses to items at the 40% probability level (in contrast to the 50% Rasch expectation) might be appropriate to flag the possibility that a respondent had deliberately missed answering questions correctly in order to be streamed into an easier second language course.

The development and maintenance of a large calibrated item pool for CAT is a large task, as is administering the exam and reporting the results. The Bergstrom and Lunz (1999) chapter provides detailed Rasch-informed insights into the issues involved in moving from a paper-and-pencil test to computer adaptive format.

JUDGED SPORTING PERFORMANCES

Some Olympic games events provide the quintessential example of how we have come to routinely, and even passively, accept subjectivity in judgments of human performance. Although, performance-enhancing drugs aside, there is rarely any dispute about who wins gold in, say, the 1,500-m freestyle, the 100-m track, or the team bobsled, a few of us can be drawn into the occasional argument about the medal winners in platform diving or on the beam. Better still, let's take the winter Olympics women's figure skating as an example of a judged event. For the first skater about to go out on the ice, the announcer dramatically whispers something to the effect, "She must be upset because being the first skater on this program puts her at a disadvantage." Surely, we have all wondered why, in the attempts to at least create *the appearance* of objectivity in judging, we could openly admit and accept that the order in which one skates actually influences the judges' ratings! Even if you haven't noticed that particular example of lack of objectivity in the rating of performers, you would really be hard-pressed not to admit what appears to be nationalistic or political alliance biases among the judges, where judges tend to favor skaters from their own countries (e.g., Eastern Bloc judges rate Western Bloc skaters less favorably and vice versa). In spite of these phenomena having been well documented in the literature (Bring & Carling, 1994; Campbell & Galbraith, 1996; Guttery & Sfridis, 1996; Seltzer & Glass, 1991; Whissel, Lyons, Wilkinson, & Whissell, 1993), the judgment by median rank approach has been maintained as the best method for minimizing this bias (Looney, 1997) because it is held to minimize the effect of extreme rankings from any one judge in determining any skater's final score.

The median rank approach has two problems, however (Looney, 1997). First, the judges are required to give different ratings to each skater, that is, no two skaters may receive the same score from the same judge. This violates the principle of independence of irrelevant alternatives (Bassett & Persky, 1994; Bring & Carling, 1994), meaning that each skater, rather than being rated independently, is directly compared with others who skated before her. This can result in a situation where skater A is placed in front of skater B, but can then be placed *behind* skater B once skater C has performed (see Bring & Carling, 1994, for an example; Looney, 1997). It is then clear why it is unfortunate to be the first skater—the judges tend to "reserve" their "better" scores in case they need them for a later performer! Second, the subjective meanings of the scores may differ from judge to judge, that is, "a 5.8 may represent the best skater for Judge A, but the third best skater for Judge B" (Looney, 1997, p. 145). This variation in meaning is what we refer to in chapter 8 when discussing how some judges are routinely more severe or lenient than others—a judge effect that certainly cannot be corrected simply by calculating the median score.

In an attempt to illustrate how one could create a set of objective, interval-level measures from such ordinal-level rankings, Looney (1997) ran a many-facets Rasch analysis for the scores from the figure skating event from the 1994 winter Olympics. Many will recall this controversial event in which Oksana Baiul won the gold medal over Nancy Kerrigan, who won silver.

Looney (1997) obtained scores from the nine judges' ratings of 27 skaters on both components: Technical Program (composed of required elements and presentation) and Free Skate (composed of technical merit and artistic impression). Rasch analysis allowed her to calibrate these scores on an interval scale, showing not only the ability ordering of the skaters, but also the distance between each skater ability estimate. With many-facets Rasch analysis, Looney was also able to estimate judge severity and component difficulty (the component elements nested within each of the two items) in the same measurement frame of reference.

Although in most of the examples throughout this book we place more interest in the ordering and estimation of items (i.e., to examine how well our survey/examination is working), here the researcher was far more interested in estimations based on the ordering of the skaters and the severity of the judges. Of course, valid component ordering is a prerequisite to the interpretation of the other facets, but the emphasis here is more on the placement of persons (given the preset required components and their rating scales) and the impact of the judges on those placements.

The Rasch estimates showed remarkably good fit to the model for all facets of the measurement problem: the four skating components, the judge ratings (with the exception of the judge from Great Britain), and skater ability (with the exception of Zemanova, the lowest ranked skater). Consequently, Looney would have been justified in feeling confident of her interpretation of the Rasch-based placements. By estimating all of these facets in an objective frame of measurement, summing these judge ratings, and weighting each component its appropriate item weight, Looney found the top four skaters in order to be Kerrigan, Baiul, Bonaly, and Chen (Looney, 1997, p. 154). (The Olympic medals went to Baiul [Ukraine], Kerrigan [USA], and Chen [China], with Bonaly fourth.)

Upon closer examination of the fit statistics for the judges, Looney discovered that judge idiosyncrasies did not affect the results of the Technical Program, but they did affect the results of the Free Skate. Since the Free Skate holds more weight in determining the final placement of skaters, these judge idiosyncrasies subsequently affected who won the gold medal. In fact, Looney (1997) concluded:

> All of the judges with an Eastern block or communistic background not only ranked Baiul better than expected, but ranked Kerrigan worse. The same trend was seen for Western Block judges. They ranked Baiul worse and Kerrigan better than expected. When the median of the expected ranks is determined, Kerrigan would be declared the winner. Before the free skate began, all the judges knew the rank order of the skaters from the technical program and the importance of the free skate performance in determining the gold medal winner. This may be why some judging bias was more prevalent in the free skate than in the technical program. (p. 156)

Looney's investigation of the effect of judges' ratings on the final placement of skaters objectively validates what a chorus of disbelieving armchair judges had suspected. The median rank system cannot remove the effect of judge bias in close competitions because it focuses on between-judge agreement. The many-facets Rasch model, however, shifts that focus to within-judge consistency (Linacre, 1994, p. 142) so that individual judge effects, including bias, can be detected and subsequently accounted for in the final placement decisions.

PREDICTING BASKETBALL SUCCESS

Researchers at the MESA Psychometric Laboratory (University of Chicago) sought to create a set of objective measures for predicting the success and failure of NCAA Division I men's basketball teams. The measures were created using the paired-comparisons method (by using the log odds of a win for a home team [H] over a guest team [G]), using only the win–loss records for each team, the opponent, and whether the games were at home or on the road (Linacre, 1999c, p. 18):

$$\text{Log} \frac{\text{Probability of Win by H}}{\text{Probability of Loss by H}} =$$

$$\text{H's Proficiency} + \text{Home Court Advantage} - \text{G's Proficiency}$$

The MESA group downloaded a list of teams from the Web, along with accurate daily results. For those teams with perfect records at the start of the season, MESA imputed scores for wins against notional bad teams and losses against notional good teams (Linacre, 1999c). (This harks back to the ideas raised in chapter 9 for calculating estimates for perfect scores on a multiple-choice test.) Using this process, MESA was able to publish daily measures for the entire basketball season. These orderings were compared to those posted by the Associated Press (AP).

Both MESA's and AP's orderings were very similar for the top 20 teams. However, MESA provided estimates for all 315 teams, thereby providing more accurate predictions for more teams. One of the most interesting inconsistencies between the AP rankings and the MESA rankings was shown in the predictions for the New Mexico team. New Mexico was consistently ranked in the top 25 by AP. Apparently, AP's ranking was based on a series of wins at the start of the season and further strengthened when they beat a 13th-ranked team (Arizona). What AP apparently did not figure into this ranking, however, was the fact that these initial wins were against weak teams and with the home-court advantage, and that the Arizona victory was an unexpected result (i.e., showed misfit in the MESA analysis). Using an objective measurement system, MESA rated New Mexico in approximately the 75th spot (Linacre, 1999c). This placement was later reinforced when New Mexico was defeated by number 242 (Hawaii). Furthermore, MESA's predictions for wins and losses were accurate to about 72%, similar to rates of professional tipsters (Linacre, 1999c). However, MESA made predictions for every team for every game of the entire basketball season, not just select games.

EQUATING PHYSICAL
FUNCTIONING SCALES

In the long term, the use of the Rasch model to perform joint calibration of measures of the same underlying construct will be an extremely productive means to further our scientific endeavors. The following example of equating physical functioning scales demonstrates a key step toward an indispensable goal in human science research: the creation of universal measures. Again, the need for universal measures in the human sciences is made obvious from research in the physical sciences, and made possible by fundamental measurement techniques grounded in Rasch analysis. Take for example the measurement of temperature that we have used previously. It is still the case that most everyday reports of temperature are scale dependent: 32°F, 0°C, and 276°K refer directly to the particular temperature scale being used, in these cases, degrees of Fahrenheit, Celsius, and Kelvin, respectively.

In the same way, creating universal measures in the human sciences would help us to avoid unnecessary duplication of efforts in variable construction and move research toward the construction of common metrics for specific constructs, much as in the physical sciences. One aim of "psychosocial metrology," as Fisher described it, would be the establishment of a single measurement scale of units for each human variable of interest: a logit-based equal-interval set of values that would apply regardless of which appropriate test was used with any appropriate subject (Fisher, 1993, 1999, 2000).

The most prominent work in creating universal measures in the human sciences has been done with physical functioning scales. This work begins by equating various physical functioning scales with one another, then gradually builds a common item pool with specific units. The equating study by Fisher, Eubanks, and Marier (1997) serves as a model of a single step in this ongoing process.

Fisher et al. (1997) pointed out that physical functioning often is used as a medical rehabilitation index, but argued that the use of such tests is restricted when a patient's score interpretation is dependent on which physical functioning test the patient took. They thus undertook the step of equating the physical functioning subscales of the Medical Outcomes Study Short Form 36 (SF-36; Haley, McHorney, & Ware, 1994; McHorney, Haley, & Ware, 1997; Stucki, Daltroy, Katz, Johanneson, & Liang, 1996) and the Louisiana State University Health Status Instruments–Physical Functioning Scale (LSUHSI–PFS; Fisher et al., 1997). The SF-36 has a 10-item physical functioning scale with three ordered categories yielding 20 distinctions, whereas the PFS has 29 items and six ordered categories yielding 145 distinctions.

The equating process depended, in the first instance, on the theoretical argument that the two scales to be equated represent the same underlying construct or variable. Then, each set of items was analyzed separately using Rasch analysis. Equating examines the extent of the concurrence between the two scales; that is, can a common meaningful interval scale be constructed?

The methodology used to answer this question consisted of using two types of equating methods to compare both scales in terms of their item difficulties, person measures, mean square and standardized fit statistics, as well as separations and reliabilities. The first equating procedure compared estimates from the separate scale analyses (steps for conducting common item equating are outlined in chapter 5 of this volume). The second procedure was a co-calibration, or combining all data from both scales. The co-calibration provided a common metric from which it was possible to anchor the difficulty estimates in any subsequent set of separate scale analyses. Estimates from these comparisons are then compared in the same manner as the first equating procedure. The authors used both approaches to equating in order to examine the effect of the different numbers of items and rating-scale points for the two scales and whether the items were positioned in meaningful relation to one another. Once equivalence was established between the scales, inspection of the combined item set showed that measures on one scale could be translated directly to the other scale, as is done routinely with the Celsius and Fahrenheit temperature scales.

Of course, it takes more than this first set of steps to establish a universal metric, but in the field of medical rehabilitation, the future is very promising indeed. Fisher (1997) had reported earlier that the construct of physical functional independence shows a remarkable measurement convergence across a wide range of instruments, samples, and areas of physical functional independence. He emphasized the importance of this opportunity to build scale-free measures in transforming the economics of health care to evidence-based preventive care. This effort shows the way in which each of our own human science disciplines can benefit from the establishment of a common meaning (i.e., a common metric) for behaviors, attitudes, symptoms, and abilities.

DIAGNOSIS IN MEDICAL SETTINGS

Perkins, Wright, and Dorsey (2000) illustrated the use of Rasch measurement to produce a clear, simple picture of the relation between laboratory abnormalities in the diagnosis of gout. Ninety-six sets of medical record observations were submitted for analysis—half for patients diagnosed with gout and half for nongout patients. Each observation had values recorded for indicators usually considered in the diagnostic process for gout: uric acid, gender, age, diabetes, hypertension, weight, height, body surface area, nephrolithiasis, diuretics, cholesterol, triglyceride, blood urea nitrogen, and creatinine. Rasch measurement techniques were used in an attempt to establish a single dimension for diagnosing gout. Because blood chemistries in mg/dl, height, and weight are recorded as continuous variables, each of the physical science data points (X) was rescored linearly to its nearest integer code, using the conversion $Y = (X - \text{Min. Value})/((\text{Max. Value} - \text{Min. Value})/9)$. The resultant coding, which simplifies the physical science metrics to 10 equal-size steps, has a monotonic relation with the original physical science variables.

Usual Rasch analysis procedures (estimates and fit indices) were followed by the deletion of items that did not contribute useful information. In this case, Perkins et al. (2000) then used the WINSTEPS principal component analysis of measure residuals to identify significant relations among the diagnostic items (see the end of chapter 12). The plot of factor loadings of residuals against the Rasch item measures in Fig. 10.5 shows a clear separation of the male corpulence cluster from the blood chemistry cluster. Note that the "gout" diagnosis is located in the center of the blood chemistry cluster at the bottom. The triglyceride variable was also removed from the measurement model because person separation was improved by setting aside triglyceride information (see chapter 11). In the end, a medical variable defined by the three blood chemistries (uric acid, blood urea nitrogen, and creatinine) was established, proving the best linear variable for predicting gout that the data could support. This allows the probabilities for gout diagnosis to be read off for any particular blood chemistry results, as well as the identification of both gout and nongout patients who do not fit the gout variable.

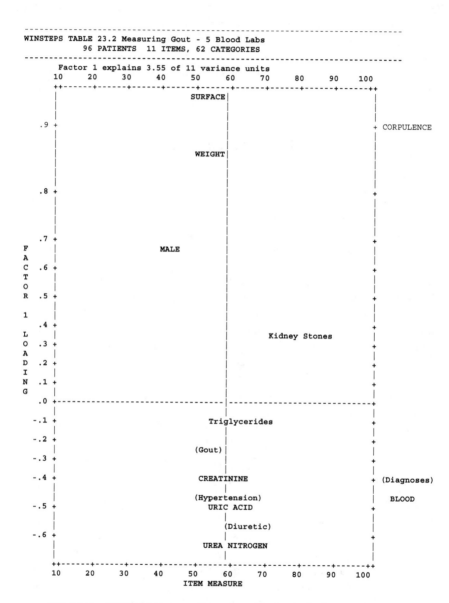

FIG. 10.5.   WINSTEPS map of Rasch residual principal components.

APPLICATIONS TO PHYSICAL THERAPY

Throughout this book we have emphasized the advantages of the Rasch measurement model over classical test theory in many ways. Because one of our greatest emphases has been on using the model to establish the construct validity of an instrument, it seems appropriate to end this chapter with an exceptional example of such an application. We briefly summarize a study by Campbell, Kolobe, Osten, Lenke, and Girolami (1995), in which they examined the construct validity of the Test of Infant Motor Performance (TIMP). Their article was proclaimed the best published in the journal *Physical Therapy* for that year (Campbell, 1996).

The TIMP is intended for use by physical therapists to detect deviations from an infant's normal path of development. These detections must be made as early as possible in order that effective interventions can be quickly implemented. Detection of deviations involves close contact between the therapist and baby, during which the therapist observes "both spontaneous and provoked actions of babies ranging in age from premature to 4 months old" (Campbell, 1996). The therapist then rates these actions according to a strict protocol learned during training.

Using therapist ratings of videotaped babies of a variety of ages, impairment levels, and racial origins, Campbell et al. (1995) constructed measures with a many-facets Rasch model. They plotted measures of development separately for normal and high-risk children. The comparison of the two sets of measures revealed that although high-risk babies start lower on the scale and grow more slowly, the difference was slight, indicating the critical importance of precise measurement at this stage (Campbell et al., 1996). Moreover, their research provided empirical validation of a key theory of fetal development: The plots revealed that 7.5 months after conception is a pivotal point in motor development.

Although it is true that analyses based on the use of the Rasch family of measurement models do have potential required by the researcher who faces the pragmatic task of trying to make a silk purse of measures out of a sow's ear of underconceptualized data, the future for many of the human sciences lies in the intelligent application of Rasch measurement to the theory–practice nexus of empirical research. Our key argument remains: Empirical research must incorporate the principles and procedures of Rasch modeling if researchers are to derive the benefits of fundamental measurement necessary for the development of rational quantitative human sciences. Substantive theory about the human condition provides detail of empirical outcomes that are subjected to the requirements of genuine measurement. Discrepancies between anticipated findings and the actual empirical outcomes are mutually informative: Theory informs practice— and practice informs theory.

11

Rasch Modeling Applied: Rating Scale Design

The process of responding to a rating scale should be viewed as a communication between the test developer's intentions (as expressed in the items and their associated response categories) and the respondents' record of their attitudes, behaviors, or achievement on the construct of interest. It is common knowledge that the way each rating scale is constructed has a great influence on the quality of data obtained from the scale (Clark & Schober, 1992). That is, some categorizations of variables yield higher quality measures than other categorizations (Linacre, 1999a; Wright & Linacre, 1992). Thus, rating scales not only should reflect careful consideration of the construct in question, but they also should be conveyed with categories and labels that elicit unambiguous responses. Even after great care has been taken to develop an unambiguous rating scale, the assumptions about both the quality of the measures and the utility of the rating scale in facilitating interpretable measures should be tested empirically.

This chapter expands on the analysis of rating scale data presented in chapter 6 by discussing guidelines for investigating empirically the utility of rating scales in the development of high-quality measures. Such investigations give explicit consideration to the influence of both the number and the labeling of categories in this process. We address these issues to demonstrate specifically how the design of rating scales has a large impact on the quality of the responses elicited, and to show how the Rasch model provides an appropriate framework for carrying out such investigations.

NUMBER OF CATEGORIES

Say, for example, respondents are asked to rate the extent to which they agree with the statement, "My boss is supportive of my work." Both the type of elicited responses and the inferences made about perceived supervisor support will depend on how many and what kind of response options are provided. We examine the following three options:

Option A		Disagree		Agree	
Option B		Disagree	Neutral	Agree	
Option C	Strongly disagree	Disagree	Neutral	Agree	Strongly agree

Option A is designed as a yes or no (dichotomous) type: My boss is either supportive or not. Option B allows for a middle of the road response to be included so respondents are not forced into choosing either of the extremes. Option C allows for more definition to the variable of interest (i.e., it depicts perceived support as a continuum). By designing rating scales as in the options, the test developers are conveying their ideas about perceived support to the respondents. The respondents are now required to express their perceptions within the restrictions imposed by this scale, and to the extent that the respondents can effectively communicate their perceptions within those restrictions, the quality of the measures will be enhanced.

At this point, we go beyond the careful design of our rating scale and begin to question how well our scale actually worked. Do the respondents need more categories to express themselves (as provided in option C)? Will they actually use more categories if more categories are offered as alternatives? These questions focus on the important empirical issue: What is the appropriate number of response categories for the optimal measurement of this variable?

A considerable amount of research literature examines the question of how to determine the appropriate number of rating scale categories. Typically, the criterion for judging the optimal number has been the reliability of the responses. Results have shown mixed conclusions, with the following range of assertions about reliability: that it is independent of number of response categories (Bendig, 1953; Brown, Widing, & Coulter, 1991; Komorita, 1963; Remington, Tyrer, Newson-Smith, & Cicchetti, 1979), or that it is maximized with a 7-point scale (Finn, 1972; Nunnally, 1967; Ramsay, 1973; Symonds, 1924), a 7-point scale plus or minus two (Miller, 1956), a 5-point scale (Jenkins & Tabler, 1977; Lisitz & Green, 1975; Remmers & Ewart, 1941), a 4-point scale (Bendig, 1954b), or a 3-point scale (Bendig, 1954a).

Here is a common 7-point scale as an example:

Option D	Strongly disagree	2	3	4	5	6	Strongly agree

Would this rating scale communicate more effectively than options A through C? Is it actually useful to add more response categories, or do the distinctions between, say, five and six categories now become blurred, hence introducing confusion for the respondents and ultimately lowering the meaningfulness of the scores (Fox, Gedeon, & Dinero, 1994)?

There is research suggesting that although the addition of response categories generally increases reliability, it does so only if these additional categories are not arbitrary (Linacre, 1995; Wright & Linacre, 1992). As explained by Chang (1994), the increase in the number of response alternatives might introduce error by allowing respondents to draw more freely on divergent frames of reference. In such a situation, it is difficult for a "common language" (Lopez, 1996) to be shared between the respondent and the investigator via the rating scale. In short, two people might perceive the same level of supervisor support, yet one may check a 5 and the other a 6, simply because the introduction of too many response options muddles the definition of the variable in question. With options A or B, the category definition and meaning is much more precise than it is in option C.

The fact is, there is no definitive optimal number of response categories that applies to all rating scales. Whereas five response categories might work for accurately measuring one construct, a simple yes-or-no type of response might be best for another. It is therefore the job of the test developer to determine empirically the optimal number of response categories every time a new rating scale is developed or when an existing rating scale is used with a new population. Thus, the analyst must discover empirically, rather than assert, the optimal number of rating scale categories for measuring a given construct (Lopez, 1996).

CATEGORY LABELS

A different, but closely related, empirical question involves the labeling of these response categories (Dunham & Davison, 1990; Frisbie & Brandenburg, 1979; Klockars & Yamaagishi, 1988; Lam & Klockars, 1982; Lam & Stevens, 1994; Ory, 1982; Spector, 1976). Variation in labeling includes choice of category labels, use of anchors, and positive and negative packing of the scale, to name a few.

Consider options E and F as follows:

| Option E | Strongly disagree | 2 | 3 | 4 | Strongly agree |
| Option F | Strongly disagree | Disagree | Somewhat agree | Agree | Strongly agree |

Option E is ambiguous in that it is missing labels for several categories, whereas option F is stacked, or positively packed, in its labeling of responses because it includes three agree options but only two disagree response options.

Rating scale examples A through F all encompass certain assumptions about how the construct is perceived by the respondents, and how that perception can best be communicated through the rating scale. We argue that these assumptions can and should be routinely tested empirically. The principles for investigating the quality of the measures is similar for both assumptions, and the Rasch model provides a set of diagnostics to help us with this task.

RATING SCALE DIAGNOSTICS

The strategy for determining the optimal number of response categories requires examination of Rasch measurement diagnostics. Statistics guide us in assessing how the categories are functioning to create an interpretable measure. Here we fall back on the principles espoused throughout this volume: Do we have reliable data for persons and items? Do the categories fit the model sufficiently well? Do the thresholds indicate a hierarchical pattern to the rating scale? Are there enough data in each category to provide stable estimates?

If any problems are diagnosed in the existing rating scale, the suggested general remedy is to reduce the number of response options by collapsing problematic categories with adjacent, better-functioning categories, and then to reanalyze the data. Diagnostics from the new analysis then are compared with those from the original analysis, and a determination is made to see whether the collapsing helped to improve variable definition. The goal is to produce the rating scale that yields the highest quality measures for the construct of interest. The WINSTEPS software provides a wide variety of output formats that are virtually indispensable for investigating rating scale quality, whereas the RUMM software provides interactive opportunities for this purpose.

CATEGORY FREQUENCIES
AND AVERAGE MEASURES

The simplest way to assess category functioning is to examine category use statistics (i.e., category frequencies and average measures) for each response option (Andrich, 1978c, 1996; Linacre, 1995, 1999a). Category frequencies indicate how many respondents chose a particular response category, summed for each category across all items. These category frequencies provide the distribution of responses across all categories, providing a very quick and basic examination of rating scale use.

Two features are important in the category frequencies: shape of the distribution and number of responses per category. Regular distributions such as uniform, normal, bimodal, slightly skewed distributions are preferable to those that are irregular. Irregular distributions include those that are highly skewed (e.g., distributions having long tails of categories with low responses; Linacre, 1999a).

Categories with low frequencies also are problematic because they do not provide enough observations for an estimation of stable threshold values. Such infrequently used categories often indicate unnecessary or redundant categories. Hence, these are the categories that should be collapsed into adjacent categories. Exactly how these collapsing decisions should be made is detailed later in the chapter. The recommended minimal number of responses per category is 10 (Linacre, 1999a).

Average measures are useful for "eyeballing" initial problems with rating scale categories. They are defined as the average of the ability estimates for all persons in the sample who chose that particular response category, with the average calculated across all observations in that category (Linacre, 1995). For example, if for category 1, the average measure were recorded as −2.5, that −2.5 can be interpreted as the average ability estimate, or logit score, for persons who chose category 1 on any item in the questionnaire. These average measures are expected to increase in size as the variable increases. They increase monotonically, indicating that on average, those with higher ability/stronger attitudes endorse the higher categories, whereas those with lower abilities/weaker attitudes endorse the lower categories. When this pattern is violated, as indicated by a lack of monotonicity in the average measures, collapsing categories again is recommended.

Table 11.1 shows sample output for a well-functioning four-category (three-threshold) rating scale. The category frequencies (i.e., the observed count) show a negatively skewed distribution, with at least 10 responses in each category. Average measures appear in the next column. The average measure for category 1 is −1.03, meaning that the average agreeability estimate for persons answering 1 across any item is −1.03 logits. For the persons who answered 2 on any item, the average agreeability estimate is +0.34 (i.e., these persons are more agreeable on average than the persons who answered 1). We can see that these average measures function as expected (i.e., they increase monotonically across the rating scale).

TABLE 11.1
Category Frequencies and Average Measures
for Well-Functioning Four-Category Rating Scale

Category Label	Observed Count	Average Measure
1	63	−1.03
2	341	+0.34
3	884	+1.57
4	1,179	+3.12

THRESHOLDS AND CATEGORY FIT

In addition to category frequency and the monotonicity of average measures, other pertinent rating scale characteristics include thresholds, or step calibrations, and category fit statistics (Lopez, 1996; Wright & Masters, 1982). As explained in chapter 6, step calibrations are the difficulties estimated for choosing one response category over another (e.g., how difficult it is to endorse "strongly agree" over "agree"). Like the average measures, step calibrations should increase monotonically. Thresholds that do not increase monotonically across the rating scale are considered disordered.

The magnitudes of the distances between the threshold estimates also are important. Threshold distances should indicate that each step defines a distinct position on the variable. That is, the estimates should be neither too close together nor too far apart on the logit scale. Guidelines indicate that thresholds should increase by at least 1.4 logits, to show distinction between categories, but not more than 5 logits, so as to avoid large gaps in the variable (Linacre, 1999a). Diagnostics presented in Table 11.2 illustrate that our rating scale meets these criteria.

One visual method of inspecting the distinction between thresholds is to examine the probability curves, which show the probability of endorsing a given rating scale category for every agreeability–endorsability (B–D) difference estimate. Each category should have a distinct peak in the probability curve graph, illustrating that each is indeed the most probable response category for some portion of the measured variable. Categories observed to be "flat" on the graph are never the most probable, and hence do not aid in defining a distinct point on the variable. Therefore, thresholds that are disordered or too close will show up visually, with flat probability curves, as being problematic.

The graph in Fig. 11.1 illustrates the probability of responding to any particular category, given the difference in estimates between any person ability and any item difficulty. For example, if a person's ability were 1 logit lower than the difficulty of the item (-1 on the x axis), that person's probability of endorsing a 4 is close to 0, of endorsing a 1 or a 3 is close to 0.2, and of endorsing a 2 is close to 0.55 on that item. This person therefore is most likely to endorse category 2 on this item. For persons with ability estimates higher than the given item difficulty (e.g., $+3$ on the x axis), the most probable response is a 4. This graph

TABLE 11.2
Thresholds for a Well-Functioning Four-Category Rating Scale

Category Label	Threshold
1	None
2	−2.05
3	−0.01
4	+2.06

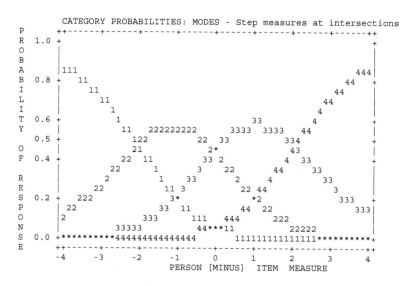

```
       CATEGORY PROBABILITIES: MODES - Step measures at intersections
 P      ++------+------+------+------+------+------+------+------++
 R   1.0 +                                                        +
 O       |                                                        |
 B       |                                                        |
 A       |111                                               444   |
 B   0.8 +  11                                            44      +
 I       |    11                                        44        |
 L       |      11                                    44          |
 I       |        1                                  4            |
 T   0.6 +         1                      33        4             +
 Y       |          11    222222222    3333  3333  44            |
     0.5 +            122           22  33        334             +
 O       |            21            2*            43              |
 F   0.4 +           22  11        33 2         4  33             +
         |          22    1       3    22     44    33            |
 R       |         2       1    33      2    4        33          |
 E       |        22        11 3         22 44          3         |
 S   0.2 +    222            3*            *2             333     +
 P       |  22             33  11        44  22             333   |
 O       | 2             333       111  444      222          333 |
 N       |2             33333      44***11         22222          |
 S   0.0 +**********444444444444444      1111111111111111**********+
 E       ++------+------+------+------+------+------+------+------++
         -4      -3     -2     -1      0      1      2      3      4
                        PERSON [MINUS]  ITEM   MEASURE
```

FIG. 11.1.   Probability curves for a well-functioning four-category rating scale.

shows that each response category in turn is the most probable across some section of the variable.

The threshold estimates in Table 11.2 correspond to the intersection of rating scale categories in Fig. 11.1. Each threshold estimate represents a distinct point on the measured variable. Thus each response category is the most probable category for some part of the continuum. It should be noted that each threshold estimate from Table 11.2 is represented visually by the intersection of probability curves in Fig. 11.1, the point at which there is an equal probability of choosing either of two adjacent response category options. For example, the first threshold in Table 11.2 is −2.05. A vertical line drawn from the intersection of the 1 and 2 probability curves in Fig. 11.1 intersects with the x axis at −2.05. You should take a few minutes to find the corresponding point in Fig. 11.1 for each of the other two thresholds seen in Table 11.2.

Fit statistics provide another criterion for assessing the quality of rating scales. Outfit mean squares greater than 2 indicate more misinformation than information (Linacre, 1999a), meaning that the particular category is introducing noise into the measurement process. Such categories warrant further empirical investigation, and thus might be good candidates for collapsing with adjacent categories. Table 11.3 shows the fit of each rating scale category to the unidimensional Rasch model, meeting the criterion of mean square statistics less than 2.0 (Linacre, 1999a).

The rating scale diagnostics discussed earlier include category frequencies, average measures, threshold estimates, probability curves, and category fit.

TABLE 11.3
Category Fit for a Well-Functioning Four-Category Rating Scale

Category Label	Outfit Mean Square
1	1.10
2	1.11
3	0.81
4	1.02

These diagnostics should be used in combination. Typically, they tell the same story in different ways. For example, if one category has a very low frequency, the thresholds are likely to be disordered, and the probability curves will not have distinct peaks for each of the rating scale categories. Likewise, the average measures might be disordered, and the fit statistics will be larger than expected. This will not be the case in every situation, but these diagnostics, when used in combination, are very useful in pointing out where we might begin to revise the rating scale to increase the reliability and validity of the measure.

REVISING THE RATING SCALE

When rating scale diagnostics indicate that some categories were used infrequently or inconsistently by respondents, adjacent categories should be combined and the data reanalyzed. The aim here is to eliminate noise and improve variable clarity (Fox et al., 1994; Linacre, 1999a; Wright & Linacre, 1992). Look again at the example in option D at the beginning of the chapter. Do we understand the intended difference between a 5 and a 6 on this rating scale? Is it possible that given two respondents with the same attitude, one might circle 5 and the other circle 6? If respondents cannot make a distinction between the meaning of categories 5 and 6 and hence use them in an inconsistent manner, unreliability is introduced into the measure, and category diagnostics will show us where we went wrong in the development of the rating scale. On the basis of this information, collapsing categories together will, in most cases, improve the representation and interpretation of the measure.

AN EXAMPLE

In this example, 221 elementary science teachers were asked to rate the frequency with which they used different pedagogic strategies for teaching science (e.g., writing reflections in journals, developing portfolios, working to solve real-world problems, engaging in hands-on activities). The rating scale categories were labeled as follows:

1	2	3	4	5
Never	Rarely	Sometimes	Often	Always

The rating scale diagnostics are shown in Table 11.4 and Fig. 11.2. The first obvious problem we see in Table 11.4 is that category 4 has only seven observations in all, across all prompts. This problem also is reflected in the average measure values, the step calibrations, and the probability curves. The average measures for categories 4 and 5 are disordered. Respondents who endorse "always" (category 5) on average have lower measures (agreeability estimates) on this variable than do respondents who endorse "often." This is counterintuitive, and also is reflected in the threshold calibrations, in which thresholds 3 and 4 are disordered, and in Fig. 11.2, in which the probability curve for category 4 is flat (i.e., it never is the most probable category).

TABLE 11.4
Diagnostics for Problematic Rating Scale

Category Label	Observed Count	Average Measure	Infit Mean Square	Outfit Mean Square	Threshold Calibration
1	190	−2.08	0.77	0.83	None
2	207	−0.86	0.93	1.01	−1.51
3	179	0.15	1.13	1.88	−0.36
4	7	1.71	0.33	0.90	3.57
5	113	1.18	1.45	1.47	−1.70

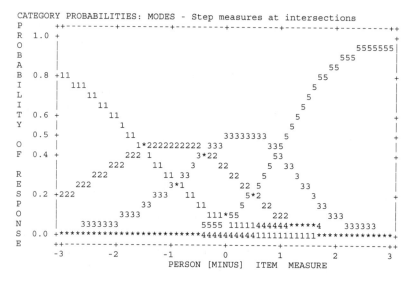

FIG. 11.2. Probability curves for problematic rating scale.

These problems with the rating scale impede our interpretation of the construct frequency of pedagogic strategies. When it is easier on average to endorse "always" than to endorse "often," we have direct empirical evidence that our rating scale is not being used by respondents in the way we intended. This warrants the collapsing of rating scale categories to improve variable construction and interpretation.

GUIDELINES FOR COLLAPSING CATEGORIES

The first and foremost guideline in collapsing rating scale categories is that what we collapse must make sense (Wright, 1996; Wright & Linacre, 1992). That is, will the new pivot point between, say, agree/disagree and rarely/often responses be based on something substantive? In the example described, our infrequently used category was labeled "often." Does it make sense to collapse this category with "sometimes"? Does it make sense to collapse this category with "always"? In this particular example, there does not seem to be a compelling substantive reason to do either, so which do we do? Do we collapse the "often" category up or down?

A second guideline for collapsing data indicates that we should attempt to create a uniform frequency distribution (Linacre, 1995, 1999a). This suggests that category 4 should be joined, or collapsed, into category 5. The software codes for collapsing category 4 upward into category 5 are "12344," indicating that we want to analyze four categories instead of five, with the last two categories (4 and 5) being analyzed as the same response (4 and 4). The complete software commands are found at the end of the chapter.

Table 11.5 and Fig. 11.3 present the results from this recategorization of the variable (i.e., with "frequently" and "always" treated as the same response). With four categories instead of five, we now have enough observations in each of the response categories. The average measures and step calibrations are now monotonic, and the probability curves show that each category represents a distinct portion of the underlying variable. Thus, collapsing categories 4 and 5 has improved our rating scale diagnostics.

TABLE 11.5
Diagnostics for 12344 Collapsing

Category Label	Observed Count	Average Measure	Infit Mean Square	Outfit Mean Square	Threshold Calibration
1	190	−2.5	0.72	0.79	None
2	207	−0.83	0.97	0.92	−1.74
3	179	+0.79	0.88	1.35	−0.12
4	120	+1.96	1.39	1.31	+1.86

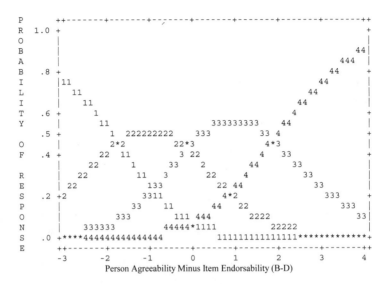

```
P       ++-------+-------+-------+-------+-------+-------+-------++
R   1.0 +                                                         +
O       |
B       |                                                      44|
A       |                                                   444 |
B    .8 +                                                 44     +
I       |11                                             44       |
L       |  11                                         44         |
I       |    11                                     44           |
T    .6 +      1                                   4             +
Y       |       11                  333333333    44             |
     .5 +        1   222222222   333          33  4              +
O       |         2*2          22*3            4*3              |
F    .4 +        22  11        3  22        4     33             +
        |       22    1        33    2       44      33          |
R       |     22      11    3       22    4         33           |
E       | 22           133          22 44            33          |
S    .2 +2            3311            4*2               333       +
P       |             33     11       44    22              333  |
O       |          333       111 444       2222              33 |
N       |    333333        44444*1111           22222           |
S    .0 +****444444444444444        111111111111111*************+
E       ++-------+-------+-------+-------+-------+-------+-------++
         -3      -2      -1       0       1       2       3       4
              Person Agreeability Minus Item Endorsability (B-D)
```

FIG. 11.3.   Probability curves for 12344 collapsing.

In addition to the guidelines found in the literature, we would also suggest collapsing the original category 4 downward into category 3 for comparison purposes (12334). We suggest this because the guidelines for collapsing are just that—guidelines. This is a common precept for Rasch modeling: Analysis is undertaken to develop and measure the meaning of a concept in practice. There can be no fixed rules to which we must adhere whereby the meaning or significance of a result becomes completely void when an arbitrary value is passed. Therefore, it is important to remain scientific about our investigations and explore several categorizations before settling on the preferred one. Table 11.6 and Fig. 11.4 show the results from collapsing category 4 downward into category 3 (12334).

It is clear that the collapsing improved category definition in both cases. Collapsing each way (12344 then 12334) resulted in monotonic step ordering and distinct category definitions. But how do we know which is the better of the two?

When comparing several categorizations of the same rating scale, we also can look at indicators other than category diagnostics. For example, we can assess

TABLE 11.6
Diagnostics for 12334 Collapsing

Category Label	Observed Count	Average Measure	Infit Mean Square	Outfit Mean Square	Threshold Calibration
1	190	−2.49	0.72	0.79	None
2	207	−0.84	0.94	0.90	−1.74
3	186	+0.83	0.87	1.27	−0.15
4	113	+1.91	1.43	1.34	+1.88

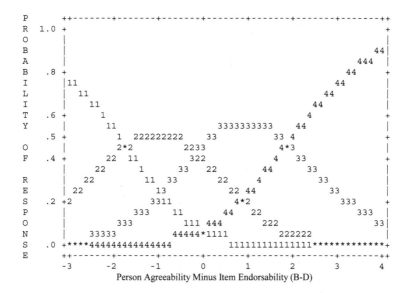

```
P     ++-------+-------+-------+-------+-------+-------++
R  1.0 +                                                +
O      |
B      |                                             44|
A      |                                          444  |
B   .8 +                                        44     +
I      |11                                    44       |
L      |  11                                44         |
I      |   11                             44           |
T   .6 +     1                           4             +
Y      |    11              3333333333   44            |
    .5 +      1  222222222  33        33 4             +
O      |       2*2        2233         4*3             |
F   .4 +      22 11        322          4   33         +
       |     22    1       33   22        44   33      |
R      |   22      11  33       22    4        33      |
E      | 22          13         22  44          33     |
S   .2 +2            3311        4*2              333   +
P      |           333    11      44   22            333|
O      |          333        111 444       222        33|
N      |   33333         44444*1111       222222         |
S   .0 +****444444444444444      11111111111111**************+
E      ++-------+-------+-------+-------+-------+-------++
       -3      -2      -1       0       1       2       3       4
              Person Agreeability Minus Item Endorsability (B-D)
```

FIG. 11.4. Probability curves for 12334 collapsing.

the quality of the various reliability and validity indices for the variable, and compare these across each categorization (Lopez, 1996; Wright & Masters, 1982). Chapter 3 argues that person and item separation should be at least 2, indicating that the measure separates persons, items, or both into at least two distinct groups. Table 11.7 shows that categorization 12344 yielded the higher reliability for both persons and items.

With respect to validity, we can look at both the item order and fit. That is, does one categorization of the variable result in a better ordering of the underlying variable, one that is more consistent with the theory that generated the items in the first place? Do more items misfit with one categorization than another? These reliability and validity issues are addressed in previous chapters, but the same principles apply here as well. Here they help us gain a fuller picture of how we can best define the rating scale. Thus, whereas the rating scale diagnostics help

TABLE 11.7
Comparison of Three Categorizations

Categorization	Average Measures	Fit	Step Calibrations	Person Separation	Item Separation
12345	Disordered	<2.0	Disordered	1.36	6.91
12344	Ordered	<2.0	Ordered	2.06	8.23
12334	Ordered	<2.0	Ordered	1.90	8.16

us in determining the best categorization, knowledge of Rasch reliability and validity indices tells us how the measure is functioning as a whole.

THE INVARIANCE OF THE MEASURES ACROSS GROUPS

A final step in investigating the quality of the new measure is to compare the estimates across two or more distinct groups of interest (e.g., male/female, Christian/Jewish, employed/unemployed, married/divorced/never married) to examine whether the items have significantly different meanings for the different groups. This is called differential item functioning (DIF). We take the same example as before, the reported frequency of pedagogic strategies among elementary science teachers. Suppose we want to compare the frequency of use with a sample of mathematics teachers. We can use the data for common item equating, plotting item estimates for science teachers against those for mathematics teachers to examine whether the frequency of usage is significantly different for science and mathematics teachers. Any difference in the frequency of pedagogic strategies between the groups can be examined more closely to see why any particular strategy was not rated the same for both groups (Fig. 11.5).

Examination of DIF follows the same procedures as those outlined in chapter 5 on common person equating. Instead of comparing persons across two tests to determine the invariance of the ability estimates, however, DIF (based on common item equating principles) models the invariance of item difficulty estimates by comparing items across two or more samples. The procedure requires that

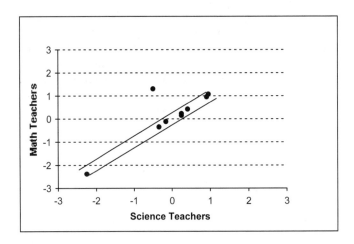

FIG. 11.5. Differential item functioning (DIF): math versus science teachers.

item difficulties be estimated for each sample separately, and that the item calibrations be plotted against each other.

The model for invariance of item estimates is represented by a straight line with a slope equal to 1 (i.e., 45°) through the mean item difficulty estimates from each sample (i.e., 0 logits for each). Control lines show which items do not display invariance, within the boundaries of measurement error, across the person samples (see Wright & Masters, 1982, pp. 114–117). Given that the model requires that relative item estimates remain invariant across appropriate samples of persons, items revealing DIF should be investigated closely to determine what might be inferred about the underlying construct, and what that implies about the samples of persons detected. In achievement testing, for example, DIF is regarded as prima facie evidence of item bias. However, it takes detailed knowledge about the construct and the samples of relevant persons to determine just what can be learned from DIF, how it can be avoided, and whether it should be. The evidence of DIF might just be the very information that is central to your investigation.

Software Commands

WINSTEPS:

```
&INST
TITLE='Collapsing Categories'
NI=15
ITEM1=5
NAME1=1
MODEL=R
CODES=12345
NEWSCOR=12334
RESCOR=2
&END
Item  1
Item  2
.
.
.
Item 15
END NAMES
```

Line 1 contains a command that must begin every WINSTEPS file.
Line 2 provides a title for the output.
Line 3 indicates the number of items in the test.
Line 4 identifies the starting column for the data.
Line 5 identifies the starting column for the person identification number.

Line 6 specifies the rating scale model.

Line 7 identifies all possible rating scale scores in the data set.

Line 8 specifies the new codes, joining categories 3 and 4 together to make a four-category rating scale.

Line 9 tells the program to do the rescoring for all of the items in the scale.

12

The Question
of Model Fit

It would be difficult to deny the claim that the most contentious issue in Rasch measurement circles is that of fit. Outside Rasch measurement circles, we continue to perplex the rest of the world of measurement by insisting that our task is to produce data that fits the Rasch model's specification rather than talk of fit in the usual way (i.e., that the model should fit the data). Of course, the concept of fit must be considered hand-in-hand with that of unidimensionality. The concept of unidimensionality reflects the focus of the Rasch model on the process of fundamental measurement. The argument is that even in the most complex measurement situations, individual attributes should be measured one at a time.

The Rasch model is a mathematical description of how fundamental measurement should appear. Its task is not to account for the data. Indeed, the special measurement properties of the Rasch model, including the production of equal interval measures that can be added together meaningfully, apply to the results only when the Rasch model expectations are sufficiently well met in practice.

There is no doubt that mathematical models do not hold in the real world. They describe an unattainable idealization, just as they do in all sciences. Empirical data describe what the imperfect real world is like. In Rasch measurement, we use fit statistics to help us detect the discrepancies between the Rasch model prescriptions and the data we have collected in practice.

THE DATA, THE MODEL, AND RESIDUALS

In a number of places so far, we have used an item–person matrix to show the interactions between person ability and item difficulty. Each cell in the complete matrix would have an entry, x_{ni}, representing the actual observed score (either 0 or 1) that resulted when person n took item i. Table 12.1 shows a portion of the

TABLE 12.1
Some Actual or Observed Scores (x_{ni}) From Table 2.3 (Ordered)

| | Items | | | | | Person |
Persons	i	a	b	. . .	g	Total
J	1	1	1		1	9
C	1	1	1		0	8
E	1	0	1		0	7
. . .						. . .
H	0	1	0		0	2
Item Total	11	10	7	. . .	1	

ordered matrix of actual observed scores from Table 2.3 where schoolchildren A–N answered math questions a–l. When we order that matrix according to the difficulty of the items and the ability of the persons, we have the opportunity to compare the Rasch model prescriptions with what we find in the data set. The estimation procedure in Rasch analysis has two distinct phases: first, calibration of the difficulties and abilities, and second, estimation of fit.

In the dichotomous model, the Rasch parameters, item difficulty and person ability, are estimated from the pass-versus-fail proportions for each item and each person. (The pass/fail proportion = number correct/number incorrect: $n/[N - n]$.) For item difficulty, the estimate is calculated from the proportion of the sample that succeeded on each item. Person ability is calculated from the proportion of items on which each person succeeded. The result of that iterative process is a set of all the item calibrations (i.e., one for each item) and a set of all possible person measures (i.e., one for every possible total score).

If we then take a second, same-size but empty matrix, we can substitute the estimated Rasch person measures in place of the n/N proportion for each person, and the Rasch estimated item measures in place of the n/N proportion for each item (see the ability and difficulty estimates in Table 12.2). Given that there is a direct curvilinear transformation of n/N proportions into logit values, the items and persons will maintain their exact orders. Next, we take the corresponding pair of parameter values for, say, person n and item i and substitute those values into the Rasch model (formula 3 in Appendix A), thereby obtaining an expected response value, E_{ni}, for that particular item–person pair (i.e., the expected response value when person n encounters item i). By repeating that calculation for every item–person pair and entering the resultant value in the appropriate cell, we use the Rasch model to generate a complete matrix of expected response values based on the previously estimated person and item calibrations. Table 12.2 shows the Rasch-modeled correct response probabilities (E_{ni}) for persons J, C, E, . . . , H encountering items i, a, b, . . . , g (E_{ni} is the expected response value for person n on item i).

TABLE 12.2
Rasch Expected Response Probabilities (E_{ni}) Based on Item and Person Estimates

Persons	Items					Ability Estimate
	i	a	b	$\ldots$	g	
J	0.26	0.50	0.77		0.95	+1.52
C	0.20	0.40	0.70		0.94	+1.19
E	0.12	0.27	0.56		0.89	+0.58
...						...
H	0.02	0.04	0.14		0.50	−1.52
Difficulty Estimate	+2.59	+1.59	+0.32	$\ldots$	−1.52	

RESIDUALS

The difference between the actual observed score in any cell $(x_{ni}$—Table 12.1) and the expected response value for that cell $(E_{ni}$—Table 12.2) is the response residual $(y_{ni}$—Table 12.3). If the expected response value for a cell is high, say, estimated at 0.95 (i.e., $E_{Jg} = 0.95$), then we can calculate the unstandardized residual in which the actual score is 1 $(x_{Jg}$—we observed that person J actually scored 1 on item g). So capable person J performed as expected on rather easy item g, and scores 1 (i.e., $x_{Jg} = 1$). Then: $y_{Jg} = x_{Jg} - E_{Jg} = 1 - 0.95 = +0.05$ (a very small residual), whereas if person J had unexpectedly scored 0 for item g (i.e., $x_{Jg} = 0$), then $y_{Jg} = x_{Jg} - E_{Jg} = 0 - 0.95 = -0.95$ (a very large residual). For the first case, the residual is low, indicating that the actual response was close to the model's expectation. The alternative scenario, with the much larger residual, indicates that such an actual performance would be quite different from the Rasch modeled expectation.

It then is easy to imagine a third similarly sized matrix that for each person–item pair contains the score residual for that cell (y_{ni}) when the expected response value (E_{ni}) is subtracted from the actual score (x_{ni}). Table 12.3 is a matrix

TABLE 12.3
Matrix of Response Residuals $(y_{ni} = x_{ni} - E_{ni})$

Persons	Items					Residual Total (Person)
	i	a	b	$\ldots$	g	
J	0.74	0.50	0.23		0.05	low
C	0.80	0.60	0.30		−0.93	high
E	0.88	−0.27	0.44		−0.89	high
...						...
H	−0.02	0.96	−0.14		−0.50	modest
Residual Total (Item)	high	modest	low	$\ldots$	high	

of response residuals (y_{ni}) derived from Table 12.1 actual scores (x_{ni}) and Table 12.2 expected response values (E_{ni}). When the person's ability is the same as the item's difficulty, the residual value will be +0.50 if the answer given is correct $(1 - 0.50 = +0.50)$, or −0.50 if the person gets that item wrong $(0 - 0.50 = -0.50)$. Whereas residual values range from −1 to +1, negative values are always derived from incorrect (0) responses and positive residual values from correct (1) responses.

There is an obvious problem (one very frequently encountered in statistics) in trying to aggregate a total residual score for any item or any person. Because any actual score (x_{ni}) will be either 0 or 1, and every expected response value (E_{ni}) will be a decimal fraction $(0 < E_{ni} < 1)$, the residual will always be a negative fraction for all actual scores of 0 and a positive fraction for all actual scores of 1. Just adding those residual values for any item or person string will result in totals of 0.0 for every person and every item. However, squaring those residual values will result in all positive values (e.g., $+0.05^2 = +0.0025$ and $-0.95^2 = +0.9025$). These squared residual values can then be aggregated by summing along any relevant item residual column or any person residual row. Although the expected residual is an impossible-to-achieve 0, residual values outside of ±0.75 are seen as unexpected. In practice, each raw residual (y_{ni}) is standardized by using the variance of that residual, and it is the standardized residual (z_{ni}) that is used to calculate fit statistics.

FIT STATISTICS

Rasch himself suggested the use of chi-square fit statistics to determine how well any set of empirical data met the requirements of his model. Rasch analysis programs usually report fit statistics as two chi-square ratios: infit and outfit mean square statistics (Wright, 1984; Wright & Masters, 1981).

Outfit is based on the conventional sum of squared standardized residuals, so for person n, each standardized residual cell is squared and the string of those squared residuals, one for each and every item encountered by person n, is summed and its average (mean) found by dividing by the number of items to which person n responded, hence "mean squares."

Infit is an information-weighted sum. The statistical information in a Rasch observation is its variance, the standard deviation (SD) of that estimate squared (SD^2), which is larger for well-targeted observations and smaller for extreme observations. To calculate infit, each squared standardized residual value in the response string, say, the residual z_{ni} for each of the items encountered by person n, is weighted by its variance and then summed. Dividing that total by the sum of the variances produces the same distribution as outfit, but leaves the differential effects of the weightings in place.

Therefore, infit and outfit statistics are reported as mean squares in the form of chi-square statistics divided by their degrees of freedom, so that they have a ratio scale form with an expected value of +1 and a range from 0 to positive infinity. Infit and outfit mean square values are always positive (i.e., >0). In this form, the mean square fit statistics are used to monitor the compatibility of the data with the model.

An infit or outfit mean square value of 1 + x indicates 100x% more variation between the observed and the model-predicted response patterns than would be expected if the data and the model were perfectly compatible. Thus, an infit mean square value of more than 1, say, 1.30 (i.e., 1 + 0.30) indicates 30% (100 × 0.30) more variation in the observed data than the Rasch model predicted. An outfit mean square value of less than 1, say, 0.78 (1 – 0.22 = 0.78) indicates 22% (100 × 0.22) less variation in the observed response pattern than was modeled.

The idea of the response string showing more variation than expected is a concept with which most are comfortable. This happens when a person's responses are more haphazard than expected: A capable person gets easier items unexpectedly wrong (e.g., 0010011110, where items are ordered easiest to most difficult), or a less able person gets harder items unexpectedly correct (e.g., 1101000110).

EXPECTATIONS OF VARIATION

However, the Rasch model is a stochastic or probabilistic model and, from that viewpoint, a perfect Guttman response pattern, 1111100000, is unrealistically and unexpectedly perfect and shows too little variation (i.e., much less variation than the Rasch model predicts). A Guttman response string would have a mean square value considerably less than 1. According to the probabilistic principles incorporated in the heart of the Rasch model, a more realistic and expected response pattern would look more like this: 1110101000, and the mean square fit value would be much closer to +1. (All of these exemplar response strings have a score of five answers correct.)

Infit and outfit statistics also are reported in various interval-scale forms (e.g., t or z) in which their expected value is 0. For example, both of these mean square fit statistics can be transformed into an approximately normalized t distribution by applying the Wilson–Hilferty transformation. These normalized versions of the statistics are referred to as the infit t and the outfit t in QUEST (Adams & Khoo, 1992, p. 79). When the observed data conform to the model, the t values have a mean near 0 and a standard deviation near 1. Using the commonly accepted interpretation of t values, infit and outfit t values greater than +2 or less than –2 generally are interpreted as having less compatibility with the model than expected ($p < .05$). Normalized or standardized infit and outfit statistics could have either positive or negative values. Negative values indicate less vari-

TABLE 12.4
Fit Statistics and Their General Interpretation

Mean Squares	t	Response Pattern	Variation	Interpretation	Misfit Type
>1.3	>2.0	Too haphazard	Too much	Unpredictable	Underfit
<0.75	<2.0	Too determined	Too little	Guttman	Overfit

ation than modeled: The response string is closer to the Guttman-style response string (all easy items correct then all difficult items incorrect). Positive values indicate more variation than modeled: The response string is more haphazard than expected (Table 12.4).

Therefore, rather than talking about fit statistics, we really should talk about the estimation of misfit. In any cells wherein the empirical data do not match the Rasch model prescription, the difference between the data and prescription, the residual, contributes toward misfit.

Our conception of misfit must include the idea that every response string is actually possible in practice, although some response strings are more probable than others. Although the Guttman pattern remains the most probable, all other patterns are probable, although some are highly improbable. The Rasch model, as a probabilistic or stochastic model, regards the perfect Guttman pattern as too rigid. The Rasch expectation is that there will be a zone of uncertainty or unpredictability around the person's level of ability. Linacre and Wright (1994a) described the following response strings and provided infit and outfit mean square values for each (Table 12.5).

TABLE 12.5
Diagnosing Misfit

Response String Easy ... Items ... Hard	Diagnosis	Infit Mean Square	Outfit Mean Square
111 ... 0110110100 ... 000	Modeled	1.1	1.0
This would be regarded as an ideal Rasch model response string.			
111 ... 1111100000 ... 000	Deterministic	0.5	0.3
This is an example of a Guttman or deterministic pattern. Note that the outfit and infit mean square statistics are too low to be believed.			
011 ... 1111110000 ... 000	Carelessness	1.0	3.8
This suggests carelessness with an easy item.			
000 ... 0000011111 ... 111	Miscode	4.3	12.6
This response string is too bad to be believed and suggests that the responses might be miscoded.			
111 ... 1111000000 ... 001	Lucky guessing	1.0	3.8
On the other hand, unexpected success on the most difficult item suggests lucky guessing.			
111 ... 1000011110 ... 000	Special knowledge	1.3	0.9
This highly improbable pattern suggests the presence of special knowledge, either the knowledge that is missing in the string of failures or special knowledge that allowed the unexpected string of successes.			

TABLE 12.6
Some Reasonable Item Mean Square Ranges for Infit and Outfit

Type of Test	Range
Multiple-choice test (High stakes)	0.8–1.2
Multiple-choice test (Run of the mill)	0.7–1.3
Rating scale (Likert/survey)	0.6–1.4
Clinical observation	0.5–1.7
Judged (where agreement is encouraged)	0.4–1.2

The interpretation of fit statistics, more than any other aspect of Rasch modeling, requires experience related to the particular measurement context. Then "[w]hen is a mean-square too large or too small? There are no hard-and-fast rules. Particular features of a testing situation, e.g., mixing item types or off-target testing, can produce idiosyncratic mean-square distributions. Nevertheless, here, as a rule of thumb, are some reasonable ranges for item mean-square fit statistics" (Wright & Linacre, 1994b; Table 12.6).

Whereas such a set of general guidelines will be helpful for researchers embarking on Rasch modeling, a considerable bibliography of relevant material exists. Articles published by Smith (e.g., 1991a, 1994, 2000) provide good starting points for a more thoroughly informed view of issues concerning fit statistic interpretation.

FIT, MISFIT, AND INTERPRETATION

The kidmap for student 1 (Fig. 12.1) summarizes that student's performance according to the Rasch model's expectations. In the kidmap option in the QUEST software, the item difficulties are displayed in the usual Rasch fashion, with the easiest items at the bottom of the map and the most difficult items at the top. The items located on the left side of the map are those on which this particular child was successful, and the items on the right side of the map are those that the child did not complete successfully. The child's ability estimate of -0.40 logits is plotted in the center column, with the dotted line on the left indicating the upper bound of the ability estimate (ability estimate plus one standard error: $b_n + s_n$) and the dotted line on the right indicating its lower bound (ability estimate minus one standard error: $b_n - s_n$). The fit index, an infit mean square value of 0.92, indicates a pattern of performance that closely approximates the predicted Rasch model response pattern based on the child's ability estimate: The expected fit value is $+1.0$. Item 10.3 is correct despite a less than 50% probability of success, whereas item 7.2 is incorrect, a little against the Rasch expectation of a slightly more than 50% probability of a correct response. The 0.92 infit mean

```
Middle School Math Project
---------------------------- K I D M AP ---------------------------------------
Student #1                                              ability:    -.40
  group:     all                                        fit:         .92
  scale:     all                                        % score:   40.00

------------Harder Achieved --------------------Harder Not Achieved --------



                                                │ │
                                                │ │
                                                │ │
                                                │ │
                                          18.3  │ │

                                          18.2  │ │


                                          23.3  │ │


                                          8.3   │ │
                                          3.3   │ │  23.2
                                          3.2   │ │   4.3    22.3
                                          8.2   │ │  21.3
                             10.3         4.2   │ │  22.2
                                          9.3   │ │  21.2
                                          17.2  │ │
.................................10.2.........  │ │  2.3    11.3
                             14.3               │ │  9.2    19.3
            16.3     14.2     2.2               │ │ 12.3    19.2
                             15.3          │XXX│  11.2    20.3
                                                │ │  7.3    12.2
                             16.2         ..................................................
                             6.3                │ │
                     20.2    15.2               │ │  7.2
                             6.2                │ │

                             5.3                │ │
                      1.3    1.2                │ │

                             5.2                │ │

                             13.3               │ │


                             13.2               │ │




            4.1     3.1    2.1     1.1          │ │
------------Easier Achieved --------------------Easier Not Achieved --------
     Some items could not be fitted to the display
================================================================================
```

FIG. 12.1. Kidmap for student 1 showing good fit to the model.

180

square value indicates a performance close to that of the Rasch model, and the kidmap corroborates that visually.

The infit mean square value of +1.78 for student 16 indicates that the pattern of responses shown in the Fig. 12.2 kidmap is more haphazard than the Rasch model would indicate for an estimated ability of +0.45 logits. Following the principles outlined in the previous interpretation, we can detect the unexpected responses made by student 16: Item 3.3 is the only item that the student gets unexpectedly correct, but the difficulty estimate of this item step is so close to the upper bound of the estimated ability for student 16 that it could just be disregarded in terms of affecting misfit. The items that are unexpectedly incorrect, however, paint a different picture: These are the source of the misfit, estimated at 78% (1.78 − 1.0 × 100%) more variation than the Rasch-modeled expectation.

But how can this be of value diagnostically to the investigator? A comparison between the two kidmaps is a good place to start. Student 16 was completely unsuccessful at a group of items that were quite below that student's ability level (revealed by this testing). Student 1 has considerably less ability overall, as revealed by this investigation, but this student was able successfully to complete all the items in groups 14, 15, 16, and 19. In terms of Table 12.5, the response pattern of student 16 is consonant with that shown as "special knowledge missing." To the child's teacher, however, this indicates the possibility of a developmental gap in this child's understanding of fundamental mathematical concepts. Of course, the teacher would first ensure that the child actually was present at school on the occasions when this material was covered in school lessons before going on to investigate further the reasons behind this apparent deficiency.

New teaching that did not account for this lack of understanding would not be as effective as teaching that first successfully undertook learning experiences aimed at remediation.

There is an interesting sidelight to these kidmaps and the issue of fit that could help us further understand the qualitative–quantitative nexus in the investigation of human behavior. The orginal researcher who had undertaken the qualitative interview of each student in this middle school mathematics investigation asked the data analyst to explain the meaning of the Rasch output. During that process, kidmaps 1 and 16 were generated solely on the basis of the fit statistics shown in the group output. Kidmap 1 was chosen as the first student in the output with unremarkable fit values, whereas kidmap 16 was chosen as the very first where misfit seemed apparent. The segments of output for those two students are shown in Table 12.7. When shown what the high misfit value for student 16 revealed in terms of unexpected errors in the response pattern, the interviewer took out the handwritten case notes for that student. The top of the page was annotated with an expression of the interviewer's surprise that an apparently capable student had performed so poorly on a whole group of obviously easier questions. The investigator was both surprised and delighted that the misfit value had alerted the data analyst to a case on quantitative grounds that the investigator had noted while conducting the qualitative interview.

```
Middle School Math Project
----------------------------- K  I  D  M  A  P--------------------------------
  Candidate: 16                                       ability:      .45
  group:     all                                      fit:         1.78
  scale:     all                                      % score:    62.22

-----------Harder Achieved --------------------Harder Not Achieved --------
                                    │ │
                                    │ │
                                    │ │
                                    │ │
                            18.3    │ │
                            18.2    │ │
                                    │ │
                                    │ │
                            23.3    │ │
                                    │ │
                             8.3    │ │
                  3.3        23.2   │ │
..........22.3.....4.3.....3.2..........│ │
                             8.2      21.3
        22.2   10.3    4.2          │ │
                9.3            XXX│  21.2
                                    │ │ 17.2
        11.3   10.2    2.3   .........................................
                9.2          14.3    19.3
               12.3    2.2   14.2    16.3     19.2
               20.3   11.2   15.3
               12.2    7.3
                             16.2
                      6.3
        20.2    7.2          15.2
                      6.2
                      5.3
                1.3    1.2
                      5.2
                     13.3
                     13.2
                                    │ │
                                    │ │
                                    │ │
                                    │ │
    4.1    3.1    2.1    1.1    │ │
-----------Easier Achieved --------------------Easier Not Achieved --------
  Some items could not be fitted to the display
================================================================================
```

FIG. 12.2. Kidmap for student 16 showing inadequate fit to the model.

182

TABLE 12.7
Case Statistics for Students 1 and 16

Case ID No.	Actual Score	Possible Score	Ability (Logits)	Error	Infit Mean Square	Outfit Mean Square	Infit t	Outfit t
01	18	23	−0.41	0.30	0.93	0.68	−0.19	−0.17
16	28	23	+0.45	0.30	1.78	1.50	2.41	0.82

FIT: ISSUES FOR RESOLUTION

Notwithstanding the important distinction raised earlier about the relation between the data and the Rasch model, Rasch analysis procedures share a number of general features with other data-modeling techniques. After the initial estimation of approximate item difficulties, these values are used to estimate the first round of person abilities. This iterative process is repeated for the purpose of reducing the item and person residuals to their lowest values. Generally speaking, WINSTEPS estimation iterations continue until the amount of change in residuals brought about by an iteration reaches the default level of 0.5 score points (while the largest change in any person or item estimate is less than 0.01 logits). The default value in QUEST is 0.005 logit change in estimate value.

The matrix of residuals then is used in the fit estimation procedures. It should be noted that the estimation procedures cannot be iterated until the residuals finally disappear (i.e., actually reach 0). However, in other data-modeling techniques, including the two- and three-parameter item response theory (IRT) models, the second and third parameters might be manipulated just to further reduce the residuals to their lowest possible values. Therefore, the criterion by which the iteration of estimation procedures is terminated cannot be the attainment of some admirably low average residual value. With poorly fitting data, the value will never reach that low. Iterations cease when an acceptably small change (reduction) in residuals is recorded.

This leads to a rather counterintuitive paradox: A test made up of two equal-size, but unrelated, sets of items can produce more acceptable fit estimates than a test attempting to measure one attribute that includes a small number of poorly constructed items. Think of it this way. In the example of the "two different halves" test, there is no single underlying attribute on which person performance is being measured. The estimation iterations simply will be repeated until the default change in residual values is recorded, and perhaps all items will "fit." For a well constructed test, in which two or three items are not working as well as the others, the underlying latent attribute is defined, psychometrically, by the performances of the persons on the large number of items. The interactions between the persons and the large number of good items will dominate the estimation process, and when the residuals are reduced as far as possible for the bulk of the data set, the two or three less adequate items will show evidence of misfit.

This leads us back, conveniently, to the value of theory-driven research. Misfit indicators are likely to be less reliable when data collection devices have been assembled haphazardly. How can data analysis be expected to discriminate between equally poor items? It is not unreasonable to suggest, however, that misfit indicators could be very useful in helping the investigator to understand where the theory-driven measurement intentions went astray in empirical practice: A small number of less satisfactory items might be detected against a backdrop of a larger number of successful items.

MISFIT: A MORE FUNDAMENTAL ISSUE?

In recent work, Karabatsos (1999a, 1999b, 2000) argued that the problem with the whole range of the fit statistics used in Rasch analysis is far more fundamental than merely the question of which fit statistics do the best job. Although he cites approximately a dozen issues of real concern with the use and calculation of residual-based fit statistics for the Rasch model, two central issues appear both important and indicative of a direction for solution. Crucially, in the calculation of the matrix cell residual (z_{ni}), the actual response of person n to item i (x_{ni}) is always discrete, either 0 or 1 in the dichotomous case, and the Rasch-modeled expectation (E_{ni}) is always continuous, in this case, $0 < E_{ni} < 1$. Therefore, x_{ni} (categorical) uses a crisp, true/false definition of set membership, whereas E_{ni} (continuous) uses "fuzzy" set membership. Then, x_{ni} and E_{ni} are, strictly, incompatible. Therefore, the "true" distance between these two terms (i.e., z_{ni}) is unattainable.

Moreover, the plot of function z_{ni} (residual) against $\beta_n - \delta_i$ (ability–difficulty) shows that z_{ni} is a nonlinear function of $\beta_n - \delta_i$ (Andrich, 1988, p. 82, Fig. 6.5b). Karabatsos (1999) claimed then that we can make only nonlinear judgments about fit to linear Rasch measurement models when we use any residual-based fit statistic. In terms of the indicators of misfit currently available, Karabatsos (2000) commends "statistically optimal" indexes such as Klauer's "uniformly most powerful" person fit statistics (Klauer, 1995). Because the analyst has to specify (or model) in advance the particular type(s) of misfit to be detected, such models are indicative of both that misfit exists and the likely source of the measurement disturbance.

PARTIAL SOLUTION 1: A LOGIT FIT INDEX

From Karabatsos's (1999) perspective then, it would be much wiser to find a way to express misfit magnitude on a logit scale, establishing a unit of measure for misfit just as we have for ability and difficulty. The obvious, but ill-informed, solution would be to perform a log transformation on already-calculated residual values, or worse still, on mean square estimates, because according to the preceding argument, both the residuals and the mean square estimates are inaccurate to begin with.

Karabatsos (1999b) suggested that the solution to finding a "logit scale" that expresses misfit magnitude on the same logit scale as $\beta_n - \delta_i$ is encapsulated in the following: Consider the case of a person with an ability estimate (B) of +1 logits who encounters an item with a difficulty estimate (D) of +3 logits. The Rasch model would predict an incorrect (0) response rather than a correct (1) response. If the person made the expected incorrect (0) response (i.e., actual response = predicted response), then the fit value would be 0, or "0.0 logits misfit." If the person unexpectedly answered this item correctly, the difference between the expected response and the actual response would be calculated in terms of the difference between the person ability estimate (B = 1) and the item difficulty estimate (D = 3; i.e., it could be stated that the person "performed 2 logits above what was expected by the model"). In that case misfit has occurred, and the size of the misfit for this response could be quantified as B − D = +2. The average of the logit fit values across all that person's responses on the test items would constitute a logit measure of person misfit. Of course, the averaging calculation also could be completed for items to yield a measure of item misfit (Karabatsos, 1999b).

COMPLETE SOLUTION 2: AXIOMATIC CONJOINT MEASUREMENT

In part of the next chapter, we review the relation between the Rasch measurement model and the requirements for fundamental measurement in the social sciences following the prescriptions for axiomatic conjoint measurement (Luce, 1995; Luce, Krantz, Suppes, & Tversky, 1990; Michell, 1999) and look at Karabatsos's (1999) arguments maintaining that axiomatic measurement theory helps to decide which IRT models actually contribute to the construction of measures, and that axiomatic tests, rather than residual fit statistics, are more informative about the violation of the unidimensionality principle. Indeed, Karabatsos argues, following Cliff (1992), that the axioms of conjoint measurement require the parallel Item Characteristic Curves (ICCs) that are central to Rasch measurement.

IN THE INTERIM

One interesting sidelight to come from the never-ending search for ways of detecting important deviations from the important undimensionality requirement of Rasch modeling has been the application of factor analysis techniques to the residual matrices (Wright, 1996). If the Rasch-modeled person–item interaction information extracted from the data matrix leaves a random dispersion of residuals, then the claim is that the solution is accounting for just one dimension. The presence of factor loadings in the analysis of residuals would suggest the presence of more than one underlying test dimension. WINSTEPS facilitates this analysis and interpretation in Tables 23.3 and 24.3, Principal Components Analysis of Residuals, which decomposes the matrix of item or person correlations based on residuals to identify other possible factors (dimensions) that might be affecting response patterns (Linacre, 1998; Smith, 2000). Alternatively, CONQUEST software (Wu, Adams, & Wilson, 1998) provides methods for assessing whether a single Rasch dimension, or two or more closely related Rasch dimensions, provide the most parsimonious summary of data–model fit.

13

A Synthetic Overview

The human condition is, by almost any definition, exceptionally complex. Although we remain amazed at the range of individual differences that distinguish each and every one of us from the others, one of the purposes central to the human sciences has been the generation of laws and theories to describe the common features of human existence. It seems as though those of us who try to understand the human condition must struggle to deal with the tension that exists between trying to describe, explain, and predict the common attributes of human beings on the one hand, and appreciating and accounting for idiosyncratic individual differences on the other.

Although many paradigms exist across the human sciences for studying and explaining the human condition, the work presented in this book is essential to the position that psychology, for example, is a quantitative rational science. In spite of the many other paradigms that contribute to our understanding of human nature, social interaction, health, behavior, intellectual development, and school achievement, it is not unreasonable to claim that in the 20th century, the social sciences have been dominated by those determined to quantify the important aspects of human behavior.

There are those who appear willing to accept all human behavior at its face value: What you see is what you get (wysiwyg). Latent trait theorists, however, regard observable behavior merely as the outward indicator of human states that remain, for the most part, unknowable. It would not be difficult to defend the idea that it is impossible for me to know myself, and even more so, for me to understand my fellows. When the day at the beach or the park is spoiled by bad weather that had not been predicted, we are somewhat consoled by the meteorologists' claim that weather systems are far too complex to predict accurately. Yet we express our disappointment that the behavior of a particular person cannot be predicted from what we already know about that person's past and the current situation. Although we might, in a moment of frustration, complain that the weather seems to have a mind of its own, few of us would really believe that. Although most of us would admit that, unlike the weather, humans have the capacity to influence their own behavior, we remain frustrated at the attempts of psychology, philosophy, sociology, medicine, and the like to predict human outcomes in the way that we expect the physical sciences to predict and explain the behavior of objects.

In his text, *Measurement in Psychology: A Critical History of a Methodological Concept*, Michell (1999) argued that measurement in psychology has failed because psychologists, unable to meet the stringent requirements of measurement as it existed in the physical sciences, invented their own definitions of what psychological measurement would be. He maintained that these definitions ignore two fundamental steps in the measurement process. First, it is necessary to argue that the particular human trait under investigation is, in fact, quantifiable. Second, it then is necessary to construct a measure of this trait so that the numbers indicating the variety of values of the trait may be subjected lawfully to the mathematical computations that we routinely use in statistical analyses. It is not good enough, Michell claimed, to allocate numbers to behavior, and then to assert that this is measurement.

Indeed, Michell argued that psychology must remain a mere pseudoscience if it does not deal with the almost complete absence of fundamental measurement from its discipline. It is not sufficient to allocate numbers to events merely on the basis of some accepted conventions such as the nominal, ordinal, interval, ratio scales of Stevens (1946) that were designed to allow psychology to appear scientific when, in fact, it was not.

CONJOINT MEASUREMENT

Duncan Luce and his colleagues have outlined the principles and properties of conjoint measurement that would bring the same sort of rigorous measurement to the human sciences as the physical sciences have enjoyed for a considerable time. It seems that psychologists are determined to avoid the work required to implement fundamental measurement as the cornerstone of a quantitative rational science of the human condition (e.g., Luce, 1972; Luce & Tukey, 1964; Suppes, Krantz, Luce, & Tversky, 1989). They seem determined to be satisfied with Stevens's (1959) convention, peculiar to their own world, that measurement is the allocation of numbers according to a rule (p. 19), and to accept at face value his distinction between the nominal, ordinal, interval, and ratio scales.

This, of course, is unwelcome news to those countless thousands who teach courses in measurement and statistics, who have spent lifetimes doing quantitative research based on the Stevens principles, or who have millions of dollars invested in testing procedures that produce mere numbers and not measures. The argument is that all the sophisticated statistical analyses conducted in psychology, in educational outcomes, in medical rehabilitation, and the like are wasted if the data that form the input for these analyses do not adhere to the principles of fundamental measurement common in the physical sciences and described for us by Luce and Tukey (1964).

For those who have listened to Ben Wright from the University of Chicago as he makes his expositions on Rasch analysis, Michell's critique of quantitative psychology is not news at all. Wright's ever-present teaching aid is a 1-foot rule that he carries around in his back pocket and uses as his model of what measurement in the physical sciences is like, and what measurement in the human sciences must be like. It is clear that, at least for the present, the Rasch model is the only technique generally available for constructing measures in the human sciences. Andrich (1988), Fisher (1994), Perline, Wright, and Wainer (1979), Wright (1985, 1999), and others have demonstrated that the Rasch model produces the sort of measurements we expect in the physical sciences when it is applied to measurement construction in the social sciences. The claim is that the Rasch model instantiates the principles of probabilistic conjoint measurement to produce interval measures in which the principles of concatenation apply.

The claim we are making is that the construction of fundamental measures is the first task in any of the human sciences in which real quantification is required. This is not to suggest that the Rasch model supersedes all that we learned in our statistics courses at college. The use of the Rasch model is, however, the precursor of any statistical analyses we want to conduct. It could be argued that the term "psychometrics" is terminally flawed, that the current practices have a lot to do with the "psycho" and very little to do with the "metrics." We can highlight the problem by looking at one of the classic texts used in postgraduate measurement classes, that of Hays (1994). In the Introduction to his book, *Statistics*, he explains:

Controlled experimentation in any science is an attempt to minimize at least part of the accidental variation or *error* in observation. Precise techniques of measurement are aids to scientists in sharpening their own rather dull powers of observation and comparison among events. So-called exact sciences, such as physics and chemistry, thus have been able to remove a substantial amount of the unwanted variation among observations from time to time, place to place, observer to observer, and hence often are able to make general statements about physical phenomena with great assurance from the observation of limited numbers of events. . . . In the biological, behavioral, and social sciences, however, the situation is radically different. In these sciences, the variations between observations are not subject to the precise experimental controls that are possible in the physical sciences. Refined measurement techniques have not reached the stage of development that have obtained in physics and chemistry. . . . And yet the aim of the social or biological science test is precisely the same as that of the physical scientist—arriving at general statements about the phenomena under study. (p. 4)

Hays then follows on with the rest of his text, explaining how the statistics part is performed and relegating the measurement part to oblivion. His position seems to be that, because measurements of human phenomena are underdeveloped, we should drop that agenda and get on with the doable task of executing inferential statistical analyses. Of course, Hays is not peculiar in this regard. His approach to measurement, or his lack of approach to measurement, is quite typical in the field. Michell (1997) lists a large number of standard texts in the field in which the measurement aspect of research is so treated. The general approach is that because the sort of measurement taken for granted in the physical sciences is beyond the reach of the human sciences, psychology's own idiosyncratic view of what measurement is will have to suffice.

The relegation of measurement to the sidelines is lamented by Pedhazur and Schmelkin (1991):

> Measurement is the Achilles' heel of sociobehavioral research. Although most programs in sociobehavioral sciences . . . require a medium of exposure to statistics and research design, few seem to require the same where measurement is concerned. . . . It is, therefore, not surprising that little or no attention is given to the properties of the measures used in many research studies. (pp. 2–3)

Unfortunately, neither the authors nor those who quote them (Kieffer, 1999) seem to understand that an essential property of useful measures is the linearity and additivity inherent in measures used in the physical sciences.

Our claim is a much stronger one: The construction of measures is a prerequisite of statistical analyses. The standard for scientific measurement is that which has been the servant of the physical sciences. Those measurement principles can be applied to the human sciences via probabilistic conjoint measurement. Currently, the Rasch model is the only model that provides for the construction of measures meeting these criteria. Rasch modeling does not replace statistical analysis; it precedes it.

Therefore, those involved in the measurement of latent traits must deal with two difficulties. First, latent traits are not directly observable; only their consequent behaviors are. Second, measurement is not the mere allocation of numbers to events, but the result of a deliberative process.

MEASUREMENT AND ITEM RESPONSE THEORY

Of the few textbooks that deal with the Rasch model, most tend to lump it together with two- and three-parameter models under the general heading, Item Response Theories. In that context, the Rasch model is referred to as the one-parameter item response theory (IRT) model. The two-parameter IRT model includes a parameter for item discrimination, and the three-parameter IRT model adds parameters for item discrimination and guessing. Proponents of the two- and three-parameter models contend that data fit generally improves when these techniques are used. We should not be surprised that this is often, though not always, the case. The values of the second and the third parameters of these models are introduced or manipulated expressly for that purpose: to maximize the fit of the model to the data.

The Rasch model, however, is used for another purpose: the construction of fundamental measures. In this context, fit statistics are used to indicate where the principles of probabilistic conjoint measurement have been sufficiently realized in practice to justify the claim that the results can be used as a measurement scale with interval measurement properties. In this case, the Rasch model question is: How well do the empirical data fit to the measurement model requirements? For the two- and three-parameter IRT models, there is another focus: How can the additional parameters be manipulated to maximize the fit of the model to the data? How can the empirical data be most completely explained? Indeed, as we see later in this chapter, it is precisely the addition of the extra parameters that robs the data output of its fundamental measurement properties.

In this context, the comments of a longtime Rasch critic, Harvey Goldstein (1979), are both informative and illustrative: " 'The criterion is that items should fit the model, and not that the model should fit the items.' This is an extremely radical proposal" (p. 15). Goldstein's comment presupposes that the sole objective of data analysis is to manipulate the data analytical procedures until the amount of variance that cannot be explained is reduced to a minimum. This approach to quantification is shared by many factor analytical techniques as well as the two- and three-parameter IRT models. From this perspective, the primacy of the empirical data is paramount. The task of data analysis is to account for the idiosyncrasies of the data.

From the fundamental measurement perspective, the requirements of the measurement model are paramount. The idiosyncrasies of the empirical data are of secondary importance. The measurement ideal, encapsulated in the Rasch model, has primacy. The researcher's task is to work toward a better fit of the data to the model's requirements until the match is sufficient for practical measurement purposes in that field.

CONSTRUCT VALIDITY

The foregoing discussion highlights another important issue for our consideration. The primacy of empirical data over the theoretical model in the sphere of measurement often is accompanied by a parallel regard for the primacy of data over substantive theory. This perspective has its philosophical roots in positivism, but often reveals itself in practice as short-sighted pragmatism. In this regard, Rasch practitioners often have been as guilty as any other. It frequently is the case that data have been collected in an undisciplined manner, using a poorly crafted instrument, and that Rasch measurement techniques are brought to bear on the assembled mess with the aim of making a silk purse out of a sow's ear. Although it has been possible to develop quite useful measurement outcomes from this technique, it does not capitalize on the role that Rasch measurement can and should play as a tool of construct validity.

In his American Psychological Association (APA) presentation, *Construct Validity: A Forgotten Concept in Psychology?*, Overton (1999) detailed the importance of Fisher's (1994) claim that the Rasch model is an instrument of construct validation. The term "construct validity," introduced by Cronbach and Meehl (1955) according to Overton, is the "extent to which [a] . . . test [or score] may be said to measure a theoretical construct or trait." Construct validation should serve to focus our "attention on the role of psychological [or other guiding] theory" (Anastasi & Urbina, 1997, p. 126).

Therefore, given some theoretical claim about a construct, the Rasch model permits the strong inference that the measured behaviors are expressions of that underlying construct. Even in the text quoted earlier, construct validity then becomes a comprehensive concept that includes the other types: content validity, face validity, concurrent validity, and so on (Messick, 1989, 1995). In the research world, where empirical data has primacy, the process of validating tests involves showing their concurrence with existing data collection devices. It is the process of induction that leads us from the data we have collected to the summary statements or explanations we can make about them (Overton, 1998a, 1999).

In the situation positing a substantive theory about human behavior, education achievement, or posttrauma rehabilitation, the role of the investigator is to identify an appropriate construct or latent trait, and to use that construct as a guide in deciding which observable aspects of the human condition should be operationalized as part of a data collection device. The investigator's understanding of the construct will allow for the prediction of the measurement outcomes to a considerable extent. Given that the measurement of the construct is the first goal, the investigator will ensure that the test items, prompts, observational checklist, or the like both validly represent the theoretical construct and meet the requirements for fundamental measurement.

Overton (1998a) used the Drawing Hands illustration of the famous graphic artist M. C. Escher to show the dialectical nature of the theory–practice interface. As the right hand draws the left, the left hand simultaneously draws the right. As theory tells the investigator how to go about the data collection process, the result of that process informs about theory. The process of construct validation works at the interface between the development of a data collection device and the empirical data so collected. Rasch measurement works hand in hand with the investigator to determine the extent to which the data actually measure the construct under examination.

THE RASCH MODEL
AND PROGRESS OF SCIENCE

Michell (1999) asserted that it is the lack of attention to fundamental measurement in psychology that has hampered its development as a science during the 20th century. It is not the case, however, that the construction of measures will, in and of itself, pave the way for progress in the human sciences. Too often, those working in research methods, data analysis, and even Rasch measurement are called on to give advice after the data have been collected, sometimes even after the first few attempts at data analysis have failed. Instead of being involved in the research methodology and instrument design process from the very beginning, number crunchers often are called in at the last minute to advise a soon-to-graduate doctoral student on how to analyze and present the results of the data already collected. In another scenario, a colleague, an external contracting agency, or a professional licensing board rushes in to take last-minute advice on how to save a project that, on reflection, looks rather poorly conceived from the start.

These one-shot research projects, it seems, are going nowhere. They are designed merely to satisfy some course requirement or to fulfill some institutional reporting obligation or the like, and often are one-time research consultancies. We have Rasch measurement colleagues who insist that their nonnegotiable requirement for becoming involved in such post hoc situations is that Rasch measurement techniques will be used to see what sort of measures can be constructed (salvaged?) from the assembled data. This is a well-grounded, but rather pragmatic, approach to the situation. Indeed, much of the advice given in the preceding chapters is quite applicable under these circumstances, which involve knowing how to make a silk purse out of a sow's ear.

However, where researchers have a long-term commitment to a substantive area of research with human subjects, in which they are consulted at the conceptualization of the project, the approach can be somewhat different. In these circumstances wherein researchers intend for their work to have some impact in the area under investigation, their understanding of the substantive (theoretical) area can work hand in hand with the Rasch models of fundamental measurement toward progress in that area of human science. Whereas Michell (1999) castigated psychologists for their persistence in avoiding the scientific measurement imperative, Mauran (1998) warned us that although measurement might be a necessary condition for scientific investigation, without a substantive theoretical orientation, it will never be sufficient.

The contrast between the pragmatic use of the Rasch model and its incorporation at the very beginning of a research project became clear in the graduate measurement course we taught together in 1999 in the College of Education at the University of Toledo. Most of our students had made considerable progress in doctoral programs. Some, in fact, were taking their last courses before writing and defending their dissertations. In the measurement course, they were required to demonstrate competency with appropriate use of Rasch analysis software, and to demonstrate sufficient understanding of Rasch measurement principles for drawing reasonable conclusions and inferences from the data they had analyzed. For those students considering their dissertation proposals, we urged each to look at one small but important area of understanding, and to work toward advancing the state of the field in that area.

For the measurement coursework assessment, any minimally satisfactory data set was fair game. As long as a modest-size item–person data matrix was available, Rasch modeling could be used to see the quality of the measures, if any, that could be constructed from the existing data. For the most part, practical considerations ruled while short timelines existed. For dissertation purposes, however, students started consulting us about how fundamental measurement principles could be built into projects they already had in mind, or how measures could be constructed in their particular fields of interest. Some students, of course, made the best of both worlds, using the measurement course assessment requirement as the trial for the investigative devices they were intending to develop in their doctoral research projects.

BACK TO THE BEGINNING
AND BACK TO THE END

It was obvious to Ben Wright, in seeing some early presentations of Rasch measurement applied to Piagetian theory, that the apparent ease with which these developmentalists were able to develop a variety of data collection techniques to produce person and item measures, was in part, because of their reliance on a broad, thoughtfully constructed developmental theory expressed in thousands of Piagetian chapters and journal articles. To the developmentalists, it seemed as though the chief strength of the Rasch approach to data analysis came primarily from the role that ordinality played in the construction of item and person measures. Indeed, for developmentalists, Guttman scaling held out a promise for developmental assessment that was only ever rarely satisfied in empirical practice (Kofsky, 1966). With hindsight, we can see that the key problem of the Guttman ordering for developmental studies was its deterministic or true-score nature. Clearly, the observation and recording of human performance is plagued by both systematic and random errors. A deterministic ordering model, like that of Guttman, has expectations that rarely can be met in empirical practice.

To developmentalists, the Rasch principles incorporate the attractive ordering features of the Guttman model and complement them with a more realistic probabilistic, or stochastic, framework. Indeed, this takes us back to the beginning work on this volume, which was intended to be a sort of self-help book for developmental and educational psychologists who were trying to make some measurement sense of their data. However, a confluence of originally quite diverse circumstances shows that the value of the Rasch model is not coincidental. Neither is it of benefit only to developmental and educational psychologists. The benefits to those who use Rasch modeling in constructing fundamental measures of some aspect of human existence derive from the model's expectation that good measurement should satisfy the axiomatic principles of conjoint measurement (Luce & Tukey, 1964).

It is clear from the work of Andrich (1988), Fisher (1994), Michell (1999), Perline, Wright, and Wainer (1979), and others that the axioms of conjoint measurement theory provide the only satisfactory prescription for scientific measurement and, that in terms of widespread application to the human sciences, Rasch measurement is the only game in town. In a brief but elegant American Educational Research Association paper, Karabatsos (1999a) succinctly summarized the axioms of conjoint measurement: where extensive measurement is achieved and when the requirements of transitivity, connectivity, monotonicity, restricted solvability, positivity, associativity, and the Archimedean condition are satisfied. As Karabatsos (1999a) said:

> The properties of extensive measurement are the logical rules underlying explicit physical measurement. Obviously, in situations where measurements are not directly observable, such as achievement or intelligence, the structures are not explicit. *But this does not mean that structure cannot be used to verify the measurement of latent traits.* The theory of additive conjoint measurement makes fundamental measurement a possibility in the social sciences, where all observations are ordinal. Within the psychometrics framework, this theory proves that when the axioms of independence and double cancellation are satisfied, then the numbers assigned to persons and items represent a common linear (interval) style, measured on a single dimension. Furthermore, person measurement is independent of the items used, and item calibrations are independent of which persons they measure. (pp. 8–9)

By constructing a 5 × 7 conjoint matrix of Rasch correct response probabilities based on an ordered set of five person ability estimates and seven item ability estimates, Karabatsos (1999a) was able to demonstrate the independence of items in relation to persons, arguing that such independence is a necessary condition for the double cancellation proof that is central to conjoint measurement. By demonstrating the double cancellation requirement for the set of correct response probabilities based on Rasch person and item estimates, Karabatsos was able to conclude that such independence, a basic requirement of measurement invariance, was the basic property of the Rasch measurement model.

However, it would be just as unexpected for any real data from the human sciences observation to satisfy the deterministic conjoint measurement axioms as it would be for them to attain a perfect Guttman structure. "However, because the axioms of additive conjoint measurement define measurement linearity, they should be considered as rules which data must statistically approximate" (Karabatsos, 1999a, p. 12).

Using simulated data to generate 100 4 × 4 conjoint matrices for each of the Rasch, two-parameter (2PL), and three-parameter (3PL) models, the theoretical probability values for each of the 300 matrices were checked for violations of the independence and double cancellation axioms of conjoint measurement. Karabatsos (1999a) concluded:

> There is strong support that almost 100% of the time, the parameters of the 2 PL and 3 PL violate interval scaling. On the other hand, the theoretical probabilities of Rasch models will always support a stable, interval scale structure. If the intention is to construct stable interval measurement, data should approximate uniform item-characteristic curves. The argument that 2 PL and 3 PL are advantageous because they are less restrictive alternatives to Rasch models (Hambleton & Swaminathan, 1985; van der Linden & Hambleton, 1997) does not recognize the connections between linear measurement requirements and uniform ICCs [Item Characteristic Curves]. . . . This study is not needed to prove that Rasch models satisfy conjoint measurement axioms. However, it seems that the field of item response theory does not recognize the mathematical requirements of measurement. (p. 18)

The question that we called "fit" in the previous chapter could now be considered fruitfully in terms of the extent to which actual response probabilities in any Rasch-modeled data sets violate the conjoint measurement axioms. Details of the necessity and requirements of conjoint measurement are canvassed in several places (Cliff, 1992; Fisher, 1994; Michell, 1986, 1990, 1997, 1999; Narens & Luce, 1993).

CONCERNS OVER USING THE RASCH MODEL WITH REAL DATA

From the perspective taken in developing the arguments contained in this textbook, we are now in a much better position to react to concerns expressed about the use of the Rasch model in educational and other human science measurement spheres. These concerns are variously expressed, but the following concerns, based loosely around excerpts from a number of measurement discussion lists, will serve to illustrate. The first concern has its primacy in the role of test specifications in the assessment process. This concern goes something like this: It does not matter at all how well scored and how statistically sophisticated the results are, if the test is not valid, in the sense that it does not measure what it was intended to measure, it cannot be reliable. Moreover, in the final analysis, validity is determined by panels of experts in the subject area(s) being tested or by the final end users of whatever is being tested.

Furthermore, according to this concern, it follows that before we examine the fit of test items to the Rasch model, we should first examine the fit of the Rasch model to the test framework. It is obvious that in the case of many assessment devices, the construct the test is supposed to assess is multidimensional. For example, nearly all mandated state education assessments in writing and mathematics reflect multidimensional constructs. From this viewpoint, the candidates and the items or tasks are supposed to involve more than a single dimension, and sometimes more than a small number of dimensions. The same can be said of tests in many other domains such as medical licensure and professional certification testing.

The perception is that test developers then "fit a Rasch model to the test data" from the apparently multidimensional assessment specification and promptly delete the items that do not fit the model. The claimed result is that test developers, wedded to the Rasch model, have sacrificed content validity in favor of the Rasch model requirement, because the original argument for content validity was based on the test framework, and the internal structure of the test no longer reflects the test framework. The consequence is a set of scale scores with wonderful technical properties but no validity.

Under any circumstances, we should always be concerned about the applicability of Rasch measurement to the rich concerns of school achievement or any other human attribute. However, following up on the school achievement thread for simplicity, whenever we make a decision either to measure and compare the achievement levels of different individuals in a particular area of school achievement, or to measure and monitor any individual's growth or development in an area of school achievement over time, we already have made the main assumption of Rasch measurement. Not only that, but we also have placed ourselves in a situation wherein a method for testing and validating this Rasch measurement assumption is essential.

When researchers, examination boards, licensing authorities, rehabilitation specialists, survey analysts, and the like summarize any human attribute in a single score, they always face a risk of being misled if the data collection and analysis process is not supervised by a unidimensional measurement model capable of identifying threats to meaningful comparison, and perhaps the need for augmentation by some qualifying descriptive data. Such supervision is especially important if comparisons are to be made across different instruments, which explains why serious attempts to measure, say, school achievement (e.g., the Third International Mathematics and Science Study, and the Program for International Student Assessment) insistently specify such a model (G. N. Masters, personal communication, January 26, 2000: posting to the Rasch measurement electronic forum [rasch@acer.edu.au]).

IN SUMMARY

Attempts at measurement in the human sciences are best grounded in a well-articulated conceptualization of the construct or attribute under investigation. Argument should establish the hypothesis that the attribute is quantifiable. Progress toward measurement should proceed for one attribute at a time.

The Rasch model for measurement should supervise the construction of measures because its prescriptions instantiate the principles of probabilistic conjoint measurement of items and persons, each independently of the distribution of the other.

Progress to measurement is an iterative dialectical process in which the dialogue between construct conceptualization and the results of measurement attempts informs subsequent iterations and involves all partners in the measurement processes.

Although all sorts of analytical techniques may be used on many sorts of data, the wide range of powerful statistical techniques in the psychometrician's repertoire are most fruitfully applied to measures as they are heretofore described.

What is perhaps new, is that with the application of the Rasch model, the boundaries between the use of statistical analyses and substantive analyses is more clear than with the application of other models: When the Rasch model is intended to hold a because of its special measurement properties, failure of the data to conform to the model implies further work on the substantive problem of scale construction, not on the identification of a more complex model that might account for the data. (Andrich, 1988, p. 86)

APPENDIX A:
Technical Aspects
of the Rasch Model

RASCH FAMILY OF MODELS

Dichotomous Model

Georg Rasch developed a mathematical model for constructing measures based on a probabilistic relation between any item's difficulty and any person's ability. He argued that the difference between these two measures should govern the probability of any person being successful on any particular item. The basic logic is simple: All persons have a higher probability of correctly answering easier items and a lower probability of correctly answering more difficult items. For example, the simplest member of the Rasch family of models, the dichotomous model, predicts the conditional probability of a binary outcome (correct/incorrect), given the person's ability and the item's difficulty. If correct answers are coded as 1 and incorrect answers are coded as 0, the model then expresses the probability of obtaining a correct answer (1 rather than 0) as a function of the size of the difference between the ability (B) of the person (n) and the difficulty (D) of the item (i).

The starting point for creating measures begins with a calculation of the percentage correct for each person (the number of items successfully answered divided by the total number of items) and each item (the number of persons successfully passing the item divided by the total number of persons) when the test is administered to an appropriate sample. These raw score totals are ordinal-level data, yet they are both necessary and sufficient for estimating person ability (B_n) and item difficulty (D_i) measures, as shown by Andersen (1973), Douglas and Wright (1986), and Wright and Douglas (1986).

The first step in estimating B_n (the ability measure of person n) is to convert the raw score percentage into odds of success, which are estimated by calculating the ratio of each person's percentage correct (p) over the percentage incorrect (1 − p). For example, a raw score of 40% correct is divided by the percentage incorrect (1 − p), that is, 60%, to obtain the ratio 40/60. The natural log of these odds (ln 40/60 = −0.4) then becomes the person ability estimate. The procedure is exactly the same for items, estimating D_i (the difficulty measure of item i), that is, dividing the percentage of people who answered the item correctly by the percentage of people who answered the item incorrectly and taking the natural log of that value.

These item difficulty (D_i) and person ability (B_n) estimates then are expressed on a scale of log odd ratios, or logits. The average logit is arbitrarily set at 0, with positive logits indicating higher than average probabilities and negative logits indicating lower than average probabilities. The Rasch model calculations usually begin by ignoring, or constraining, person estimates, calculating item estimates, and then using that first round of item estimates to produce a first round of person estimates. The first round of estimates then are iterated against each other to produce a parsimonious and internally consistent set of item and person parameters, so that the B − D values will produce the Rasch probabilities of success described more fully later. The iteration process is said to converge when the maximum difference in item and person values during successive iterations meets a preset convergence value. This transformation turns ordinal-level data (i.e., correct/incorrect responses) into interval-level data for both persons and items, thereby converting descriptive, sample-dependent data into inferential measures based on probabilistic functions.

Once we have estimated ability (B_n) and difficulty (D_i), the probability of correctly answering an item can be expressed mathematically as the general statement:

$$P_{ni}(x = 1) = f(B_n − D_i),\qquad(1)$$

where P_n is the probability, x is any given score, and 1 is a correct response. This equation therefore states that the probability (P_n) of person n getting a score (x) of 1 on a given item (i) is a function (f) of the difference between a person's ability (B_n) and an item's difficulty (D_i).

By using the Greek symbols commonly used in statistics to indicate the parameters being estimated, as opposed to the values calculated, the formula is expressed as follows:

$$\pi_{ni}(x_{ni} = 1) = f(\beta_n − \delta_i),\qquad(2)$$

where π (pi) represents response probability, β (beta) denotes person ability, and δ (delta) stands for item difficulty.

Given B_n and D_i, we then can expand on equation 1 to demonstrate that the function (f) expressing the probability of a successful response consists of a natural logarithmic transformation of the person (B_n) and item (D_i) estimates. This relation can be expressed mathematically as follows:

$$P_{ni}(x_{ni} = 1/B_n, D_i) = \frac{e^{(B_n - D_i)}}{1 + e^{(B_n - D_i)}}, \qquad (3)$$

where $P_{ni}(x_{ni} = 1/B_n, D_i)$ is the probability of person n on item i scoring a correct ($x = 1$) response rather than an incorrect ($x = 0$) one, given person ability (B_n) and item difficulty (D_i). This probability is equal to the constant e, or natural log function (2.7183) raised to the difference between a person's ability and an item's difficulty ($B_n - D_i$), and then divided by 1 plus this same value. Therefore, for example, if a person's ability is estimated at 3 logits and the difficulty of the item at 1 logit, then

$$P_{ni}(x = 1/B(3), D(1)) = \frac{2.7183^{(3-1)}}{1 + 2.7183^{(3-1)}} = \frac{2.7183^2}{1 + 2.7183^2} = 0.88, \qquad (3.1)$$

the person has an 88% chance of successfully passing the item.

If that same person ($B = 3$) were given an item with a difficulty estimate of 2 logits ($D = 2$), the expected probability of correctly answering that item would necessarily be lower than 0.88:

$$P_{ni}(x = 1/B(3), D(2)) = \frac{2.7183^{(3-2)}}{1 + 2.7183^{(3-2)}} = \frac{2.7183^1}{1 + 2.7183^1} = 0.73 \qquad (3.2)$$

(i.e., the probability would be 73%).

By following the same procedure in equations 3.1 and 3.2, we can see how an item perfectly targeted for that person (i.e., an item with a difficulty estimate [e.g., $D = 3$] equal to the ability estimate of the person [$B = 3$]) results in a 50/50 chance of that person successfully passing that item:

$$P_{ni}(x = 1/B(3), D(3)) = \frac{2.7183^{(3-3)}}{1 + 2.7183^{(3-3)}} = \frac{2.7183^0}{1 + 2.7183^0} = 0.50. \qquad (3.3)$$

Similarly, encountering a more difficult item (e.g., $D = 4$) would result in less than a 50/50 chance of passing:

TABLE A.1
Probability of Passing an Item for Various Differences
Between Item Difficulty and Person Ability

$B_n - D_i$	$P_{ni}(x = 1)$
−3.0	0.05
−2.5	0.08
−2.0	0.12
−1.5	0.18
−1.0	0.27
−0.5	0.38
0.0	0.50
+0.5	0.62
+1.0	0.73
+1.5	0.82
+2.0	0.88
+2.5	0.92
+3.0	0.95

$$P_{ni}(x = 1/B(3), D(4)) = \frac{2.7183^{(3-4)}}{1 + 2.7183^{(3-4)}} = \frac{2.7183^{-1}}{1 + 2.7183^{-1}} = 0.27. \qquad (3.4)$$

Table A.1 shows the probabilities of passing an item for a variety of difference values between B_n and D_i. If the values in the ability – difficulty ($B_n - D_i$)
column are placed in equation 3, the probabilities of success will match the $P_{ni}(x = 1)$ column in Table A.1. Note that when item difficulties are greater than person abilities (negative $B_n - D_i$ values), persons have a lower than 50% probabil-
ity of correctly answering the item. Likewise, when item difficulties are lower
than person abilities (positive $B_n - D_i$ values), persons have a higher than 50%
probability of correctly answering the item.

Parameter Separation. Taking the right-hand expression of equation 3
(i.e., the probability of success on any item, given a person's ability and an
item's difficulty), and dividing it by the probability of failure on any item (i.e., 1
minus the probability of success), and taking the natural log of this expression,
we get something quite interesting:

$$\ln\left(\frac{\dfrac{e^{(B_n - D_i)}}{1 + e^{(B_n - D_i)}}}{1 - \left(\dfrac{e^{(B_n - D_i)}}{1 + e^{(B_n - D_i)}} \right)} \right) = B_n - D_i. \qquad (4)$$

Equation 4 shows that taking the natural log of the odds (i.e., the division of two
probabilities) of successfully passing an item results in the direct comparison be-

tween a person's ability and an item's difficulty. The ability of the Rasch model to compare persons and items directly means that we have created person-free measures and item-free calibrations, as we have come to expect in the physical sciences; abstract measures that transcend specific persons' responses to specific items at a specific time. This characteristic, unique to the Rasch model, is called *parameter separation*. Thus, Rasch measures represent a person's ability as independent of the specific test items, and item difficulty as independent of specific samples within standard error estimates. Parameter separation holds for the entire family of Rasch models.

Rating Scale Model

The rating scale model is an extension of the dichotomous model to the case in which items have more than two response categories (e.g., Likert scales). For example, if an item has four response choices (0 = strongly disagree, 1 = disagree, 2 = agree, 3 = strongly agree), it is modeled as having three thresholds. Each item threshold (k) has its own difficulty estimate (F), and this estimate is modeled as the threshold at which a person has a 50/50 chance of choosing one category over another. The first threshold, for example, is modeled as the probability of choosing a response of 1 (disagree) instead of a response of 0 (strongly disagree), and is estimated with the following formula:

$$P_{ni1}(x = 1/B_n, D_i, F_1) = \frac{e^{(B - [D_i + F_1])}}{1 + e^{(B - [D_i + F_1])}}, \tag{5}$$

where P_{ni1} is the probability of person n choosing "disagree" (category 1) over "strongly disagree" (category 0) on any item (i). In this equation, F_1 is the difficulty of the first threshold, and this difficulty calibration is estimated only once for this threshold across the entire set of items in the rating scale. The threshold difficulty F_1 is added to the item difficulty D_i (i.e., $D_i + F_1$) to indicate the difficulty of threshold 1 on item i. Given that $B_n - (D_i + F_1)$ has the same value as $B_n - D_i - F_1$, and helps to show more easily the shared bases of the Rasch models, the latter is used in the following explanations of the rating scale model.

Modeling subsequent thresholds in the rating scale follows the same logic. The difficulty of endorsing category 2 (agree) instead of category 1 (disagree) is modeled as follows:

$$P_{ni2}(x = 2/B_n, D_i, F_2) = \frac{e^{(B_n - D_i - F_2)}}{1 + e^{(B_n - D_i - F_2)}}, \tag{6}$$

where B_n is the person ability, D_i is the difficulty of the entire item, and F_2 is the difficulty of the second threshold, estimated across all items. Thus, the general form of the rating scale model expresses the probability of any person choosing any given category on any item as a function of the agreeability of the person n (B_n) and the endorsability of the entire item i (D_i) at the given threshold k (F_k) (Wright & Masters, 1982).

$$P_{nik} = \frac{e^{(B_n - D_i - F_k)}}{1 + e^{(B_n - D_i - F_k)}} . \tag{7}$$

Furthermore, if these probabilities are converted to odds, parameter separation can be demonstrated for the rating scale model as well:

$$\ln\left(\frac{P_{nik}}{1 - P_{nik}}\right) = B_n - D_i - F_k . \tag{8}$$

By using the Greek symbols commonly used in statistics to indicate the parameters estimated (as opposed to the values calculated), the formula is expressed as:

$$\ln\left(\frac{\pi_{nik}}{1 - \pi_{nik}}\right) = \beta_n - \delta_i - \tau_k , \tag{9}$$

where β_n is the person ability, δ_i is the item difficulty, and τ_k is the difficulty of the kth threshold.

The thresholds for a set of rating scale items can be depicted as the intersection of item probability curves for each response option (see Fig. A.1). Fig. A.1 shows F_1 as the threshold for choosing category 1 over category 0, F_2 as the threshold for choosing 2 over 1, and F_3 as the threshold for choosing 3 over 2. The x axis expresses the difference between person ability (B_n) and item difficulty (D_i). So, for example, a person whose agreeability is 3 logits lower than the endorsability of the item as a whole ($B_n - D_i = -3$) has a greater than 50% chance of choosing category 0. If, however, a person's agreeability is, for example, 3 logits higher than the endorsability of the item ($B_n - D_i = 3$), category 3 is clearly the one most likely to be endorsed.

Partial Credit Model

The partial credit model can be seen as a version of the rating scale model in which the threshold estimates, including the number of thresholds, are not constrained; that is, they are free to vary from item to item. When the partial credit model is used to model rating scale data, it allows each item to vary in its threshold estimates. Whereas the rating scale model used one set of threshold estimates that applies to the entire set of items (an example was depicted in Fig.

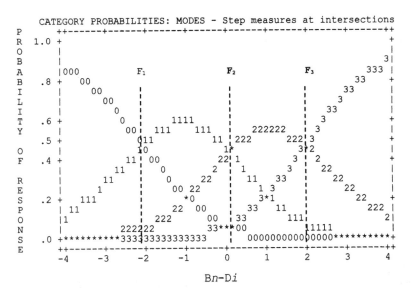

FIG. A.1. Category probability curves for a rating scale item with three thresholds.

A.1), the partial credit model provides a set of individual threshold (k) estimates for each item (i):

$$\ln\left(\frac{P_{nik}}{1 - P_{nik}}\right) = B_n - D_{ik}. \tag{10}$$

Therefore, the D_{ik} replaces the $(D_i - F_k)$ from equation 8, signifying that in the partial credit model, each set of threshold estimates is unique to its own individual item (i.e., threshold k for item i), instead of being estimated as a separate set of threshold estimates (F_k) for the entire set of items.

The partial credit model not only allows for an empirical test of whether the distances between response categories are constant for each item, but, more importantly, it allows the option for each item to vary in its number of response categories. A test or survey, for example, could comprise a mix of response formats, with some questions having two response options, some five, and some seven. This model would be ideal for situations in which partial marks are awarded for answers, such as essay examinations.

Many-Facets Rasch Model

The many-facets Rasch model adds yet more flexibility for estimating fundamental aspects of the measurement process. If we can imagine another aspect of the testing process (in addition to person ability and item difficulty) that might

TABLE A.2
Notation for the Rasch Family of Models

Values Calculated	Parameter Estimated	Definition
B	β (beta)	Person ability/measure
D	δ (delta)	Item difficulty/calibration
F	τ (tau)	Category threshold/calibration
C	λ (lambda)	Facet difficulty
P	π (pi)	Probability
n		Person
i		Item
k		Threshold
j		Facet
x		Response

systematically influence persons' scores, for example, individual raters, specific tasks within an item, time of day the test is given, and method of testing (paper and pencil vs. computer), we can estimate the impact of that facet on the measurement process. A difficulty estimate for each facet is calibrated, for example, the severity (C) of rater j. This severity is considered in the probability estimate of any person (n) responding to any item (i) for any category threshold (k) for any rater (j):

$$P_{nikj} = \frac{e^{(B_n - D_i - F_k - C_j)}}{1 + e^{(B_n - D_i - F_k - C_j)}}, \tag{11}$$

and is a function of the ability of the person (B_n), the difficulty of the item (D_i), the difficulty of the threshold (F_k), and the severity of the rater (C_j).

This model adheres to the principles of parameter separation:

$$\ln\left(\frac{P_{nikj}}{1 - P_{nikj}}\right) = B_n - D_i - F_k - C_j. \tag{12}$$

The symbols for the Rasch family of models are summarized in Table A.2.

RASCH MODEL ASSESSMENT

Reliability Indices

In the Rasch model, reliability is estimated both for persons and for items. The *person separation reliability* (R_P) (Wright & Masters, 1982) is an estimate of how well one can differentiate persons on the measured variable. That is, it estimates the replicability of person placement across other items measuring the same construct. The estimate is based on the same concept as Cronbach's alpha. That is, it is the percentage of observed response variance that is reproducible:

$$R_P = \frac{SA_P^2}{SD_P^2}. \tag{13}$$

The denominator (SD_P^2) represents total person variability, that is, how much people differ on the measure of interest. The numerator (SA_P^2) represents the reproducible part of this variability (i.e., the amount of variance that can be reproduced by Rasch model). This amount of variance that is reproducible with the Rasch model is called the *adjusted person variability* (SA_P^2). The adjusted person variability is obtained by subtracting error variance from total variance $(SD_P^2 - SE_P^2 = SA_P^2)$. This reproducible part then is divided by the total person variability (SD_P^2) to obtain a reliability estimate for persons (R_P), with values ranging between 0 and 1 (Wright & Masters, 1982).

An alternative index for estimating the spread of persons on the measured variable is the *person separation index* (G_P). This is estimated as the adjusted person standard deviation (SA_P) divided by the average measurement error (SE_P), where measurement error is defined as that part of the total variance that is not accounted for by the Rasch model:

$$G_P = \frac{SA_P}{SE_P}. \tag{14}$$

Thus, person reliability is expressed in standard error units (Wright & Masters, 1982, p. 92). Unlike the person separation reliability, the person separation index is not bound by 0 and 1, hence proving more useful for comparing reliabilities across several analyses. For example, in order to separate the persons into statistically distinct ability strata, using 3 standard errors to define each strata, then the formula ([4G + 1]/3) will indicate the number of ability strata defined in the sample (Wright & Masters, 1989, p. 92).

Reliability and separation for items are estimated in the same manner as for persons, with item variance being substituted for person variance,

$$G_I = \frac{SA_I}{SE_I}, \tag{15}$$

and the number of statistically distinct difficulty strata can be calculated in the same way.

Fit Statistics

Because the Rasch model is a strict mathematical expression of the theoretical relation that would hold between all items and all persons along a single underlying continuum, no items and persons will ever perfectly fit the model. We are interested, however, in identifying those items and persons whose pattern of responses deviate more than expectations, resulting in fit statistics for all persons and all items in the data matrix.

The estimation of fit begins with the calculation of a response residual (y_{ni}) for each person n when each item i is encountered. That is, how far does the the actual response (x_{ni}) deviate from Rasch model expectations (E_{ni}) (Wright & Masters, 1982)?

$$y_{ni} = x_{ni} - E_{ni}.$$ (16)

Because there are too many person–item deviations, or residuals (y_{ni}), to examine in one matrix, the fit diagnosis typically is summarized in a fit statistic, expressed either as a mean square fit statistic or a standardized fit statistic, usually a z or t distribution. Additionally, these two fit statistics are further categorized into (a) those that have more emphasis on unexpected responses far from a person's or item's measure (outfit statistics), and (b) those that place more emphasis on unexpected responses near a person's or item's measure (infit statistics).

The outfit statistic is simply an average of the standardized residual (Z_{ni}) variance, across both persons and items. This average is unweighted. That is, it is not influenced by (multiplied by) any other information. This results in an estimate that gives relatively more impact to unexpected responses far from a person's or item's measure (Wright & Masters, 1982):

$$\text{outfit} = \frac{\Sigma Z_{ni}^2}{N}.$$ (17)

The infit statistic, on the other hand, is a weighted standardized residual, in which relatively more impact is given to unexpected responses close to a person's or item's measure. Residuals are weighted by their individual variance (W_{ni}) to lessen the impact of unexpected responses far from the measure:

$$\text{infit} = \frac{\Sigma Z_{ni}^2 W_{ni}}{\Sigma W_{ni}}.$$ (18)

When these infit and outfit values are distributed as mean squares, their expected value is 1. Guidelines for determining unacceptable departures from expectation include flagging items or persons as misfits when mean square infit or

TABLE A.3

Notation and Definition for Model Assessment

Notation	Definition
R_P	Person reliability index; bound by 0 and 1
SA_P^2	Person variance, adjusted for measurement error
SD_P^2	Person variance, unadjusted
SE_P	Standard error for persons
SA_P	Standard error for persons, adjusted for measurement error
G_P	Person separation index; in standard error units
R_I	Item reliability index; bound by 0 and 1
SA_I^2	Item variance, adjusted for measurement error
SD_I^2	Item variance, unadjusted
SE_I	Standard error for items
SA_I	Standard error for items, adjusted for measurement error
G_I	Item separation index; in standard error units
y	Residual
x	Observed score
E	Expected score from the Rasch model
Z_{ni}	Standardized residual for each person on each item
W_{ni}	Variance for an individual across a given item

outfit values are larger than 1.3 for samples less than 500, 1.2 for samples between 500 and 1,000, and 1.1 for samples larger than 1,000 (Smith, Schumacker, & Bush, 1995).

When reported simply as standardized t values, the fit statistics have an expected mean of 0 and a standard deviation of 1. Here the recommended cutoff for flagging misfits includes t values outside of ±2.0 (Smith, 1992).

The four types of fit statistics (mean square, t, infit, outfit) can be used separately or in combination for making fit decisions. Generally speaking, more emphasis is placed on infit values than on outfit values in identifying misfitting persons or items. The issues surrounding the estimation and interpretation of misfit are more thoroughly canvassed in chapter 12. Table A.3 provides a summary of symbols and definitions for the model assessment formulas.

APPENDIX B:
Rasch Resources

COMPUTER SOFTWARE FOR RASCH MEASUREMENT

Each of the software packages that follows implements estimation and fit procedures for more than one of the Rasch family of measurement models. Each of the estimation procedures has its own band of rather devoted adherents, but each has its shortcomings as well.

JMLE: Joint Maximum Likelihood Estimation (sometimes called UCON)
MMLE: Marginal Maximum Likelihood Estimation
PAIR: Pairwise Estimation

Similarly, each of the Rasch software programs has its own disciples, but no one program incorporates the advantages of all the packages, or avoids the tolerable shortcomings of its own particular estimation procedure. For the members of the Rasch family of models dealt with in detail in this textbook—the models for dichotomous, partial credit, and rating scale data—the usual Rasch analytical procedures, as they are implemented in the software packages listed here, produce estimates that are generally equivalent, for all practical analytical purposes. Sometimes pragmatic considerations are foremost in the practitioner's mind: Macintosh users have one obvious option—Quest—all the rest run on PCs; RUMM takes full advantage of the Windows platform; Winsteps is Windows compatible and has lots of diagnostics; Bigsteps is free; ConQuest has more analytical potential than most mere mortals can imagine; and so on. (However, adventurous Mac users can run even facets-type analyses using PC emulation software on, say, a G3 or G4.)

Australian Council for Educational Research—Melbourne

Quest—The Interactive Test Analysis System (Adams & Khoo): Joint Maximum Likelihood Estimation

Quest claims to offer a comprehensive test and questionnaire analysis environment by providing access to Rasch measurement techniques as well as a range of traditional test analysis procedures. It combines a rather easy-to-use control language with flexible and informative output. Quest can be used to construct and validate variables based on both dichotomous and polytomous observations.

The Rasch analysis provides item estimates, case estimates, and fit statistics; the results from this analysis can be accessed through a variety of informative tables and maps. Traditional analyses report counts, percentages, and point-biserials for each possible response to each item and a variety of reliability indices.

Quest runs in batch mode, interactive mode, or a combination of the two. The batch mode conveniently allows a one-step submission of more routine analysis jobs, whereas the interactive environment facilitates exploration of the properties of test data. In interactive mode, Quest allows analysis results to be viewed on the screen as the analysis proceeds.

Quest allows the user to define subgroups and subscales so that analyses can be performed for any combination of subgroup and subscale. It has the usual Rasch flexibility for dealing with missing data and allows for item and case estimate anchoring to facilitate test equating and item banking. The software supports export of results to facilitate importation into database, analysis, and spreadsheet programs. The Quest Compare command provides Mantel–Haenszel and Rasch tests of differential item functioning.

Quest has been implemented on several platforms, including IBM PCs or compatibles running PC-DOS or MS-DOS, Apple Macintosh, Windows 95, Windows NT (console mode), and Vax/VMS. In its desktop form it handles up to 10,000 cases and 400 items with up to 10 response categories per item. A total of 10 subgroup–subscale combinations are permitted.

ConQuest (Adams, Wu, & Wilson): Marginal Maximum Likelihood Estimation

ConQuest is able to fit a much more extensive range of item response models than any of the other programs described here. Perhaps it is easiest to describe this package at two levels. First, at the level of Rasch analysis software, it can not only fit the standard dichotomous and polytomous Rasch models, but can be used for facets-type analyses and what ConQuest refers to as LLTM-type item response models as well. ConQuest does most of what Quest does, offering access to Rasch measurement techniques as well as a range of traditional test analysis procedures. At this level it is directly related to the content of this textbook and is suited to the entry-level Rasch measurement practitioner.

At the next level, directed specifically to those with more advanced analytical needs, ConQuest is a very versatile and powerful general modeling program that can also fit multidimensional item response models and both unidimensional and multidimensional latent regression models (i.e., multilevel models) as well as generate plausible values for the solution of difficult measurement problems. It uses a special keyword syntax to define the very wide range of item response models just described. Beyond that, it includes a method of defining special models using a design matrix approach, which makes it extremely flexible for more experienced users.

ConQuest is available for standard Windows and UNIX operating systems. It can be run from either a GUI (Windows) interface or a console interface. It combines a rather easy-to-use control language with flexible and informative output. In terms of output from Rasch and traditional analyses, as well as operation modes, ConQuest provides the same features detailed for the Quest package.

Demonstration versions and supporting material are available at ftp://www.ACER.edu.au/Rasch.

MESA Laboratory—Chicago

Winsteps (Linacre & Wright): Joint Maximum Likelihood Estimation

Winsteps constructs Rasch measures from simple rectangular data sets, usually of persons and items, with up to 1,000,000 cases and 10,000 items using JMLE. Each item can have a rating scale of up to 255 categories; dichotomous, multiple-choice, and multiple rating scale and partial credit items can be combined in one analysis. The developers of Winsteps use the program daily in their own work, and are continually adding new features as a result of their own experience and feedback from users. Winsteps is designed as a tool that facilitates exploration and communication.

Winsteps provides for powerful diagnosis of multidimensionality, using principal components analysis of residuals to detect and quantify substructures in the data. The working of rating scales can be examined thoroughly, and rating scales can be recoded and items regrouped to share rating scales as desired. Measures can be anchored at preset values. Training seminars are held regularly at MESA. A free student/evaluation version, limited to 100 cases and 25 items, is available at www.winsteps.com. An earlier DOS-based Rasch program, Bigsteps, with a capacity of 20,000 persons and 1,000 items, can also be downloaded free.

Facets (Linacre): Joint Maximum Likelihood Estimation

Facets is designed to handle the more complex applications of unidimensional Rasch measurement and performs many-facets Rasch measurement handling up to 1 million examinees and up to 255 response categories using JMLE. Facets constructs measures from complex data involving heterogeneous combinations of examinees, items, tasks, and judges along with further measurement and structural facets. All facet summary "rulers" are provided so the user can view all facets in the same frame of reference. It is designed to handle flexibly combinations of items of different formats in one analysis. Measures can be fixed-anchored individually or by group mean, facilitating equating and linking across test sessions. Quality-control fit evaluation of all measures is provided, and bias, differential item functioning, and interactions can be estimated. Weighting schemes can be implemented.

Since organizing the data for input to Facets and then interpreting its output can be challenging, it is recommended that simpler approaches be tried first. Training seminars are held regularly at MESA. A free student/evaluation version of Facets can be downloaded from www.winsteps.com.

RUMM Laboratory—Perth

RUMM 2010: Pairwise Conditional Estimation

RUMM 2010 is an interactive Rasch software package for Windows 95/98 and WinNT platforms, which uses a variety of graphical and tabular displays to provide an immediate, rapid, overall appraisal of an analysis. RUMM 2010 is entirely interactive, from data entry to the various analyses, permitting rerunning analyses based on diagnosis of previous analyses, for example, rescoring items, eliminating items, carrying out test equating in both raw score and latent metrics. The RUMM laboratory recommends 64 Mb of RAM and up to 12 Mb free hard disk space to make good use of the extensive graphic capabilities (128 Mb is a good idea for large data sets).

RUMM handles 5,000 or more items with the number of persons limited by available memory. It allows up to 9 distractor responses for multiple-choice items, a maximum of 64 thresholds per polytomous item, and up to 9 person factors such as gender, grade, age groups for group comparisons, DIF detection, and the like. The software employs a range of special Template files for allowing the user to customize analyses adding convenience and speed for repeated, related, and future analyses.

RUMM 2010 implements the Rasch models for dichotomous and polytomous data using a pairwise conditional estimation procedure that generalizes the equation for one pair of items in which the person parameter is eliminated to all pairs of items taken simultaneously. The procedure is conditional estimation in the sense that the person parameters are eliminated while the item parameters are estimated (Zwinderman, 1995). The procedure generalizes naturally to handling missing data.

Given that we have included all the Quest and Winsteps control files for the major analyses we have conducted for this book, we have included at the end of this appendix a sample snippet from the procedures used to set up an analysis using RUMM.

THE CLASSIC REFERENCE TEXTS

The following texts have been absolutely indispensable to the progress of Rasch measurement and to the writing of this book. Inevitably, each should become part of the the serious Rasch practitioner's reference library.

The foundation stone of the Rasch family of models:

Rasch, G. (1980). *Probabilistic models for some intelligence and attainment tests* (Expanded ed.). Chicago: University of Chicago Press. (Reprinted 1992, Chicago: MESA Press) This is Georg Rasch's seminal work on measurement that describes the theory, simple applications, and mathematical basis of the model. Many claim that in this prescient work, Rasch outlines the problems and principles that underlie even the latest developments in Rasch measurement.

The dichotomous model reference:

Wright, B. D., & Stone, M. H. (1979). *Best test design.* Chicago: MESA Press. (Also available in Spanish)

In *Best Test Design*, Wright and Stone outline the principles of Rasch measurement and apply the analytical techniques to dichotomous data. This instructional text on Rasch measurement introduces very straightforward estimation procedures as well as more complex estimation methods. Chapter 1: "What Is Measurement?" Chapter 2: "How to Measure?" shows how to perform by hand a Rasch analysis of the "Knox Cube Test." The chapter on "How Well Are We Measuring?" introduces the concept of data-to-model fit.

The polytomous models reference:

Wright, B. D., & Masters, G. N. (1982). *Rating scale analysis.* Chicago: MESA Press.

In *Rating Scale Analysis,* Wright and Masters discuss the philosophy behind linear, interval measurement and extend the application of the Rasch model to rating scales as part of the family of Rasch models for different polytomous applications, including Poisson counts, binomial, Bernoulli trials, and partial credit responses. In keeping with the principles behind *Best Test Design, Rating Scale Analysis* derives the major estimation methods and investigates data-to-model fit.

The many-facets Rasch model:

Linacre, J. M. (1989). *Many-facet Rasch measurement.* Chicago: MESA Press.

Judges, tasks, time-points, and other facets of the measurement situation can be parameterized with the many-facets Rasch model. Since these extensions are hard to conceptualize and difficult to manage, they are usually avoided whenever possible. But, these extensions can be crucial, for instance, in the adjustment of candidate measures for the severity of the judges they encountered. This book outlines the theory and application of this methodology.

An elegant, succinct account emphasizing Rasch measurement properties:

Andrich, D. (1988). *Rasch models for measurement.* Newbury Park, CA: Sage.

How psychologists willfully ignored the requirements for fundamental measurement and why the delusion continues to the present:

Michell, J. (1999). *Measurement in psychology: Critical history of a methodological concept.* New York: Cambridge University Press.

OTHER RASCH-BASED TEXTS

A good introduction to Rasch measurement (esp. chapters 6, 7, & 9):

McNamara, T. F. (1996). *Measuring second language performance.* New York: Longman.

George Ingebo contrasts the results of Rasch methods with conventional statistics for assessing student responses to basic skills testing and shows the advantages of Rasch measurement for school district testing programs.

Ingebo, G. S. (1997). *Probability in the measure of achievement*. Chicago: MESA Press.

Key papers from the International Objective Measurement Workshops have been issued in an important series of reference texts:

Wilson, M. (1992). *Objective measurement: Theory into practice, Vol. 1.* Norwood, NJ: Ablex.

Wilson, M. (1994). *Objective measurement: Theory into practice, Vol. 2.* Norwood, NJ: Ablex.

Engelhard, G., & Wilson, M. (1996). *Objective measurement: Theory into practice, Vol. 3.* Norwood, NJ: Ablex.

Wilson, M., Engelhard, G., & Draney, K. (Eds). (1997). *Objective measurement: Theory into practice,* Vol. 4. Norwood, NJ: Ablex.

Wilson, M., & Engelhard, G. (Eds.). (2000). *Objective measurement: Theory into practice, Vol. 5.* Stamford, CT: Ablex.

Each volume appears approximately 18 months after the workshop, and the next one, based on the IOMW in New Orleans, April 2000, will be edited by George Engelhard and Mark Wilson. The selection of papers always includes a set of papers describing interesting applications. There are also usually themed sections exploring topics such as rating scale analyses, facets-type analyses, and multidimensional measurement.

SEMINAL PAPERS

Physicist Norman Campbell's Theory of Fundamental Measurement as described for psychologists by Thomas Reese (1943) is available at www.rasch. org/rm8.htm

Sample-Free Test Calibration and Person Measurement. Ben Wright. 1967.

This presentation at the 1967 Educational Testing Service Invitational Conference launched Rasch measurement in the United States. Available at www. rasch.org/ memo1.htm

The Structure and Stability of the Functional Independence Measure (FIM)™. Linacre, Heinemann, Wright, Granger, Hamilton, 1994.

This paper demonstrated the efficacy of Rasch measurement in clarifying and solving measurement problems in survey and diagnosis situations. Available at www.rasch.org/memo50.htm

A History of Social Science Measurement. Ben Wright. 1997.

This paper addresses the main threads in the conceptualization of measurement (as opposed to mere numeration) in the Social Sciences, and relates them to the Rasch model. Available at www.rasch.org/memo62.htm

OTHER PUBLICATIONS

Rasch Measurement Transactions, under the continuing editorial hand of Mike Linacre, is a quarterly publication of the Rasch Measurement Special Interest Group of the American Educational Research Association. Back issues have been bound into volumes and published by MESA Press. *RMT* contains short research notes addressing many of the key issues and questions raised in the theory and practice of Rasch analysis. It is also available at www.rasch.org/rmt

MESA Research Memoranda by Ben Wright and several others form a collection of many of the foundational papers in Rasch measurement. The entire text of the pivotal MESA Research Memoranda are available at www. rasch.org/memos.htm

Popular Measurement magazine and the quarterly *Newsletter of the IOM* are publications of the Institute for Objective Measurement.

WEB SITES

Access to the Web site that supports this volume and provides the data sets and control files so readers can try the analyses for themselves is available at:

www.jcu.edu.au/~edtgb

The major Web site for Rasch measurement organizations and practitioners:

www.rasch.org

The Rasch listserv:

http://www.rasch.org/rmt/index.htm#Listserv

The Rasch Measurement Practitioners' online directory:

http://www.ACER.edu.au/Rasch/email.html

RASCH MEASUREMENT ORGANIZATIONS

Institute for Objective Measurement

The Institute for Objective Measurement (IOM) is a nonprofit, tax-exempt corporation whose mission is to develop, teach, promote, and make available the practice of objective measurement. It is in the business of problem solving through education and the promotion of objective measurement.

The IOM sees itself as a "public" organization whose orientation and focus is outward to the world as well as inward to the professional growth and support of its members. Its members constitute measurement professionals who live in many countries throughout the world. While the majority of members are employed by universities and other organizations that concern themselves with some aspect of measurement, about one third of the IOM's membership are students.

IOM provides support for programs in objective measurement that are far-reaching and implemented throughout various countries of the world. There are at least three categories of these offerings. The first includes large international conferences, such as the International Outcomes Measurement Conferences (IOMC) and the International Objective Measurement Workshops (IOMW). The second incorporates smaller regional workshops such as the New England Objective Measurement Workshops (NEOM), the South Central Objective Measurement Seminars (SCOMS), Midwest Objective Measurement Seminars (MOMS), and the Chicago Objective Measurement Talks (COMET). The third includes those educational programs offered by local IOM chapters. For the latter two groups, the IOM offers financial support in the form of stipends.

In addition to providing persons interested in objective measurement access to IOM's Web site at www.Rasch.org, the IOM provides its members with issues of *Popular Measurement* and quarterly *Newsletters of the IOM*.

A 12-member Board of Directors and three standing committees (Executive, Program, and Development) are responsible for the governance of the IOM. The IOM can be contacted by e-mail at: InstObjMeas@Worldnet.att.net or at www.Rasch.org

American Educational Research Association Rasch SIG

The Rasch Measurement Special Interest Group (SIG) of the American Educational Research Association is an international forum that allows Rasch measurement practitioners to place interesting measurement problems into a semi-public professional arena, as well as to share advice and techniques and to discuss theoretical and practical issues. The Rasch SIG sponsors several paper presentation sessions at each annual meeting of the American Educational Research Association. The SIG sponsors a Listserv that facilitates international discussions of measurement-related issues via e-mail. The SIG publishes *Rasch Measurement Transactions*, a quarterly newsletter that includes abstracts, reviews, and brief notes on the theory and practice of Rasch measurement. To join the SIG, go to <http://www.rasch.org>. Back issues of *RMT* can be accessed from this site as well. The SIG serves to maintain a sense of community among Rasch practitioners.

RASCH-BASED PROFESSIONAL MEETINGS

International Objective Measurement Workshops

The International Objective Measurement Workshops began in the spring of 1981, to develop and inspire cooperative and innovative work in the field of objective measurement as a tribute to the memory of Georg Rasch. The first workshop was held in Judd 111 at the University of Chicago by a small group of researchers, many of whom had worked closely with Georg Rasch (Ben Wright, Geoff Masters, David Andrich, Graham Douglas, George Morgan, Richard Smith, Barry Kissane, and Pender Pedler). The presentations at IOMW1 ranged from "Simplicity in Calibrating and Measuring" to "Bayes Estimation of Rasch Measurement." IOMW3 was held at the same time as the American Educational Research Association meeting in the spring of 1985, and in 1989 the tradition of holding IOMW around the same time as AERA was established as a means of expediting participation.

Currently, the International Objective Measurement Workshop is held biennially at the same time and city as the American Educational Research Association annual meeting. The most recent, IOMWX, was held in 2000 in New Orleans, and the next is planned for 2002, also in New Orleans. The meeting is a gathering of researchers and practitioners interested in all aspects of Rasch and Rasch-related measurement. There are usually both research presentations (in the form of traditional-style talks and poster presentations, as well as software demonstrations) and professional development workshops on various practical approaches and analysis techniques.

Selected and edited papers presented at the IOMW have been gathered into several volumes listed above.

International Outcomes Measurement Conference

The Third International Outcomes Measurement Conference was held on the Chicago campus of Northwestern University on June 16 and 17, 2000. Hosted by IOM, the MESA Psychometrics Laboratory at the University of Chicago, and the Rehabilitation Institute of Chicago, the third conference built on the work of two previous conferences held at the University of Chicago in 1996 and 1998. The conference was organized by Allen W. Heinemann, PhD, Professor of Physical Medicine and Rehabilitation at Northwestern University Medical School, and Benjamin D. Wright, PhD, Professor, Departments of Education and Psychology at the University of Chicago. The fourth IOMC is scheduled for 2002.

RASCH-BASED RESEARCH AND DEVELOPMENT ENTERPRISES

The Australian Council for Educational Research

ACER has pioneered the application of Rasch measurement in large-scale educational testing programs, both in Australia with the Basic Skills Testing Program–NSW (1989), and worldwide with the TIMSS (1994–) and PISA (1998–) projects.

> Masters et al. (1990). *Profiles of learning—The Basic Skills Testing Program in New South Wales 1989*. Melbourne: ACER.

Masters et al. (1990) reports on the first Australian statewide testing program in which the performances of 60,000 Year 3 and 60,000 Year 6 children have been reported along qualitatively described literacy and numeracy continua. The other Australian states followed suit, and now Rasch measurement is being used to equate state and territory tests on national scales for Reading, Writing, Spelling, and Numeracy on which benchmarks of minimum acceptable performances have been established. Another relevant reference is:

> Masters, G., & Forster, M. (1997). *Mapping literacy achievement—Results of the 1996 National School English Literacy Survey*. Canberra, Australia: *Department* of Employment, Education, Training and Youth Affairs.

TIMSS

The Third International Mathematics and Science Study is undoubtedly "the most extensive investigation of mathematics and science education ever conducted," as it involved the assessment of more than half a million students in 45 countries with the aim of quantifying education achievements around the globe.

> http://ustimss.msu.edu/

Reports of the Australian/ACER perspective on TIMSS (1996, 1997, and 1999) can be found as *Mathematics and Science on the Line—Australian junior secondary students—Third International Mathematics and Science Study (TIMSS) Monographs #1 #2 and #3.*

PISA: Program for International Student Assessment

PISA is an internationally standardized assessment, jointly developed by participating countries and administered to 15-year-olds in groups in their schools. It is administered in 32 countries, of which 28 are members of the OECD. Between 4,500 and 10,000 students typically have been tested in each country. PISA assessments are presently planned for 2000, 2003, and 2006.

> http://www.PISA.oecd.org/

ACER has a special interest in developmental assessment and in the construction of educational variables for measuring growth. It maintains the Rasch listserv (http://www.rasch.org/rmt/index.htm#Listserv) and the Rasch Measurement Practitioners' online directory (http://www.ACER.edu.au/Rasch/email.html).

ACER Press is located at: http://www.acer.edu.au/acer/acerpress/index.html

Details at: http//:www.acer.edu.au

Northwest Evaluation Association (OR)

The Northwest Evaluation Association (NWEA) has been using Rasch modeling in the area of educational achievement testing since the 1970s; indeed, it has been a clear leader in the application of Rasch measurement to educational assessment in the United States. As a not-for-profit agency, NWEA has created Rasch scales in Reading, Mathematics, Language Usage, and the Sciences. These cross-grade scales include an achievement range from grade 2 to grade 10 and have used to create item banks with thousands of items in each content area. These item banks have allowed the development of customized achievement-level tests and adaptive tests used in over 300 school districts in the United States. As a direct result of the influence of NWEA, many Oregon state educational assessments are now reported in RITS (Rasch logITS).

The assessments developed by NWEA benefit from Rasch modeling in several ways. First, the measurement instruments are designed for efficiency through the selection of items based on their difficulty estimates, resulting in tests that are optimally challenging for each student. Second, the scale is designed to measure growth throughout much of a student's education, resulting in particularly useful longitudinal data. Third, the scale is permanent, so that changes may be made in test instruments without disturbing any client school's ability to study change across time.

However, the assessments that NWEA develops are just a means to an end. The primary focus for NWEA is to help all students learn more. High-quality assessments supported by Rasch modeling help accomplish this by creating a climate in which data is valued and allows achievement data to be used to inform change at the student level, as well as change at school, state, and national levels. By using the Rasch models to create quality measurement instruments, NWEA aims to help move education past reliance on educational fads to an environment in which the structure of education continually improves by using measurement to direct change.

Details at: http://www.nwea.org

Computer Adaptive Technologies, Inc.

Founded in 1984, Computer Adaptive Technologies, Inc. (CAT) became a division of the Houghton Mifflin Company in 1998, and provides testing organizations with solutions to create and deliver electronic tests worldwide. The CATGlobal Testing Network includes test delivery, via the Internet, at public and private test sites, as well as through home or office PCs.

The CAT Software system is a complete tool set for creating computer-based tests delivered in the CATGlobal Testing Network. CAT Consulting Services provide program management, test development, and psychometric consulting for computer-based tests. At the heart of CAT delivery is the Rasch model. Maximum information is obtained in the computer adaptive testing situation by incorporating the Rasch principle that the test taker will have a 50% probability of correctly answering an item that is targeted to test-taker ability.

Details at: http://www.catinc.com

The Lexile Reading Framework

The Lexile reading comprehension framework uses Rasch measurement techniques to provide a common interval scale for measuring both reader performance and the difficulty of written text (i.e., it places readers and text on the same Rasch scale). The Lexile limen is set so that when a reader has the same Lexile measure as a title, the reader should read that "targeted" title with 75% comprehension. The difference between a reader's Lexile measure and a text's Lexile measure is used to forecast the comprehension the reader will have with the text. A text measure 250L greater than a reader's measure predicts a comprehension drop to 50%, while a reader measure advantage of 250L over the text means comprehension goes up to 90%.

The technology of the Lexile Framework includes a graphical representation of reading development called the Lexile Map and, even more interestingly, a software program called the Lexile Analyzer that measures the difficulty of text. An approximation of a reader's measure can be inferred by getting the reader to read aloud from texts with known Lexile measures. For high-stakes decisions, specific tests can be used to provide more precision in reader location. The Lexile library lists tens of thousands of literature titles, magazines, newspapers, and textbooks, each of which has been assigned a Lexile measure. Chapter 1 of this book was measured at 1440L, placing it near the kind of text found on the Test of English as a Foreign Language (1400L), the Graduate Management Admissions Test (1440L), and the *Wall Street Journal* (1400L) on the Lexile map. Readers such as matriculants of first-tier U.S. universities read between 1400L and 1600L and demonstrate 75% to 90% comprehension of 1400L text. Are we on target?

Details at: www. lexile.com

SurveyMetrics (Eugene, OR)

SurveyMetrics has integrated Rasch analysis and computer interface technologies into a highly flexible measurement and reporting tool to provide measures of service utilization and satisfaction with the delivery of medical services, in particular. Data collection is implemented by a specially designed touch-screen computer kiosk that is either suitably located or is taken to patients upon discharge. The computer kiosk incorporates both carefully designed graphic interfaces for patients and item selection algorithms for Rasch precalibrated item banks.

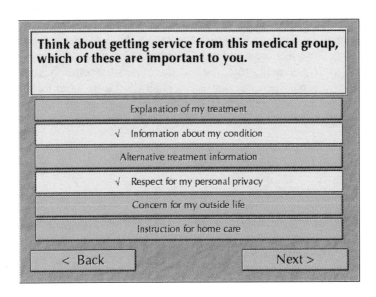

Interacting with this screen display, the patient indicates which medical service attributes are important. The computer will then loop through the set of identified important attributes only, presenting one screen per attribute to obtain satisfaction ratings.

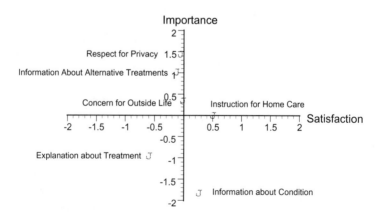

How satisfied were you with the information you received about your medical condition?

| Very Unsatisfied | **Touch Here** | Very Satisfied |

Touch the slider to show your satisfaction. It can be adjusted by touching again.

| < Back | Next > |

Both the importance and satisfaction ratings are Rasch analyzed and measures are obtained at point-of-service, and real-time reports are then provided to administrators, that is, there is no time lag between data collection and availability of results. Both the importance and the satisfaction ratings are calibrated and reported in a display like that shown in the graph. Though all medical service attributes could be rated on the satisfaction scale, SurveyMetrics claims that selecting only those that are important to the particular patient diminishes the survey time while generating more meaningful ratings. Importantly, measurement utility is enhanced when interactive computer kiosks are used to obtain these data, as there are clear indications that both measurement and sampling errors are diminished with the appropriate use of these technologies.

Details at: www.surveymetrics.net

Sample Rasch Analysis Procedure for RUMM Software

This procedure executes the rating scale model with scoring reversal on the CAIN Likert-style data that was the focus of chapter 6.

In order to specify the data format, the visual presentation displays the record of the first person twice: the first line is used to select the fields as required and the second line displays each field selected as an overlay on the record itself:

```
12723345363635515124556665541030054
** NO FIELDS ALLOCATED AT PRESENT **
```

When we shade the appropriate section of the data record in the first line to specify the field required, and then press the button to "accept," RUMM 2010 assembles the analysis details. For the CAIN analysis we will identify two segments at first: the **Person ID** and the **Item Format**.

Person ID allows for one unique selection per case, for example, an *ID number* or *Name*. To select ID field, shade the ID allocation on the first line of the record. The first person had the ID number "1" in the right-hand place of the three columns allocated for student number in the CAIN data file:

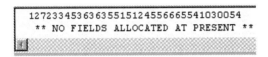

When we "accept ID," the field overlays on the record in the second line:

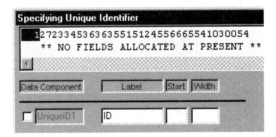

To specify the **Item Format** of the 26 CAIN items in the data file, we mark out the relevant data block by shading the the field on the first line of the record:

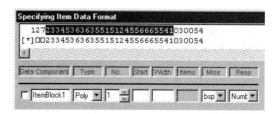

We then specify the data according to **Type**: "Poly" (i.e., Polytomous, not Multiple Choice); indicate the **Miss**ing data character as "bsp" (bsp=blank/space, rather than 1, 2, . . . x etc.) and the **Resp**onse type as "Numb" (numerical, not alpha, upper/lowercase, etc.). When we "accept Item Block," the field overlay on the record in the second line is added to the overlay for ID field already selected:

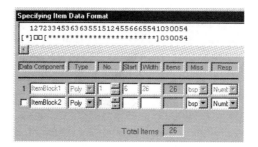

To specify the **Item Characteristics**, we can use the **Item Format** section for each Item Block by providing Labels, Response Category numbers, and Scoring Function structure details. With the CAIN data, we indicate that Item #1 has six response categories and should be scored in the direction recorded, with the 1, 2, 3, 4, 5, 6 response categories scored 0, 1, 2, 3, 4, 5.

Item Label

Code Pos01   Description Descriptor for Item 1

Category	Response	Score
1	1	0
2	2	1
3	3	2
4	4	3
5	5	4
6	6	5

No. of Response Categories 6

☐ Reverse score item

For Item #5, **Item Format** is entered to show "reverse scoring" as required by the test writers' manual:

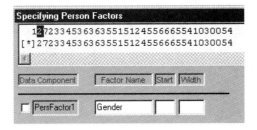

At a later point, say when we want to investigate DIF, we could use some of the nine different **Person Factors** allocations to define characteristics of the respondents such as *gender, age, school grade*. We used column 4 below to classify males (=1) and females (=2):

and column 5 to identify school grade:

Requesting a rating scale analysis constrains the Rasch model to have the effect of producing one set of threshold estimates for all items. The diagnostic RUMM item plots involve the uncentralized threshold values, that is, the set of thresholds applied to each item difficulty estimate in turn. The plot for Item #3 shows its five threshold values (for six response categories) centered on its own item location:

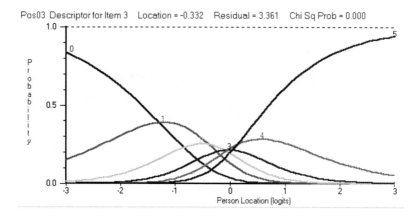

The Item #3 plot reveals a problem present around the 4th and 5th categories (i.e., threshold 4 separating categories 4 and 5). This outcome would provide grounds for rescoring these two categories because, at present, the responses in these two categories do not reflect the hierarchical ordering fundamental to the Rasch model.

Glossary

Ability estimate The location of a person on a variable, inferred by using the collected observations.

Bias The difference between the expected value of a sample statistic and the population parameter statistic estimates. It also infers the effects of any factor that the researcher did not expect to influence the dependent variable. (See DIF.)

Calibration The procedure of estimating person ability or item difficulty by converting raw scores to logits on an objective measurement scale.

Classical test theory See True score model/Traditional test theory. True score theory is classical in the sense that it is traditional.

Common person equating The procedure that allows the difficulty estimates of two different groups of items to be plotted on a single scale when the two tests have been used on a common group of persons.

Common test equating The procedure that allows the ability estimates of two different groups of people to be plotted on a single scale when they have been measured on a common test.

Concurrent validity The validity of a measure determined by how well it performs with some other measure the researcher believes to be valid.

Construct A single latent trait, characteristic, attribute, or dimension assumed to be underlying a set of items.

Construct validity Theoretical argument that the items are actual instantiations or operationalizations of the theoretical construct or latent trait under investigation; that is, that the instrument measures exactly what it claims to measure.

Counts The simple attribution of numerals to record observations. In the Rasch model, raw scores are regarded as counts.

Deterministic Characteristic of a model that implies the exact prediction of an outcome. Deterministic models explicate the relation between the observed responses and person ability as a causal pattern; for example, Guttman scaling is deterministic—the total score predicts exactly which items were correctly answered. (Cf. Probabilistic.)

Dichotomous Dichotomous data have only two values such as right/wrong, pass/fail, yes/no, mastery/fail, satisfactory/unsatisfactory, agree/disagree, male/female.

DIF (Differential item functioning) The loss of invariance of item estimates across testing occasions. DIF is prima facie evidence of item bias.

Error The difference between an observation and a prediction or estimation; the deviation score.

Error estimate The difference between the observed and the expected response associated with item difficulty or person ability.

Estimation The Rasch process of using the obtained raw scores to calculate the probable values of person and item parameters.

Facet An aspect of the measurement condition. In Rasch measurement, the two key facets are person ability and item difficulty.

Fit The degree of match between the pattern of observed responses and the modeled expectations. This can express either the pattern of responses observed for a candidate on each item (person fit) or the pattern for each item on all persons (item fit).

Fit statistics Indices that estimate the extent to which responses show adherence to the modeled expectations.

Fundamental measurement Physicist Norman Campbell showed that what physical scientists mean by measurement requires an ordering system and the kind of additivity illustrated by physical concatenation. He called this "fundamental measurement." The Rasch model is a special case of additive conjoint measurement, a form of fundamental measurement.

Identity line A line with slope = 1, plotted through the means of two sets of calibrations for the purpose of equating them. The identity line is the Rasch-modeled relation between the two sets of calibrations.

Infit mean square One of the two alternative measures that indicate the degree of fit of an item or a person (the other being standardized infit). Infit mean square is a transformation of the residuals, the difference between the predicted and the observed, for easy interpretation. Its expected value is 1. As a rule of thumb, values between 0.70 and 1.30 are generally regarded as acceptable. Values greater than 1.30 are termed misfitting, and those less than 0.70 as overfitting.

Infit statistics Statistics indicating the degree of fit of observations to the Rasch-modeled expectations, weighted to give more value to on-target observations. Infit statistics are more sensitive to irregular inlying patterns and are usually expressed in two forms: unstandardized as mean square and standardized as t.

Infit t One of the two alternative measures that indicate the degree of fit of an item or a person to the Rasch model (the other being infit mean square). The infit t (also called standardized infit) is the standardization of fit values to a distribution with a mean of 0 and variance of 1. Values in the range of -2 to $+2$ are usually held as acceptable ($p <$ .05). Values greater than $+2$ are regarded as misfitting, and those less than -2 as overfitting.

Interval scale A measurement scale in which the value of the unit of measurement is maintained throughout the scale so that equal differences have equal values, regardless of location. The 0 point on an interval scale is often regarded as arbitary or pragmatic, rather than absolute.

Invariance The maintenance of the identity of a variable from one occasion to the next. For example, item estimates remain stable across suitable samples; person estimates remain stable across suitable tests.

Item characteristic curve (ICC) An ogive-shaped plot of the probabilities of a correct response on an item for any value of the underlying trait in a respondent.

Item difficulty An estimate of an item's underlying difficulty calculated from the total number of persons in an appropriate sample who succeeded on that item.

Item fit statistics Indices that show the extent to which each item performance matches the Rasch-modeled expectations. Fitting items imply a unidimensional variable.

Item measure The Rasch estimate of item difficulty in logits.

Item reliability index The estimate of the replicability of item placement within a hierarchy of items along the measured variable if these same items were to be given to another sample of comparable ability. Analogous to Cronbach's alpha, it is bounded by 0 and 1.

Item Response Theory (IRT) A relatively recent development in psychometric theory that overcomes deficiencies of the classical test theory with a family of models to assess model–data fit and evaluate educational and psychological tests. The central postulate of IRT is that the probability of a person's expected response to an item is the joint function of that person's ability, or location on the latent trait, and one or more parameters characterizing the item. The response probability is displayed in the form of an item characteristic curve as a function of the latent trait.

Item separation index An estimate of the spread or separation of items on the measured variable. It is expressed in standard error units, that is, the adjusted item standard deviation divided by the average measurement error.

Iteration A repetition. In Rasch analysis computation, the item estimation/person estimation cycle is repeated until a specified condition (convergence criterion) is met.

Latent trait A characteristic or attribute of a person that can be inferred from the observation of the person's behaviors. These observable behaviors display more or less the characteristic, but none of the observations covers all of the trait.

Latent trait theory See Item response theory.

Likert scale (after R. Likert) A widely used questionnaire format in human science research, especially in the investigation of attitudes. Respondents are given statements or prompts and asked to endorse a response from the range of ordered response options, such as "strongly agree," "agree," "neutral," "disagree," or "strongly disagree."

Limen Threshold.

Local independence The items of a test are statistically independent of each subpopulation of examinees whose members are homogeneous with respect to the latent trait measured.

Logit The unit of measurement that results when the Rasch model is used to transform raw scores obtained from ordinal data to log odds ratios on a common interval scale. The value of 0.0 logits is routinely allocated to the mean of the item difficulty estimates.

Many-facets model In this model, a version of the Rasch model developed in the work of Mike Linacre of Chicago (esp.), facets of testing situation in addition to person ability and item difficulty are estimated. Rater, test, or candidate characteristics are often-estimated facets.

Measurement The location of objects along a single dimension on the basis of observations which add together.

Measurement error Inaccuracy resulting from a flaw in a measuring instrument—as contrasted with other sorts of error or unexplained variance.

Measurement precision The accuracy of any measurement.

Missing data One or more values that are not available for a subject or case about whom other values are available, for example, a question in a survey that a subject does not answer. The Rasch model is robust in the face of missing data.

Model A mathematical model is required to obtain measurements from discrete observations.

Muted Items or persons with infit mean square values less than 0.70 or infit t values less than –2 are considered muted or overfitting. This indicates less variability in the data than the Rasch model predicts and generally reflects dependency in the data.

95% confidence band In test or person equating, the interval within the control lines set by the investigator (at $p < .05$) requiring that 95% of measured items or persons should fit the model.

Noisy Items or persons with infit mean square values greater than 1.30 or infit t values greater than +2 are considered noisy or misfitting. This indicates more erratic or haphazard performance than the Rasch model predicts.

Nominal scale A scale in which numerals are allocated to category values that are not ordered. Although this is necessary for measurement, it is not sufficient for any form of scientific measurement. (Cf. Stevens.)

One-parameter item response model (1PL-IRT) This description of the Rasch model highlights the Rasch focus on just one item parameter—difficulty—along with the model's membership in the IRT family of data-fitting models. Such a description usually ignores the Rasch model focus on fundamental measurement.

Order The transitive relationship between values A, B, C, etc., of a variable such that A > B, B > C, and A > C, etc.

Order effect When subjects receive more than one treatment or intervention, the order in which they receive those treatments or interventions might affect the result. To avoid this problem, researchers often use a counterbalanced design.

Ordinal scale A method of comparisons that ranks observations (puts them in an order) on some variable and allocates increasing values (e.g., numerals 1, 2, 3 or letters a, b, c, etc.) to that order. The size of differences between ranks is not specified. Although this is necessary for measurement, it is not sufficient for any form of scientific measurement. (Cf. Stevens.)

Outfit statistics Unweighted estimates of the degree of fit of responses. These unweighted values tend to be influenced by off-target observations and are expressed in two forms: unstandardized mean squares and standardized t values.

Overfit See Muted.

Partial credit analysis A Rasch model for polytomous data, developed in the work of Geoff Masters (esp.), which allows the number of ordered item categories and/or their threshold values to vary from item to item.

Perfect score The maximum possible score a respondent can achieve on a given test by answering all items correctly or endorsing the highest level response category for every item.

Person ability See Person measure.

Person fit statistics Indices that estimate the extent to which the responses of any person conform to the Rasch model expectation.

Person measure An estimate of a person's underlying ability based on that person's performance on a set of items that measure a single trait. It is calculated from the total number of items to which the person responded successfully in an appropriate test.

Person reliability index The estimate of the replicability of person placement that can be expected if this sample of persons were to be given another set of items measuring the same construct. Analogous to Cronbach's alpha, it is bounded by 0 and 1.

Person separation index An estimate of the spread or separation of persons on the measured variable. It is expressed in standard error units, that is, the adjusted person standard deviation divided by the average measurement error.

Probabilistic Given that all the possible influences on person performance cannot be known, the outcomes of the Rasch model are expressed mathematically as probabilities; for example, Rasch measurement is probabilistic—the total score predicts with varying degrees of certainty which items were correctly answered. (See Stochastic.)

Raters Judges who evaluate candidates' test performances in terms of performance criteria.

Rating scale analysis A version of the Rasch model, developed in the work of David Andrich (esp.), now routinely used for the sort of polytomous data generated by Likert scales. It requires that every item in a test have the same number of response options, and applies the one set of threshold values to all items on the test.

Raw scores Scores or counts in their original state that have not been statistically manipulated.

Residual The residual values represent the difference between the Rasch model's theoretical expectations and the actual performance.

Segmentation When tests with items at different developmental levels are submitted to Rasch analysis, items representing different stages should be contained in different segments of the scale with a non-zero distance between segments. The items should be mapped in the order predicted by the theory.

Specific objectivity The measurement of any person's trait is independent of the dispersion of the set of items used to measure that trait and, conversely, item calibration is independent of the distribution of the ability in the sample of persons who take the test.

Standardized infit See Infit *t*.

Standardized outfit Unweighted estimates of the degree of fit of responses. The outfit statistic is routinely reported in its unstandardized (mean square) and standardized (*t* statistic) forms. The acceptable values for *t* range from –2 to +2 ($p < .05$). Values greater than +2 are termed misfitting, and those less than –2 as overfitting. Compared with the infit statistics, which give more weight to on-target performances, the outfit *t* statistic is more sensitive to the influence of outlying scores.

Step See Threshold.

Stochastic Characteristic of a model that expresses the probabilistic expectations of item and person performance on the construct held to underlie the observed behaviors. (Cf. Deterministic.)

Targeted The items on the testing instrument match the range of the test candidates' proficiency.

Three-parameter item response model (3PL-IRT) An item response model that estimates three item parameters—item difficulty, item discrimination, and guessing—to better fit the model to the empirical data.

Threshold The level at which the likelihood of failure to agree with or endorse a given response category (below the threshold) turns to the likelihood of agreeing with or endorsing the category (above the threshold).

Traditional test theory See True score model/Classical test theory.

True score model The model indicates that any observed test score could be envisioned as the composite of two hypothetical components: a true score and a random error component.

Two-parameter item response model (2PL-IRT) An item response model that estimates two item parameters—item difficulty and item discrimination—to better fit the model to the empirical data.

Unidimensionality A basic concept in scientific measurement that one attribute of an object (e.g., length, width, weight, temperature, etc.) be measured at a time. The Rasch model requires a single construct to be underlying the items that form a hierarchical continuum.

Validity Evidence gathered to support the inferences made from responses to explicate the meaningfulness of a measured construct through examining person fit, item fit, and item and person ordering.

Variable An attribute of the object of study that can have a variety of magnitudes. The operationalization of a scale to measure these values is termed variable construction. A variable is necessarily unidimensional.

Visual analogue scale (VAS) Scale designed to present to the respondent a rating scale with minimum constraints. Usually respondents are required to mark the location on a line corresponding to the amount they agree. The score is routinely read from the scale in millimeters.

References

Adams, R. J., & Khoo, S. T. (1993). *Quest: The interactive test analysis system* [Computer software]. Camberwell, Victoria: Australian Council for Educational Research.

Adams, R. J., Wu, M. L., & Wilson, M. R. (1998). *ConQuest: Generalised item response modelling software* [Computer software]. Camberwell, Victoria: Australian Council for Educational Research.

Anastasi, A., & Urbina, S. (1997). *Psychological testing* (7th ed.). Upper Saddle River, NJ: Prentice Hall.

Andersen, E. B. (1973). A goodness of fit for the Rasch model. *Psychometrika, 38*(1), 123–140.

Andersen, E. B. (1977). The logistic model for m answer categories. In W. E. Kempf & B. H. Repp (Eds.), *Mathematical models for social psychology*. Vienna, Austria: Hans Huber.

Andrich, D. (1978a). Application of a psychometric rating model to ordered categories which are scored with successive integers. *Applied Psychological Measurement, 2*(4), 581–594.

Andrich, D. (1978b). Rating formulation for ordered response categories. *Psychometrika, 43*(4), 561–573.

Andrich, D. (1978c). Scaling attitude items constructed and scored in the Likert tradition. *Educational and Psychological Measurement, 38*(3), 665–680.

Andrich, D. (1985). An elaboration of Guttman scaling with Rasch models of measurement. In N. B. Tuma (Ed.), *Sociological methodology* (pp. 33–80). San Francisco: Jossey-Bass.

Andrich, D. (1988). *Rasch models for measurement*. Newbury Park, CA: Sage.

Andrich, D. (1989). Distinctions between assumptions and requirements in measurement in the social sciences. In J. A. Keats, R. Taft, R. A. Heath, & S. H. Lovibond (Eds.), *Mathematical and theoretical systems: Proceedings of the 24th International Congress of Psychology of the International Union of Psychological Science* (Vol. 4, pp. 7–16). North-Holland: Elsevier Science.

Andrich, D. (1996). Measurement criteria for choosing among models with graded responses. In A. von Eye & C. C. Clogg (Eds.), *Categorical variables in developmental research: Methods of analysis* (pp. 3–35). San Diego, CA: Academic Press.

Angoff, W. H. (1960). Measurement and scaling. In C. W. Harris (Ed.), *Encyclopedia of educational research* (3rd ed., pp. 807–817). New York: Macmillan.

235

Armon, C. (1984). Ideals of the good life. In M. L. Commons, F. A. Richards, & C. Armon (Eds.), *Beyond formal operations, Volume 1: Late adolescent and adult cognitive development* (pp. 357–381). New York: Praeger.

Armon, C. (1993). Developmental conceptions of good work: A longitudinal study. In J. Demick & P. M. Miller (Eds.), *Development in the workplace* (pp. 21–37). Hillsdale, NJ: Lawrence Erlbaum Associates.

Armon, C. (1995). Moral judgment and self-reported moral events in adulthood. *Journal of Adult Development, 2*(1), 49–62.

Armon, C., & Dawson, T. (1997). Developmental trajectories in moral reasoning across the lifespan. *Journal of Moral Education, 26*(4), 433–453.

Bassett, G. W., Jr., & Persky, J. (1994). Rating skating. *Journal of the American Statistical Association, 89*(427), 1075–1079.

Bejar, I. I. (1983). *Achievement testing: Recent advances.* Beverly Hills, CA: Sage..

Bendig, A. W. (1953). Reliability of self-ratings as a function of the amount of verbal anchoring and of the number of categories on the scale. *Journal of Applied Psychology, 37*, 38–41.

Bendig, A. W. (1954a). Reliability and the number of rating-scale categories. *Journal of Applied Psychology, 38*, 38–40.

Bendig, A. W. (1954b). Reliability of short rating scales and the heterogeneity of the rated stimuli. *Journal of Applied Psychology, 38*, 167–170.

Bergstrom, B. A., & Lunz, M. E. (1992). Confidence in pass/fail decisions in computer adaptive tests and paper and pencil examinations. *Evaluation and the Health Professions, 15*(4), 453–464.

Bergstrom, B. A., Lunz, M. E., & Gershon, R. C. (1992). Altering the level of difficulty in computer adaptive testing. *Applied Measurement in Education, 5*(2), 137–149.

Boardley, D., Fox, C. M., & Robinson, K. L. (1999). Public policy involvement of nutrition professionals. *Journal of Nutrition Education, 31*(5), 248–254.

Bond, T. G. (1976/1995). *BLOT—Bond's logical operations test.* Townsville, Queensland, Australia: James Cook University.

Bond, T. G. (1980). The psychological link across formal operations. *Science Education, 64*(1), 113–117.

Bond, T. G. (1996, January). *Confirming ideas about development: Using the Rasch model in practice* [Videotape]. Invited address at the Human Development and Psychology Colloquium series, Graduate School of Education, Harvard University.

Bond, T. G., & Bunting, E. M. (1995). Piaget and measurement III: Reassessing the *méthode clinique. Archives de Psychologie, 63*(247), 231–255.

Bond, T. G., & King, J. A. (1998). *School Opinion Survey State Report.* Townsville, Australia: James Cook University. (Contracted research report with 1,200 individual site reports for Education Queensland)

Bond, T. G., King, J. A., & Rigano, D. (1997). *Parent and Student Forms for the School Opinion Survey.* Townsville, Australia: James Cook University.

Bring, J., & Carling, K. (1994). A paradox in the ranking of figure skaters. *Chance, 7*(4), 34–37.

Brogden, J. E. (1997). The Rasch model, the law of comparative judgment, and additive conjoint measurement. *Psychometrika, 42*(4), 631–634.

Brown, G., Widing, R. E., II, & Coulter, R. L. (1991). Customer evaluation of retail salespeople utilizing the SOCO scale: A replication, extension, and application. *Journal of the Academy of Marketing Science, 19*(4), 347–351.

Brunel, M.-L., Noelting, G., Chagnon, Y., Goyer, L., & Simard, A. (1993). Le profil cognitif des élèves en formation professionnelle au secondaire. In P. Goguelin & M. Moulin (Eds.), *La psychologie du travail à l'aube du XXIe siècle* (pp. 121–131). Issy-les-Moulineaux, France: EAP.

Campbell, R., & Galbraith, J. (1996, August). *Non-parametric tests of the unbiasedness of Olympic figure skating judgements.* Paper presented at the 1996 Joint Statistical Meetings, Chicago.

Campbell, S. K., Kolobe, T. H., Osten, E. T., Lenke, M., & Girolami, G. L. (1995). Construct validity of the Test of Infant Motor Performance. *Physical Therapy, 75*(7), 585–596.

Chang, L. (1994). A psychometric evaluation of 4-point and 6-point Likert-type scales in relation to reliability and validity. *Applied Psychological Measurement, 18*(3), 205–215.

Choppin, B. H. L. (1985). Lessons for psychometrics from thermometry. *Evaluation in Education, 9*(1), 9–12.

Clark, H. H., & Schober, M. F. (1992). Asking questions and influencing answers. In J. M. Tanur (Ed.), *Questions about questions: Inquiries into the cognitive bases of surveys* (pp. 15–48). New York: Russell Sage.

Cliff, N. (1992). Abstract measurement theory and the revolution that never happened. *Psychological Science, 3*(3), 186–190.

Colby, A., & Kohlberg, L. (1987). *The measurement of moral judgment: Vol. 1. Theoretical foundations and research validation.* New York: Cambridge University Press.

Crocker, L., & Algina, J. (1986). *An introduction to classical and modern test theory.* New York: Holt, Rinehart & Winston.

Cronbach, L. J., & Meehl, P. E. (1955). Construct validity in psychological tests. *Psychological Bulletin, 52*, 281–302.

Dawson, T. (2000). Moral and evaluative reasoning across the life-span. *Journal of Applied Measurement, 1*(4), 346–371.

Dinnebeil, L. A., Fox, C. M., & Rule, S. (1998). Influences on collaborative relationships: Exploring dimensions of effective communication and shared beliefs. *Infant–Toddler Intervention, 8*(3), 263–278.

Dinnebeil, L. A., Hale, L., & Rule, S. (1996). A qualitative analysis of parents' and service coordinators' descriptions of variables that influence collaborative relationships. *Topics in Early Childhood Special Education, 16*(3), 322–347.

Douglas, G., & Wright, B. D. (1986). *The two-category model for objective measurement* (Research Memorandum No. 34). Chicago: University of Chicago, MESA Psychometric Laboratory.

Draney, K. L. (1996). The polytomous Saltus model: A mixture model approach to the diagnosis of developmental differences (Doctoral dissertation, University of California at Berkeley, 1996). *Dissertation Abstracts International, 58*(02), 431A.

Duncan, O. D. (1984a). *Notes on social measurement: Historical and critical.* New York: Russell Sage Foundation.

Duncan, O. D. (1984b). Rasch measurement: Further examples and discussion. In C. F. Turner & E. Martin (Eds.), *Surveying subjective phenomena* (Vol. 2, pp. 367–403). New York: Russell Sage Foundation.

Duncan, O. D. (2000). Repudiating the Faustian bargain. *Rasch Measurement Transactions, 14*(1), 734. Available: http://www.rasch.org/rmt/rmt141e.htm. Accessed: March 15, 2000.

Dunham, T. C., & Davison, M. L. (1990). Effects of scale anchors on student ratings of instructors. *Applied Measurement in Education, 4*(1), 23–35.

Endler, L. C. (1998). *Cognitive development in a secondary science setting.* Unpublished thesis, James Cook University, Townsville, Queensland, Australia.

Engelhard, G. (1992). The measurement of writing ability with a many-faceted Rasch model. *Applied Measurement in Education, 5*(3), 171–191.

Engelhard, G. (1994). Examining rater errors in the assessment of written composition with a many-faceted Rasch model. *Journal of Educational Measurement, 31*(2), 93–112.

Ferguson, G. A. (1941). The factorial interpretation of test difficulty. *Psychometrika, 6*(5), 323–330.

Fernberger, S. W. (1930). The use of equality judgments in psychological procedures. *Psychological Review, 37*, 107–112.

Finn, R. H. (1972). Effects of some variations in rating scale characteristics on the means and reliabilities of ratings. *Educational and Psychological Measurement, 32*, 255–265.

Fischer, G. H., & Molenaar, I. W. (Eds.). (1995). *Rasch models: Foundations, recent developments, and applications.* New York: Springer-Verlag.

Fisher, R. A., & Wright, B. D. (Eds.). (1994). Applications of probabilistic conjoint measurement [Special issue]. *International Journal of Educational Research, 21*(6), 557–664.

Fisher, W. P., Jr. (1993). Scale-free measurement revisited. *Rasch Measurement Transactions, 7*(1), 272–273. Available: http://www.rasch.org/rmt/rmt71.htm. Accessed: March 15, 2000.

Fisher, W. P., Jr. (1994). The Rasch debate: Validity and revolution in educational measurement. In M. Wilson (Ed.), *Objective measurement: Theory into practice* (Vol. 2, pp. 36–72). Norwood, NJ: Ablex.

Fisher, W. P., Jr. (1997). Physical disability construct convergence across instruments: Towards a universal metric. *Journal of Outcome Measurement, 1*(2), 87–113.

Fisher, W. P., Jr. (1999). Foundations for health status metrology: The stability of MOS SF-36 PF-10 calibrations across samples. *Journal of the Louisiana State Medical Society, 151*(11), 566–578.

Fisher, W. P., Jr. (2000). Objectivity in psychosocial measurement: What, why, how. *Journal of Outcome Measurement, 4*(2), 527–563.

Fisher, W. P., Jr., Eubanks, R. L., & Marier, R. L. (1997). Equating the MOS SF36 and the LSU HSI Physical Functioning Scales. *Journal of Outcome Measurement, 1*(4), 329–362.

Fisher, W. P., Jr., Marier, R. L., Eubanks, R., & Hunter, S. M. (1997). The LSU Health Status Instruments (HSI). In J. McGee, N. Goldfield, J. Morton, & K. Riley (Eds.), *Collecting information from health care consumers: A resource manual of tested questionnaires and practical advice, Supplement* (pp. 109–127). Gaithersburg, MD: Aspen.

Fox, C., Gedeon, J., & Dinero, T. (1994, October). *The use of Rasch analysis to establish the reliability and validity of a paper-and-pencil simulation.* Paper presented at the annual meeting of the Midwestern Educational Research Association, Chicago.

Fox, C. M., & Jones, J. A. (1998). Uses of Rasch modeling in counseling psychology research. *Journal of Counseling Psychology, 45*(1), 30–45.

Frisbie, D. A., & Brandenburg, D. C. (1979). Equivalence of questionnaire items with varying response formats. *Journal of Educational Measurement, 16*(1), 43–48.

Gaulin, C., Noelting, G., & Puchalska, E. (1984). The communication of spacial information by means of coded orthogonal views. In J. M. Moser (Ed.), *Proceedings of the Annual Meeting of the North American Chapter of the International Group for the Psychology of Mathematics Education.* Madison: Wisconsin Center for Educational Research. (ERIC Document Reproduction Service No. ED 253 432).

Goldstein, H. (1979). The mystification of assessment. *Forum for the Discussion of New Trends in Education, 22*(1), 14–16.

Guild, J. (1938). Are sensation intensities measurable? In *Report of the 108th Meeting of the British Association for the Advancement of Science* (pp. 296–328). London: Association.

Gulliksen, H. (1950). *Theory of mental tests.* New York: Wiley.

Guttery, R. S., & Sfridis, J. (1996, August). *Judging bias in Olympic and World Figure Skating Championships: 1982–1994.* Paper presented at the 1996 Joint Statistical Meetings, Chicago.

Guttman, L. (1944). A basis for scaling qualitative data. *American Sociological Review, 9*, 139–150.

Hales, S. (1986). Rethinking the business of psychology. *Journal for the Theory of Social Behavior, 16*(1), 57–76.

Haley, S. M., McHorney, C. A., & Ware, J. E., Jr. (1994). Evaluation of the MOS SF-36 Physical Functioning Scale (PF-10): I. Unidimensionality and reproducibility of the Rasch item scale. *Journal of Clinical Epidemiology, 47*(6), 671–684.

Hambleton, R. K., & Swaminathan, H. (1985). A look at psychometrics in the Netherlands. *Nederlands Tijdschrift voor de Psychologie en haar Grensgebieden, 40*(7), 446–451.

Hautamäki, J. (1989). The application of a Rasch model on Piagetian measures of stages of thinking. In P. Adey (Ed.), *Adolescent development and school science* (pp. 342–349). London: Falmer.

Hays, W. L. (1994). *Statistics* (5th ed.). Fort Worth, TX: Harcourt Brace.

Inhelder, B., & Piaget, J. (1958). *The growth of logical thinking from childhood to adolescence* (A. Parsons & S. Milgram, Trans.). London: Routledge & Kegan Paul. (Original work published 1955)

Jenkins, G. D., & Taber, T. D. (1977). A Monte Carlo study of factors affecting three indices of composite scale reliability. *Journal of Applied Psychology, 62*(4), 392–398.

Karabatsos, G. (1998). Analyzing nonadditive conjoint structures: Compounding events by Rasch model probabilities. *Journal of Outcome Measurement, 2*(3), 191–221.

Karabatsos, G. (1999a, July). *Axiomatic measurement theory as a basis for model selection in item-response theory.* Paper presented at the 32nd annual conference of the Society for Mathematical Psychology, Santa Cruz, CA.

Karabatsos, G. (1999b, April). *Rasch vs. two- and three-parameter logistic models from the perspective of conjoint measurement theory.* Paper presented at the annual meeting of the American Education Research Association, Montreal, Canada.

Karabatsos, G. (2000). A critique of Rasch residual fit statistics. *Journal of Applied Measurement, 1*(2), 152–176.

Keats, J. A. (1983). Ability measures and theories of cognitive development. In H. Wainer & S. Messick (Eds.), *Principals of modern psychological measurement* (pp. 81–101). Hillsdale, NJ: Lawrence Erlbaum Associates.

Keeves, J. P. (1997, March). *International practice in Rasch measurement, with particular reference to longitudinal research studies.* Invited paper presented at the annual meeting of the Rasch Measurement Special Interest Group, American Educational Research Association, Chicago.

Kieffer, K. M. (1999). Why generalizability theory is essential and classical test theory is often inadequate. In B. Thompson (Ed.), *Advances in social science methodology* (Vol. 5, pp. 149–170). Stamford, CT: JAI.

Kindlon, D. J., Wright, B. D., Raudenbush, S. W., & Earls, F. (1996). The measurement of children's exposure to violence: A Rasch analysis. *International Journal of Methods in Psychiatric Research, 6*(4), 187–194.

King, J. (1993). Getting anxious about electronic learning. *Australian Educational Computing, 8*(2), 16–20.

King, J., & Bond, T. (1996). A Rasch analysis of a measure of computer anxiety. *Journal of Educational Computing Research, 14*(1), 49–65.

King, J. A., & Bond, T. G. (2000, April). *Measuring client satisfaction with public education: Meeting competing demands.* Paper presented at the annual meeting of the American Educational Research Association, New Orleans, LA.

Klauer, K. C. (1995). The assessment of person fit. In G. H. Fischer & I. W. Molenaar (Eds.), *Rasch models: Foundations, recent developments, and applications* (pp. 97–110). New York: Springer-Verlag.

Klinkenborg, V. (2000). The best clock in the world . . . and why we can't live without it. *Discover, 21*(6), 50–57.

Klockars, A. J., & Yamagishi, M. (1988). The influence of labels and positions in rating scales. *Journal of Educational Measurement, 25*(2), 85–96.

Kofsky, E. (1966). A scalogram study of classificatory development. *Child Development, 37*(1), 191–204.

Kolmogorov, A. N. (1950). *Foundations of the theory of probability.* New York: Chelsea.

Komorita, S. S. (1963). Attitude content, intensity, and the neutral point on a Likert scale. *Journal of Social Psychology, 61*(2), 327–334.

Küchemann, D. (1979). *PRTIII: Pendulum.* Windsor, Berkshire, England: National Foundation for Educational Research.

Lam, T. C., & Klockars, A. J. (1982). Anchor point effects on the equivalence of questionnaire items. *Journal of Educational Measurement, 19*(4), 317–322.

Lam, T. C., & Stevens, J. J. (1994). Effects of content polarization, item wording, and rating scale width on rating responses. *Applied Measurement in Education, 7*(2), 141–158.

Lawson, A. E. (1979). Combining variables, controlling variables, and proportions: Is there a psychological link? *Science Education, 63*(1), 67–72.

Levy, P. (1937). *Theorie de l'addition des variables aleatoires* [Combination theory of unpredictable variables]. Paris: Gauthier-Villars.

Linacre, J. M. (1989). *Many-facet Rasch measurement.* Chicago: MESA Press.

Linacre, J. M. (1994). Constructing measurement with a many-facet Rasch model. In M. Wilson (Ed.), *Objective measurement: Theory into practice* (Vol. 2, pp. 129–144). Norwood, NJ: Ablex.

Linacre, J. M. (1995). Categorical misfit statistics. *Rasch Measurement Transactions, 9*(3), 450–451. Available: http://www.rasch.org/rmt/rmt93.htm. Accessed: March 15, 2000.

Linacre, J. M. (1996). Year's Best Paper in *Physical Therapy. Rasch Measurement Transactions, 10*(2), 489–490. Available: http://www.rasch.org/rmt/rmt102.htm. Accessed: March 16, 2000.

Linacre, J. M. (1997). *Judging plans and facets* (Research Note No. 3). Chicago: University of Chicago, MESA Psychometric Laboratory. Available: http://www.rasch.org/rn3.htm. Accessed: March 23, 2000.

Linacre, J. M. (1998). Detecting multidimensionality: Which residual data-type works best? *Journal of Outcome Measurement, 2*(3), 266–283.

Linacre, J. M. (1999a). Investigating rating scale category utility. *Journal of Outcome Measurement, 3*(2), 103–122.

Linacre, J. M. (1999b). Paired comparison measurement with extreme scores. *Rasch Measurement Transactions, 12*(3), 646–647. Available: http://www.rasch.org/rmt/rmt1238.htm. Accessed: March 20, 2000.

Linacre, J. M. (1999c). What are the odds? Measuring college basketball. *Popular Measurement, 2*(1), 17–18.

Linacre, J. M., Engelhard, G., Tatum, D. S., & Myford, C. M. (1994). Measurement with judges: Many-faceted conjoint measurement. *International Journal of Educational Research, 21*(6), 569–577.

Linacre, J. M., & Wright, B. D. (1994a). Chi-square fit statistics. *Rasch Measurement Transactions, 8*(2), 360. Available: http://rasch.org/rmt/rmt82.htm. Accessed: March 14, 2000.

Linacre, J. M., & Wright, B. D. (1994b). Reasonable mean-square fit values. *Rasch Measurement Transactions, 8*(3), 370. Available: http://www.rasch.org/rmt/rmt83.htm. Accessed: March 22, 2000.

Linacre, J. M., & Wright, B. D. (1994c). *A user's guide to BIGSTEPS.* Chicago: MESA Press.

Linacre, J. M., & Wright, B. D. (2000). *WINSTEPS: Multiple-choice, rating scale, and partial credit Rasch analysis* [Computer software]. Chicago: MESA Press.

Lissitz, R. W., & Green, S. B. (1975). Effect of the number of scale points on reliability: A Monte Carlo approach. *Journal of Applied Psychology, 60*(1), 10–13.

Loevinger, J. (1947). A systematic approach to the construction and evaluation of tests of ability. *Psychological Monographs, 61*(4).

Looney, M. A. (1997). Objective measurement of figure skating performance. *Journal of Outcome Measurement, 1*(2), 143–163.

Lopez, W. A. (1996). The resolution of ambiguity: An example from reading instruction (Doctoral dissertation, University of Chicago, 1996). *Dissertation Abstracts International, 57*(07), 2986A.

Low, G. D. (1988). The semantics of questionnaire rating scales. *Evaluation and Research in Education, 2*(2), 69–70.

Luce, R. D. (1972). What sort of measurement is psychophysical measurement? *American Psychologist, 27*(2), 96–106.

Luce, R. D. (1995). Four tensions concerning mathematical modeling in psychology. *Annual Review of Psychology, 46*, 1–26.

Luce, R. D., Krantz, D. H., Suppes, P., & Tversky, A. (1990). *Foundations of measurement: Vol. 3. Representation, axiomatization, and invariance.* San Diego: Academic Press.

Luce, R. D., & Tukey, J. W. (1964). Simultaneous conjoint measurement: A new type of fundamental measurement. *Journal of Mathematical Psychology, 1*(1), 1–27.

Lunz, M. E., & Linacre, J. M. (1998). Measurement designs using multifacet Rasch modeling. In G. A. Marcoulides (Ed.), *Modern methods for business research* (pp. 44–77). Mahwah, NJ: Lawrence Erlbaum Associates.

Lusardi, M. M., & Smith, E. V. (1997). Development of a scale to assess concern about falling and applications to treatment programs. *Journal of Outcome Measurement, 1*(1), 34–55.

Maraun, M. D. (1998). Measurement as a normative practice: Implications of Wittgenstein's philosophy for measurement in psychology. *Theory and Psychology, 8*(4), 435–461.

Masters, G. N. (1980). A Rasch model for rating scales (Doctoral dissertation, University of Chicago, 1980). *Dissertation Abstracts International, 41*(01), 215A.

Masters, G. N. (1982). A Rasch model for partial credit scoring. *Psychometrika, 47*(2), 149–174.

Masters, G. N. (1984). DICOT: Analyzing classroom tests with the Rasch model. *Educational and Psychological Measurement, 44*(1), 145–150.

Masters, G. N. (1988). Measurement models for ordered response categories. In R. Langeheine & J. Rost (Eds.), *Latent trait and latent class models* (pp. 11–29). New York: Plenum.

Masters, G. N. (1994). Partial credit model. In T. Husén & T. N. Postlethwaite (Eds.), *The international encyclopedia of education* (pp. 4302–4307). London: Pergamon.

Masters, G. N., & Beswick, D. G. (1986). *The construction of tertiary entrance scores: Principles and issues.* Melbourne, Victoria, Australia: University of Melbourne, Centre for the Study of Higher Education.

Masters, G. N., & Wright, B. D. (1984). The essential process in a family of measurement models. *Psychometrika, 49*(4), 529–544.

McHorney, C. A., Haley, S. M., & Ware, J. E., Jr. (1997). Evaluation of the MOS SF-26 Physical Functioning Scale (PF-10): II. Comparison of relative precision using Likert and Rasch scoring methods. *Journal of Clinical Epidemiology, 50*(4), 451–461.

McNamara, T. F. (1996). *Measuring second language performance.* New York: Longman.

Mercer, A., & Andrich, D. (1997, March). *Implications when adjacent categories do not increase the trait.* Paper presented at the International Objective Measurement Workshop, Chicago.

Messick, S. (1989). Validity. In R. L. Linn (Ed.), *Educational measurement.* New York: Macmillan.

Messick, S. (1995). Validity of psychological assessment. *American Psychologist, 50*(9), 74–149.

Michell, J. (1986). Measurement scales and statistics: A clash of paradigms. *Psychological Bulletin, 100*(3), 398–407.

Michell, J. (1990). *An introduction to the logic of psychological measurement.* Hillsdale, NJ: Lawrence Erlbaum Associates.

Michell, J. (1997). Quantitative science and the definition of measurement in psychology. *British Journal of Psychology, 88*(3), 355–383.

Michell, J. (1999). *Measurement in psychology: Critical history of a methodological concept.* New York: Cambridge University Press.

Miller, G. A. (1956). The magical number seven, plus or minus two: Some limits on our capacity for processing information. *Psychological Review, 63*, 81–97.

Mislevy, R. J., & Wilson, M. (1996). Marginal maximum likelihood estimation for a psychometric model of discontinuous development. *Psychometrika, 61*(1), 41–71.

Montag, M., Simonson, M. R., & Maurer, M. (1984). *Test administrator's manual for the standardized test of computer literacy and computer anxiety index.* Ames, IA: Iowa State University, College of Education, Instructional Resources Center.

Moos, R. H. (1979). *Evaluating educational environments.* San Francisco: Jossey-Bass.

Narens, L., & Luce, R. D. (1993). Further comments on the "nonrevolution" arising from axiomatic measurement theory. *Psychological Science, 4*(2), 127–130.

Noelting, G. (1980a). The development of proportional reasoning and the ratio concept. Part I. Differentiation of stages. *Educational Studies in Mathematics, 11*(2), 217–253.

Noelting, G. (1980b). The development of proportional reasoning and the ratio concept. Part II. Problem-structure at successive stages; Problem-solving strategies and the mechanism of adaptive restructuring. *Educational Studies in Mathematics, 11*(3), 331–363.

Noelting, G. (1982). *Le développement cognitif et le mécanisme de l'équilibration.* Chicoutimi, Québec, Canada: Gaëtan Morin.

Noelting, G., Coudé, G., Rousseau, J.-P., & Bond, T. (2000). *Can qualitative stage characteristics be revealed quantitatively?* Manuscript submitted for publication.

Noelting, G., Gaulin, C., & Puchalska, E. (1985, March/April). *Levels in the ability to communicate spatial information by means of coded orthogonal views.* Paper presented at the annual meeting of the American Educational Research Association, Chicago.

Noelting, G., & Rousseau, J.-P. (in press). *Overcoming contradiction: A dialectical theory of cognitive development.* Mahwah, NJ: Lawrence Erlbaum Associates.

Nunnally, J. C. (1967). *Psychometric theory.* New York: McGraw-Hill.

Nunnally, J. C. (1978). *Psychometric theory* (2nd ed.). New York: McGraw-Hill.

Ory, J. C. (1982). Item placement and wording effects on overall ratings. *Educational and Psychological Measurement, 42*(3), 767–775.

Overton, W. F. (1998a). *Construct validity: A forgotten concept in developmental psychology?* Paper presented at the Jean Piaget Society annual symposium, Chicago.

Overton, W. F. (1998b). Developmental psychology: Philosophy, concepts, and methodology. In W. Damon (Series Ed.) & R. M. Lerner (Vol. Ed.), *Handbook of child psychology: Vol. 1. Theoretical models of human development* (5th ed., pp. 107–188). New York: Wiley.

Overton, W. F. (1999, August). *Construct validity: A forgotten concept in psychology?* Paper presented at the annual meeting of the American Psychological Association, Boston.

Parkinson, K. (1996). *Children's understanding of area: A comparison between performance on Piagetian interview tasks and school-based written tasks.* Unpublished thesis, James Cook University, Townsville, Queensland, Australia.

Pedhazur, E. J., & Schmelkin, L. P. (1991). *Measurement, design, and analysis: An integrated approach.* Hillsdale, NJ: Lawrence Erlbaum Associates.

Perkins, K., Wright, B. D., & Dorsey, J. K. (in press). Using Rasch measurement with medical data. In *Rasch measurement in health sciences.* Chicago: MESA Press.

Perline, R., Wright, B. D., & Wainer, H. (1979). The Rasch model as additive conjoint measurement. *Applied Psychological Measurement, 3*(2), 237–255.

Ramsay, J. O. (1973). The effect of number of categories in rating scales on precision of estimation of scale values. *Psychometrika, 38*(4, Pt. 1), 513–532.

Rasch, G. (1960). *Probabilistic models for some intelligence and attainment tests.* Copenhagen: Danmarks Paedagogiske Institut.

Rasch, G. (1961). On general laws and the meaning of measurement in psychology. In *Proceedings of the Fourth Berkeley Symposium on Mathematical Statistics and Probability* (Vol. 4, pp. 321–334). Berkeley: University of California Press.

Rasch, G. (1980). *Probabilistic models for some intelligence and attainment tests* (Expanded ed.). Chicago: University of Chicago Press.

Remington, M., Tyrer, P. J., Newson-Smith, J., & Cicchetti, D. V. (1979). Comparative reliability of categorical and analog rating scales in the assessment of psychiatric symptomatology. *Psychological Medicine, 9*(4), 765–770.

Remmers, H. H., & Ewart, E. (1941). Reliability of multiple-choice measuring instruments as a function of the Spearman-Brown prophecy formula, III. *Journal of Educational Psychology, 32,* 61–66.

Rogosa, D. R., & Willett, J. B. (1985). Understanding correlates of change by modeling individual differences in growth. *Psychometrika, 50*(2), 203–228.

Seltzer, R., & Glass, W. (1991). International politics and judging in Olympic skating events: 1968–1988. *Journal of Sport Behavior, 14*(3), 189–200.

Shayer, M., Küchemann, D. E., & Wylam, H. (1976). The distribution of Piagetian stages of thinking in British middle and secondary school children. *British Journal of Educational Psychology, 46*(2), 164–173.

Simonson, M. R., Maurer, M., Montag-Torardi, M., & Whitaker, M. (1987). Development of a standardized test of computer literacy and a computer anxiety index. *Journal of Educational Computing Research, 3*(2), 231–247.

Smith, R. M. (1991a). The distributional properties of Rasch item fit statistics. *Educational and Psychological Measurement, 51*, 541–565.

Smith, R. M. (1991b). *IPARM: Item and person analysis with the Rasch model.* Chicago: MESA Press.

Smith, R. M. (1992). *Applications of Rasch measurement.* Chicago: MESA Press.

Smith, R. M. (2000). Fit analysis in latent trait measurement models. *Journal of Applied Measurement, 1*(2), 199–218.

Smith, R. M., & Miao, C. Y. (1994). Assessing unidimensionality for Rasch measurement. In M. Wilson (Ed.), *Objective measurement: Theory into practice* (Vol. 2, pp. 316–327). Norwood, NJ: Ablex.

Smith, R. M., Schumacker, R. E., & Bush, M. J. (1998). Using item mean squares to evaluate fit to the Rasch model. *Journal of Outcome Measurement, 2*(1), 66–78.

Smullyan, R. (1978). *What is the name of this book? The riddle of Dracula and other logical puzzles.* Englewood Cliffs, NJ: Prentice-Hall.

Sobel, D. (1999). *Galileo's daughter: A historical memoir of science, faith, and love.* New York: Walker.

Spector, P. E. (1976). Choosing response categories for summated rating scales. *Journal of Applied Psychology, 61*(3), 374–375.

Stahl, J., Bergstrom, B., & Gershon, R. (2000). CAT administration of language placement examinations. *Journal of Applied Measurement, 1*(3), 292–302.

Stevens, S. S. (1946). On the theory of scales of measurement. *Science, 103*, 677–680.

Stevens, S. S. (1959). The quantification of sensation. *Daedalus, 88*(4), 606–621.

Stucki, G., Daltroy, L., Katz, J. N., Johannesson, M., & Liang, M. H. (1996). Interpretation of change scores in ordinal clinical scales and health status measures: The whole may not equal the sum of the parts. *Journal of Clinical Epidemiology, 49*(7), 711–717.

Suppes, P., Krantz, D. M., Luce, R., & Tversky, A. (1989). *Foundations of measurement.* San Diego, CA: Academic Press.

Symonds, P. M. (1924). On the loss of reliability in ratings due to coarseness of the scale. *Journal of Experimental Psychology, 7*, 456–461.

Thorndike, E. L. (1926). *Educational psychology.* New York: Columbia University, Teachers College.

Thorndike, E. L., Bregman, E. O., Cobb, M. V., & Woodyard, E. (1927). *The measurement of intelligence.* New York: Columbia University, Teachers College.

Thurstone, L. L. (1925). A method of scaling psychological and educational tests. *Journal of Educational Psychology, 16*, 433–451.

Thurstone, L. L. (1927). The unit of measurement in educational scales. *Journal of Educational Psychology, 18*, 505–524.

Thurstone, L. L. (1928). Attitudes can be measured. *American Journal of Sociology, 33*, 529–554.

Tucker, L. R. (1953). Scales minimizing the importance of reference groups. In *Proceedings of the 1952 Invitational Conference on Testing Problems* (pp. 22–33). Princeton, NJ: Educational Testing Service.

Van der Linden, W. J., & Hambleton, R. K. (Eds.). (1997). *Handbook of modern item-response theory.* New York: Springer.

Vogt, W. P. (1999). *Dictionary of statistics and methodology* (2nd ed.). Thousand Oaks, CA: Sage.

Wallace, J. G. (1965). *Concept growth and the education of the child.* Slough: National Foundation for Educational Research.

Whissell, R., Lyons, S., Wilkinson, D., & Whissell, C. (1993). National bias in judgments of Olympic-level skating. *Perceptual and Motor Skills, 77*(2), 355–358.

Willett, J. B. (1989). Some results on reliability for the longitudinal measurement of change: Implications for the design of studies of individual growth. *Educational and Psychological Measurement, 49*(3), 587–602.

Wilson, M. (1985). *Measuring stages of growth: A psychometric model of hierarchical development* (Occasional Paper No. 29). Hawthorn, Victoria: Australian Council for Educational Research.

Wilson, M. (1989). Saltus: A psychometric model of discontinuity in cognitive development. *Psychological Bulletin, 105*(2), 276–289.

Wilson, M., & Iventosch, L. (1988). Using the partial credit model to investigate responses to structured subtests. *Applied Measurement in Education, 1*(4), 319–334.

Wright, B. D. (1984). Despair and hope for educational measurement. *Contemporary Education Review, 3*(1), 281–288.

Wright, B. D. (1985). Additivity in psychological measurement. In E. Roskam (Ed.), *Measurement and personality assessment*. North Holland: Elsevier Science.

Wright, B. D. (1996). Comparing Rasch measurement and factor analysis. *Structural Equation Modeling, 3*(1), 3–24.

Wright, B. D. (1997). A history of social science measurement. *Educational Measurement: Issues and Practice, 16*(4), 33–45, 52.

Wright, B. D. (1998a). Estimating measures for extreme scores. *Rasch Measurement Transactions, 12*(2), 632–633. Available: http://www.rasch.org/rmt/rmt122h.htm. Accessed: October 20, 1998.

Wright, B. D. (1998b). *Introduction to the Rasch model* [Videotape]. Chicago: MESA Press.

Wright, B. D. (1999). Fundamental measurement for psychology. In S. E. Embretson & S. L. Hershberger (Eds.), *The new rules of measurement: What every educator and psychologist should know* (pp. 65–104). Mahwah, NJ: Lawrence Erlbaum Associates.

Wright, B. D., & Douglas, G. (1986). *The rating scale model for objective measurement* (Research Memorandum No. 35). Chicago: University of Chicago, MESA Psychometric Laboratory.

Wright, B. D., & Linacre, J. M. (1989). Observations are always ordinal; Measurements, however, must be interval. *Archives of Physical Measurement and Rehabilitation, 70*(12), 857–860.

Wright, B. D., & Linacre, J. M. (1992). Combining and splitting of categories. *Rasch Measurement Transactions, 6*(3), 233. Available: http://rasch.org/rmt/rmt63.htm. Accessed: March 20, 2000.

Wright, B. D., & Masters, G. N. (1981). *The measurement of knowledge and attitude* (Research Memorandum No. 30). Chicago: University of Chicago, MESA Psychometric Laboratory.

Wright, B. D., & Masters, G. N. (1982). *Rating scale analysis*. Chicago: MESA Press.

Wright, B. D., & Stone, M. H. (1979). *Best test design*. Chicago: MESA Press.

Wylam, H., & Shayer, M. (1980). *CSMS: Science reasoning tasks*. Windsor, Berkshire, England: National Foundation for Educational Research.

Zwinderman, A. H. (1995). Pairwise parameter estimation in Rasch models. *Applied Psychological Measurement, 19*(4), 369–375.

Author Index

245

Subject Index